D1686205

Susan,

My Lovely Talented Brilliant Friend!

Hillary

LEADERSHIP BEHAVIOR COACHING

The Art of Asking Purposeful Questions

Indaba Global Coaching, LLC.
5050 1st Ave N.
Saint Petersburg, FL 33710
727-327-8777

www.IndabaGlobal.com
Written by Hellen Davis   Editors: James Fryer

Copyright © 2018 Hellen Davis

All rights reserved. No part of this book, including interior design, cover design, and icons, may be reproduced or transmitted in any form, by any means (electronic, photo- copying, recording, or otherwise) without the prior written permission of the publisher.

ISBN: 978-1-58570-338-8

Printed in the United States of America.

Table of Contents

Introduction to Leadership Behavior Coaching 5
The Basis for Coaching 19
Cognitive Dissonance 31
Performance/Behavior Matrix 59
Communication During Leadership Behavior Coaching Sessions 75
The Art of Asking Purposeful Questions 79
Responses to Questions 95
Timing Questions and Responses 117
Structuring a Series of Questions 133
DISC-based Coaching Session Questions 193
Complementing Your Coaching Sessions with DISC-based Questions 209
Provide Feedback to Provoke Thoughtful Responses 250
Preparation for Your Feedback Coaching Sessions 264
Goal Setting and Behavior Coaching Accountability 288
Coaching Skills for Behavior Coaching Accountability 298
Sample Coaching Questions 322

Leadership Behavior is more than having self-awareness and striving towards self-improvement. Leadership Behavior embodies the influencing skills demonstrated in language, behavior, and actions. Leadership Behavior requires the leader to have skills and display them consistently. These are measured against leadership standards, values, and principles. Leadership Behavior insists the leader BE and DO. That is precisely what a Leadership Behavior Coach must inspire and instill in the leader coachee. ~Hellen Davis

Introduction to Leadership Behavior Coaching

Leadership Behavior is the Goal.

A Leadership Behavior Coach (whether internal to an organization or an external coach) is trained to help the client, employee, team-member, or person you are trying to coach (aka 'coachee') by addressing when changes in behavior need to happen. The goal is to have people be held accountable for their behavior. Whether the Leadership Coach is internal or external resource has little bearing on how effective a Leadership Behavior Coach can be, nor does it matter if you are a full-time coach or someone in leadership or management who has made ongoing coaching a priority for your own leadership role. A Leadership Behavior Coach helps the coachee recognize that if they don't wrap their head around any new behaviors and skills they need, and make the changes required to strive toward Leadership Behavior, their future as a leader may be limited. There's an old saying: "What got you here, isn't what will keep you here." Often, a Leadership Coach or Executive Coach can make inroads where trusted peers, employees, human resources professionals, family members, or friends cannot.

> Leadership truly is a lot of hard work. I hoped, when I was younger, that I would just be a natural leader and people would work on what I thought was awesome. Then we'd all be driving towards amazing outcomes! To a certain extent I was, but I soon learned that people follow fascinating, influencing, and fun leaders for short periods. Only when it's all happiness, sunshine, rainbows, and unicorns. When the going gets tough, that's when you have to have already built up your Leadership Currency and Trust Bank so that they stay the course with you. This building up takes skill, discipline, and determination. If you have that they'll stay with you during tough times. They'll rally when you need help. True Leadership Behavior is certainly a learned skillset rather than something you were simply born with. -Hellen Davis

WHAT IS LEADERSHIP BEHAVIOR?

Most experts agree that the best advice to give leaders is to focus on your BEHAVIOR over your FEELINGS and EMOTIONS. This doesn't mean every minute of your life, but it does mean that your behavior should be top of mind in all of your leadership efforts.

The foundation of Leadership Behavior is your actions, not your feelings and emotions. Here's a good parallel: You can be livid, fuming, furious, and ready to tear someone's head off their shoulders, but if you don't ACT on your emotions. You remain calm and self-controlled, if you restrain and control yourself, by whatever means, you are exhibiting Leadership Behavior. This means your behavior is appropriate. Understand this: You always have to control yourself and your behavior when you put on the hat of leadership. But you can rest assured that many will always have emotions that run counter to this. We are still human!

Leadership Behavior is based on the actions you take and the habits you form; guiding their thoughts, decision-making, and behaviors. If you are 'behaviorally appropriate', you consistently exhibit self-control or restraint. People might perceive your overall nature as calm, being in control, doing things in a prudent fashion, looking after the interests of the employees and the organization, abiding by appropriate boundaries, restricting or providing appropriate feedback on unwise behaviors, having command of your actions, and having a sense of self-discipline. When you exhibit Leadership Behavior you do not allow yourself to be overcome with emotion, especially negative ones.

If you lack Leadership Behavior, you might over-react – leaping to judgment, making decisions that run against leadership efforts, or those that harm relationships. Going from calm, to annoyed, to highly upset, at warp speed, it takes you a nanosecond to roar. When this happens, you are typically unable to self-regulate appropriately. You've already launched! One of the consequences: People are afraid of telling you what you need to hear. Most disturbing, you lose your ability to fine-tune your actions to the situations you face. In terms of DISCflex Factors, you've lost the ability to 'dial up' or 'dial down' your behavioral components; getting them (through self-regulation) to a place where they are behaviorally appropriate for the situation.

WHAT IS A LEADERSHIP BEHAVIOR COACH?

Behaviors often become so ingrained that a person's brain automatically turns to them, whatever the situation. Even when coachees are self-aware, many simply don't know how to modulate their behavior. As a Leadership Behavior Coach, you'll help your coachees understand their underlying natural behavior and how these can help lift them or potentially hurt their leadership efforts. Looking at the definition of Leadership Behavior, most people simply don't know where to turn to get this type of education or assistance to elevate their careers and enhance their skills. This is a fundamental reason for why people need the assistance of a Leadership Behavior Coach, with a structured and logical program, **especially if they have received feedback that something should change**.

> Before you start some work, always ask yourself three questions – "Why am I doing it?", "What might the results be?", and "Will I be successful?". Only when you think deeply and find satisfactory answers to these questions, go ahead. -Chanakya

COACHING METHODOLOGY

Certified Leadership Behavior Coaches provide a sounding board for their coachees as they progress as a leader. Most important, they provide models of excellence, a proven process, and knowledge for their coachees to follow so that they work toward better Leadership Behavior.

Unlike other coaching methodologies, we do not believe the coachee has all the answers. We believe that no one has all the answers for the things they face in their professional life. With that guiding principle, we not only ask probing questions, we help the coachee walk through options and ask them to explore the consequences of their decision making. Most importantly, we look at their behavior as a driver for attaining better Leadership Behavior. Through questioning, probing, observing, and interviewing we can provide suggestions, options, and education to help in this realm.

A LEADERSHIP BEHAVIOR COACH PROVIDES EDUCATION SO THAT COACHEES CAN ADJUST OR 'TUNE INTO' THEIR HABITS.

Flexing behavior to the situations leaders face is an extremely important skillset: Behavior is what causes action. Repeated ingrained actions are habits. Think of the way to tune into all of your habits as if you are a radio. Each station is a different habit. By raising or lowering the frequency dial ('dialing up' and 'dialing down'), you can 'set' your station (your behavior) for whatever situation you are facing. This way of thinking sets the tone for acquiring better Leadership Behavior. We have proven for more than three decades that behavioral change is possible in any arena of life – from communicating effectively, dealing with anger, handling employee concerns, working with different people, and just about professional skill imaginable. With the appropriate knowledge and guidance, coachees can acquire enhanced proficiency in Leadership Behavior.

> No one is dumb who is curious. The people who don't ask questions remain clueless throughout their lives. -Neil deGrasse Tyson

By asking questions, a Leadership Coach helps their coachees walk through their leadership and organizational goals in appropriate timelines. A Leadership Coach also stresses the need for introspection and self-examination, resulting in a rational and critical approach to solving ethical dilemmas and problems and juggling paradoxes. They help the coachee clarify their thinking by asking probing questions, listening intently for both intent and decision making that will result in actions, behaviors and habits. The coach is trained to provide clear definitions of basic concepts. They provide insight into the coachee's natural behavior patterns and explain the behaviors vital for a leader to exhibit. Most important, they track progress and provide a standard for accountability.

HISTORY

Our DISCflex™ Recovery founders started our coaching organization more than 30 years ago. Philosophically we are quite different from other coaching associations and organizations. Our foundational belief is that Certified Leadership Behavior Coaches and Executive Coaches best serve their coachees when they can fully engage; when they bring a wealth of experience to their coaching engagements. The specific goal for the coachee is to attain a working knowledge of what it takes to achieve Leadership Behavior.

LEADERSHIP BEHAVIOR COACHING PHILOSOPHY & MISSION

Philosophically as Executive Coaches and Leadership Behavior Coaches, we are quite different from other coaching associations and organizations. Our foundational belief is that a Leadership Behavior Coach best serves their coachees when they can fully engage; when they bring a wealth of experience to their coaching engagements. A Leadership Behavior Coach's mission is to encourage coachees to think about their behavior and habits; while always stressing the need for analytical self-examination, for clear definitions of basic concepts, and for a rational and critical approach to solving ethical dilemmas, approaching opportunities, and solving problems.

Leadership Behavior Coaches provide a sounding board for their coachees as they engage in philosophical dialogue tuned to leadership efforts. Most important, they provide models of behavioral excellence and knowledge for their coachees to follow so that they complete goals faster and continue with their leadership efforts. When a Leadership Behavior Coach brings their passion and wealth of their experience to the table, they often find that they perform services that are not purely in the traditional coaching realm by supplying insight, support, guidance, information, relaying material on resource providers, and recommending educational materials.

ROLES OF A LEADERSHIP BEHAVIOR COACH

You can take on various roles in your coachee's leadership efforts. If your coachee is uncertain or can't clearly see the path forward, or if there are many paths, with no 'right' answers (which is often the case), a Leadership Behavior Coach can guide them toward fleshing out their options, making sure adequate thought is taken. This process often makes a path forward appear clearer. Perhaps the leader needs a sounding board or help talking through those first critical steps in an initiative. When a coachee is ready to address their gaps or confront feedback about their Leadership Behaviors and work to change their habits, a Leadership Behavior Coach can show them alternatives that might work to preserve their personal style while enhancing the required leadership skills. You can provide insight and experience to build their hope that ongoing career success is possible for them at the level they desire. Here are some of the roles a Leadership Behavior Coach may take on:

- Listener
- Question Asker
- Educator
- Feedback Giver
- Supporter
- Advocate
- Motivator
- Accountability Person
- Alternative Suggestions
- Structure Contributor
- Courage Coach (when they need to overcome their fears)

LEADERSHIP BEHAVIOR USING A STRUCTURED AND LOGICAL APPROACH

As a Leadership Behavior Coach, you'll take your coachees through a structured program to help your coachee work to develop new and healthy behaviors. New thinking, new behavior and new habits need structure to 'gel and stick'. By working through the topic areas in the DISCflex Leadership Report and the Executive Development Suite (and with you providing insight and feedback), your coachee will put together specific actions that support their leadership efforts and professional goals. They discuss decision making and how their natural behavior patterns impact their actions and habits. With your guidance and feedback, they'll come up with alternatives to their current behaviors and habits.

MEASURING SUCCESS FOR COACHING SESSIONS

Success isn't measured by:

- The coachee's positive feelings toward and/or relationship with the Leadership Behavior Coach. **True success is measured by results of changes in behavior and ongoing adherence to behavioral parameters and goal accomplishment.**
- How well the coachee performs with the Leadership Coach's direct assistance or help. **Success is measured by how well the coachee performs when the Leadership Coach is not present.**
- How coachees 'feel' about their own progress. **Success must be measured by changes others perceive in the coachee's behavior.**

WHY USE THE LEADERSHIP BEHAVIOR PROGRAM?

We understand that Leadership Coaches are engaged by coachees for a variety of reasons and that there is no one-size-fits-all Leadership Coaching model. However, in producing this program, we discovered there is a universal 'common thread' that is found in successful leadership efforts. In particular, we have found that behavior and habits that focus on reducing cognitive dissonance, defining appropriate boundaries, goal setting, decision making, Self-Talk, and accountability are the foundations of most successful leadership efforts. The Leadership Behavior Program helps the coach lead the coachee through a logical, thoughtful and planned approach to behavior-based leadership efforts.

Our team spent years developing this behavior- and habit-based approach with the assistance and feedback from some of the best minds in the Executive Coaching and leadership communities.

WHAT MAKES THE LEADERSHIP BEHAVIOR COACHING PROGRAM DIFFERENT?

A Certified Leadership Behavior Coach's tasks are to encourage coachees to think for themselves and provide models of excellence throughout the Leadership Behavior Program. By introducing new information, we know that the coachee will experience significant amounts of cognitive dissonance. The models and activities you provide will help the coachee process through this. The DISCflex Leadership Report, the Compendium of Models and eLearning outlines a foundational program to underpin the coaching assignment by providing structure and accountability for the coachee.

We drive accountability.

USING THE PERFORMANCE/BEHAVIOR MATRIX TO ENHANCE LEADERSHIP EFFORTS

We have been training coaches for decades. We realize that while all coaching shares some common principles, Leadership Behavior Coaching focuses on two key areas that might not be as critical in management or life coaching:

1. Enhancing future Performance for the to drive motivation.
2. Increasing Behavioral Awareness and Skills to drive leadership capabilities.

By using the Performance/Behavior Accountability Matrix we can plot a coachee's progress as they work through their leadership efforts. We believe that a coachee's ability to function in the situations they encounter, as well as the behaviors they exhibit as they face these, affect performance and employee motivation and engagement.

By focusing on the Performance/Behavior Matrix, and by using cognitive dissonance principles, we provide a logical and systematic approach that provides the coachee with education and tools vital to their leadership efforts. The goal is to reduce any cognitive dissonance that occurs as a natural result of the coachee going through the Leadership Behavior Coaching Process. Together with their Leadership Behavior Coach the coachee will explore the steps necessary for their coaching goals.

HOW DOES LEADERSHIP BEHAVIOR COACHING WORK?

Increasing behavior awareness and enhancing future performance simultaneously often require a 'shift in thinking'. Often, people are never taught precisely how to make a 'behavioral shift' as well as an 'actions shift'. Often the reason that leadership efforts don't 'stick' is that these two don't line up. Even if the person wants to do both, they just don't have the knowledge, tools, or accountability coach to get there. That's why a Leadership Behavior Coach is so important. As a Leadership Behavior Coach, you'll have the tools, skills, assessments and program to hold the coachee accountable for taking on the education necessary to their journey.

As a Leadership Behavior Coach, you can help your coachees 'hold up their mirror' in a productive way that people too close to the coachee and/or the situation often can't. You'll help your coachees understand that a monumental 'shift in thinking' followed by short- and long-term shifts in behavior can indeed create healthier habits. You can help motivate them and hold them accountable because this 'shift' takes time and concentrated effort. When the coachee becomes discouraged, experiences internal anguish or loses hope again, you, as their coach, can be their sounding board, supporter, as well as their 'accountability person'. Many times, shifting these vital elements from another employee or their boss to you preserves vital relationships and allows the person to be vulnerable so they can admit they need help.

BEHAVIORAL CHANGE CREATES COGNITIVE DISSONANCE

One of the most important goals you have as a Leadership Coach's is to the monitor the levels of cognitive dissonance the coachee is experiencing. The Leadership Behavior Program will teach you precisely how this works. As a Leadership Coach, you will coach/guide/motivate the coachee towards reconciliation of the dissonance they are experiencing. Specifically, you'll take the coachee through the self-discovery process to 'square with' who the coachee was/is versus the future the coachee envisions.

BRINGING YOUR EXPERIENCE AND 'SPECIAL SAUCE' TO THE TABLE

We know that the most successful coaches in the world combine their worldly experiences with a proven process that drives coachee accountability. As a Leadership Behavior Coach, you can use the guidelines and program to bring what you have learned through formal (classroom and conventional education) and informal training (life experiences) to the table. Keeping true to your personal values and mission as a coach is vitally important to your authenticity, mission and purpose. All the knowledge and education provided in the program, including the activities, can (and should) be blended with your 'special sauce'. Your 'special sauce' is what draws coachees to you. Your unique style, personal values, purpose, and experience should always be at the core of your practice. The Leadership Behavior tools – including the Leadership Behavior Assessment and Report and all the associated educational materials - allow for you to 'be you' while providing a foundation and proven process for coaching success.

BUILD REVENUE WITH LEADERSHIP BEHAVIOR COACHING

Through our certification programs, you will grow in experience. Becoming certified in the Leadership Behavior Program will significantly enrich your coaching practice. What will set you apart from other coaches is your methodology and accountability practices including the fully validated DISCflex™ Leadership tools centered on the DISCflex Leadership Assessment and Behavior Report and recommended eLearning. By taking coachees through their coaching journey focusing on the skills and knowledge they'll gain in the Leadership Behavior Leadership Development Program, you'll be able to scale your coaching practice. You'll be able to spend more time coaching and acquiring coachees than on 'build out'. This means you'll achieve revenue goals that most coaches only dream about.

In teaching basic Leadership Behavior Coaching concepts, we point to logic and formulas within the framework of Listen & Learn, Motivate, Inspire, Coach, and Lead. We can test knowledge, but rarely do we know what will happen when the student is in the field. Will they remember the formula? Does the formula fit? Are they going to wing it? Are they going to come up with something so extraordinary that it blows conventional formulas away? In coaching, we have to literally get to the soul of the people we are dealing with, never forgetting that what we are teaching might not play out in the ways we imagined. We have to teach how to innovate and think.

The Basis for Coaching

In your first coaching session, you should have already completed your personal DISC assessment, so you know who you are. This way you know what behaviors you'll have to flex as you look at each of your coachees' DISC scores. It's important to be able to 'flex' to build trust and communicate effectively in every coaching session.

Topic of Discussion Triangle

In each coaching session, we recommend that you explain this concept and its importance.

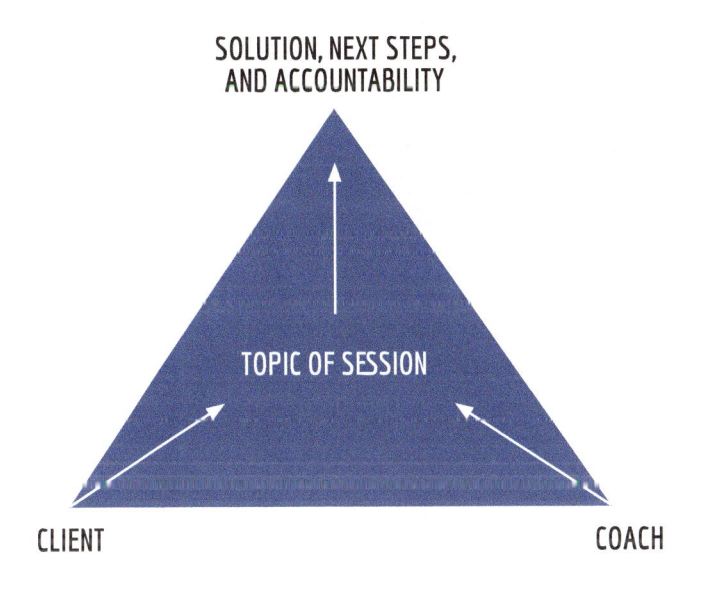

SOLUTION, NEXT STEPS, AND ACCOUNTABILITY

TOPIC OF SESSION

CLIENT **COACH**

The basis for the coaching process looks like a triangle.

THE BASE

At the base of the triangle, are two people: 1. the coachee on one side and 2. the Leadership Coach on the other. There is a distinctive separation between the two people. This is important so that the issues like transference, conflicts of interest, imposing value systems on each other, etc. do not occur.

THE CENTER OF THE TRIANGLE

Additionally, coachees might not want to talk about the topic (problem, opportunity, challenge or issue) of the session for a variety of reasons. However, where the coach focuses the session's attention has significant impact on leadership efforts. Ensuring that the topic of the session stays at the forefront will keep the coachee and coach focused on what they need to cover for that session. If a topic enters the session's discussion that is not appropriate for the topic of session or is scheduled to be discussed later up in the program, it can be handled in a variety of ways:

1. The issue can be put in a parking lot for the end of the session where specific time has been allocated for this.
2. It can be scheduled for later date.
3. Additional coaching time can be allocated.

THE APEX

At the apex of the triangle is the solution/the next steps that are mutually agreed to be the best approach and the accountability parameters around that solution. You and the coachee will discuss specific behaviors and actions that need to be accomplished for the coachee to move forward with their leadership efforts. The key to an effective coaching session, are to document the actions and desired behaviors with appropriate timelines.

The substance of the triangle is the discussion topic for the session.

- This substance could be a topic that contains a problem, opportunity, challenge or issue.
- It could be that the coachee needs to have education around the model or topic area.

Running Your Coaching Sessions

> Spectacular achievement is always preceded by unspectacular preparation. Robert H. Schuller

As a Leadership Behavior Coach, how you run and prepare for your coaching sessions is critical to yours and your coachee's success.

PREPARATION

1. Get all the information you can about your coachee prior to all your sessions and keep updating this information. How? Review their recent activity on web sites, blogs, Twitter, Facebook, and

LinkedIn. Check in with friends and family and remember the coaching guidelines for confidentiality and protocol.

2. State the purpose of the coaching sessions at the beginning of each session. Ask the coachee if they have anything to add to the coaching session agenda. Coachees may interrupt, distract, or sabotage coaching sessions or be resentful that you aren't working on topics they think are important if they're not given an opportunity to share their concerns and care-abouts. Get these concerns and care-abouts out at the start, so that the focus can then go to the coaching session's purpose. You might ask:
   a. What has transpired since we last met that you'd like to share?
   b. What goals or thoughts keep bubbling up when you think about the purpose of this coaching session?

3. State the outcome you seek for the coaching session. If you don't have a clear purpose and outcome, what's to keep your coaching sessions from going off the rails?

4. Select a venue or communication means that meets yours and your coachee's needs. Make sure that you stock it with the basics (see Checklist for Coaching Sessions Meeting Room below). Prior to every coaching session check on the room's condition prior to meeting with the coachee. Some Leadership Coaches go so far as to check for beverage preferences and to see if the room has any flickering lights beforehand. At the very least, you want to make sure that the room can accommodate your technology needs. You might also want to make sure there's sugar on hand, since glucose enhances concentration.

5. Walk through the coaching session's agenda, any meeting rules, and send out any reading material in advance that might 'tee up' the coaching session. The agenda should allocate time for each agenda item, based upon importance. Ground rules and agendas provide structure and expectations of conduct. Since coaching sessions are designed for conversation, make it clear what coachees are expected to read, bring with them, and/or review before the coaching session.

6. Always build or reestablish trust and rapport prior to launching 'the meat' of the coaching session. Craft warm-up questions that will draw out any hidden agendas or 'check ups'.
    a. We discussed the importance of providing timely feedback to employees before it becomes critical. Did you practice this since we met? How did it go?
    b. You mentioned that you thought the Sales Department head was trying to undermine your authority. You said you were going to check this out further and have a direct discussion with him using the questioning and active listening protocols we discussed last session. You also stated that you were going to remind yourself of Noble Intent so that you kept the right perspective. How did that go?

7. Prepare a list of open-ended questions to draw out opinions and ideas. Sometimes quiet coachees need a little coaxing. You might ask:
    a. What alternative approaches have we looked at that you're not fully on board with yet?
    b. What would your thoughtful response be?

THE BASIS FOR COACHING

c. How do you think one of your more outspoken colleagues respond?
  d. What if it doesn't work?
  e. Who else should we talk to before moving forward?

8. Anticipate post-meeting reluctances to follow through with commitments made, and head them off. Coachees often say what they want you to hear but when the coaching sessions is over; their actions tell what they really think. Reluctance conversations can diminish or undermine the coachee's leadership efforts. Ask a cool-down question at the end of the coaching sessions to capture the essence of coachee's thoughts and concerns about commitments they've made during the session. You might ask:
   a. As you think through what you've promised to do, what's something you wanted to address but did not see an opportunity to bring it up?
   b. What do you think will be most challenging going forward?
   c. When you go home tonight, what will you share about our coaching sessions, if anything, with others?

GROUND RULES FOR COACHING SESSIONS

Here are basic principles that should be clarified for all coaching sessions:

- Start and end on time.
- Focus on behaviors, without judgement, and facilitate honest sharing about progress.
- Respect each other's ideas, thoughts, and opinions.

- Respect confidentiality (What is discussed in the sessions, stays in the coaching sessions unless mutually agreed to share).
- Agree to participate fully during the coaching session and to be 'present'.
- Confidentiality, expectation, ethics considerations, and commitment will remain consistent throughout all coaching sessions.
- Discuss any changes to progress reporting relationships and communication parameters.
- Methods of information gathering are transparent.
- Attempt to make wise judgements, participate in prudent decision making, set objectives and monitor progress toward leadership efforts.

CHECKLIST FOR YOUR COACHING SESSION MEETING ROOM

- Silence phones.
- Water or other appropriate beverages
- Your choice of snacks/food
- Tissues
- Paper
- Pens and pencils
- Computer (to allow the coachee to take assessments and for delivering lessons/PowerPoints)
- Means for projecting educational materials
- Post the coaching sessions Ground Rules.
- Temperature should be monitored.
- Lighting should be appropriate.
- Sounds and other disturbances should be kept to a minimum.
- Ideally the venue should be private and away from 'other ears'.

ENCOURAGEMENT

> It is not the critic who counts; not the man who points out how the strong man stumbles, or where the doer of deeds could have done them better. The credit belongs to the man who is actually in the arena, whose face is marred by dust and sweat and blood; who strives valiantly; who errs, who comes short again and again, because there is no effort without error and shortcoming; but who does actually strive to do the deeds; who knows great enthusiasms, the great devotions; who spends himself in a worthy cause; who at the best knows in the end the triumph of high achievement, and who at the worst, if he fails, at least fails while daring greatly, so that his place shall never be with those cold and timid souls who neither know victory nor defeat. Shame on the man of cultivated taste who permits refinement to develop into fastidiousness that unfits him for doing the rough work of a workaday world. Among the free peoples who govern themselves there is but a small field of usefulness open for the men of cloistered life who shrink from contact with their fellows. -Theodore Roosevelt

As a Leadership Behavior Coach, it is your responsibility to encourage the coachee in building their skills. This may include giving suggestions on a variety of Leadership Behavior skills. If

Another reason for observing a coachee in their natural environment is to provide progress reports, suggestions, and feedback to the person who recommended they get coached – the coachee's sponsor. This may require you to speak on their behalf but before doing so, make sure you have read the and abide by all privacy and confidentiality laws, rules and regulations and apply to any coaching relationship/practice. As a general guideline, restrict any conversations to what is best for the coachee's growth and those statements that are designed to protect the coachee information from anyone other than who has a specific 'need to know'.

There are some exceptions when breaking cee confidentiality and confidential information. But these are limited to something akin to your knowledge that the coachee would do harm to themselves, others, or to the organization. It is strongly suggested that you become familiar with your organization's regulations, guidelines, and/or laws regarding employee confidentiality.

Cultures

Leadership Behavior Coaching serves all organizational cultures, subcultures, and even countercultures:

- An organizational culture is a set of morals, values, traditions, and practices shared by the large population or group for the greater good of an organization.
- An organizational subculture is a branch, department or team within a larger organization where a group of people have developed their own set of processes, beliefs, and values while still adhering to some of the overarching norms, guiding

your coachee wants you to see them in a leadership setting so that you can observe, they may ask you to attend an event or meeting. This is highly encouraged as it shows support and as a Leadership Coach, you can see if the skills she learned during the coaching sessions are exhibited.

In encouraging her, she may need assistance understanding why feedback is a gift. As an example, she may discount someone else's perception of her communication and influencing skills, but the feedback giver's perception is right on the money, and if not addressed will curtail her career aspirations.

THE BASIS FOR COACHING 27

principles, and/or laws of the greater culture.
- An organizational counterculture is a group of individuals within an organization whose views oppose the processes, beliefs and values of the larger organization's culture. A counterculture is defiant of the social norms that are accepted in the larger organization.

The understanding of the 3 types of organizational cultures is important for a Leadership Behavior Coach because different peoples and teams come from different environments containing different beliefs and practices. It is important during the first session of coaching to get to know the coachee and find out what type of beliefs and traditions he/she had in their formative years. A Leadership Coach should also engage in conversations about the coachee's views on the cultural elements they find most important to their success. Additionally, you should analyze whether the coachee's cultural awareness and willingness to conform to the organization's cultural norms and expectations 'fits'. Having this information can heighten the coach's awareness to be more in tune with the individual's behavior and experiences. The goal for culture discussions is to get greater insight into the coachee's background and current 'fit'. Having this insight also helps remind the coach to be respectful of the individual's preferences, norms, expectations, and experiences. Remember: Building trust with your coachee builds the foundation for them to confide in you so that you may assist them in building their leadership skills.

Bottom line: You are not to judge a person's culture, background, education, status, values or practices even if you don't agree with them.

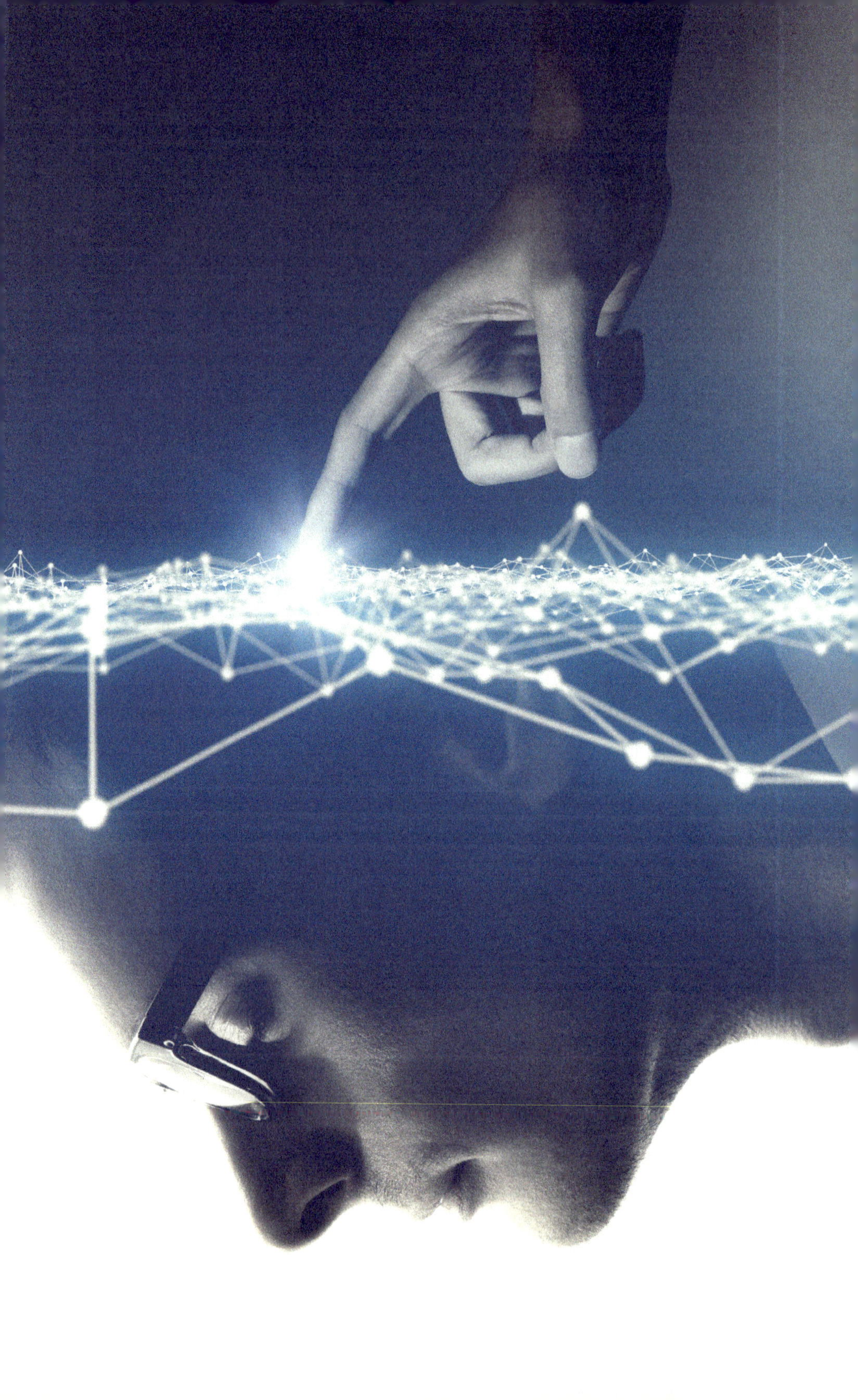

Cognitive Dissonance

What causes people to behave the way they do as they strive for new leadership behaviors?

Natural behavior patterns are set early in life. A Leadership Behavior Coach will walk their coachee through the DISCflex Leadership Behavior Report and recommended eLearning which will create awareness of the underlying natural behaviors the coachee has. These underlying natural behavior patterns are a combination of:

- Nature (traits you were born with) and
- Nurture (caused by what factors played a part in your upbringing).

These natural behaviors play a big part in how people address leadership efforts. Most important In creating new recovery-based behaviors and habits, is the roles that stress, decision making and consequence awareness play.

Critical to creating new behaviors and habits is awareness of the concept of cognitive dissonance. Cognitive dissonance is the mental discomfort (psychological stress) people feel when they have

- Choices to make,
- Things to work through that don't quite line up (especially when there's no 'win-win'), or
- When they are juggling two competing thoughts that don't 'get along together'.

> Just as your car runs more smoothly and requires less energy to go faster and farther when the wheels are in perfect alignment, you perform better when your thoughts, feelings, emotions, goals, and values are in balance. -Brian Tracy

Thoughts, choices, how-to's, consequences, etc. all fight with each other as the person tries to find a path forward causing internal stress. Often, cognitive dissonance happens a person does/has done something that goes directly against their first instincts, preferred choice, less painful option, core values, beliefs, and ideals. This is central to what happens when people are impacted by guilt for doing what is required of a leader. The person must come to terms with the consequences of their leadership choices and behaviors knowing that their personal preferences might not be in line with what they have to do for the good of the organization, stakeholders, employees or customers. A large component of the stress any leader will deal with is reconciling their actions with:

- Who they were before they had their current responsibilities,
- Their current view of who they have/will become as a consequence of working through their decision-making processes,

- How they (and those they command) execute their decisions viewed through the lens of results and consequences of the choices they've made, and
- Deciding if what they've done sits well with their value system and core beliefs.

To complicate matters in the 'becoming a better leader' process, cognitive dissonance also happens when new information is added that will impact the way a person has to begin to think or behave in their future. To function and succeed in any Leadership Development Program, people must resolve cognitive dissonance from their past professional life, and work on it to move forward to a brighter tomorrow.

COMING TO TERMS WITH THE PAST AND BUILDING A NEW FUTURE

To 'win' the internal battle and 'fix' what's causing stress, people must 'patch up' their relationship with themselves. This is difficult for someone to do when they're in the habit of beating themselves up. Leaders can be very hard on themselves and others. **Leaders must find a way to square with what they've done and where they can go in life as they move forward with their leadership efforts.** To do this, they must have dependability and consistency between their expectations of what they can do and their actions. This means they must "walk the walk, and talk the talk." To do so, a Leadership Coach can guide them through the process of systematically reducing cognitive dissonance. Cognitive dissonance will happen when words and actions don't line up. That's where a Leadership Behavior comes in. A Leadership Behavior Coach will help set up the educational components necessary to understand this concept and will build on it by supplying models to build their coachee's understanding of cognitive dissonance and the skills necessary to keep its effects low in themselves and their teams.

Being a 'cheerleader coach' isn't enough.

A Leadership Behavior Coach knows it takes a proven process to grow leadership capabilities. The Leadership Behavior Coach will explain the importance of practicing the process of 'dissonance reduction' to make sure their coachee understands how they can continually align cognitions (perceptions of the world) with their actions, attitudes, and habits. To accomplish this, they'll take their coachee through a rigorous process of self-discovery, education, and accountability, while motivating them in their leadership efforts.

MOST PEOPLE AREN'T ABLE TO LIFT THEMSELVES OUT OF STRESSFUL THINKING WITHOUT KNOWLEDGE AND HELP

Cognitive dissonance is something that most people don't even realize is happening. It's quite amazing because cognitive dissonance happens consistently whenever we are faced with something that 'seems not right', is something we are uncomfortable with, or whenever we face something we need to think through. Cognitive dissonance typically happens before making new decisions about what to do next. It's as common a mental function as breathing!

But whether you understand and recognize it or not, the ramifications of staying in a 'state of cognitive dissonance' creates mental stress and anguish. If unchecked in a leader, staying in a state of cognitive

> **As a coach, you have to prepare your clients for the certainty that cognitive dissonance will occur and provide a logical way to maneuver through it. -Hellen Davis**

What happens when you (or people you interact with) experience cognitive dissonance?

The very first thing you should do in your coaching engagement is to explain what cognitive dissonance is. When people are being coached, if you are getting through to them, they are going to experience cognitive dissonance. If coaching is working and they are being impacted, this will happen as surely as the sun rises in the East. One of the ways cognitive dissonance occurs, is when current beliefs or actions collide with new information or new ways of thinking leading to new ways of doing things (actions).

As a coach, you have to prepare your clients for the certainty that cognitive dissonance will occur and provide a logical way to maneuver through it. Understanding that your clients will become uneasy, stressed, or experience tension as they go through the changes that result from any great Coaching Program prepares them for the conversations that must occur. Recognizing that there will be a whole host of emotions (some not pleasant) sets the stage for your coaching engagement.

Also assure the coachee that experiencing cognitive dissonance is 'normal'. This will make your coaching sessions less stressful all around. This understanding will open the door for excellent questions and discussions. Most important, it will provide your clients with the knowledge that what they are experiencing when cognitive dissonance often results in poor decision making. If a leader doesn't recognize it's happening or have a way to work through it, the people on their team will begin to question or experience distrust in their decision making. They might disrespect the leader or at the very least, they'll question their leadership ability. This is precisely where a Leadership Behavior Coach can assist the coachee in understanding what is happening when cognitive dissonance is in play.

WHAT DOES COGNITIVE DISSONANCE FEEL LIKE?

The feeling of uncomfortable tension which comes from holding two conflicting thoughts in your mind at the same time. Cognitive dissonance also occurs when people do things that conflict with their core values or when they know they are in conflict with what they should be doing (behavioral misalignment).

Their Self-Talk may say things like:

- "Something's just not right here…"
- "That's annoying… Why am I doing that?"
- "I don't know what it is, but I feel it…"
- "I thought I liked her, but she was unfair to John…I'm usually a pretty good judge of character."
- "He is so good with his team but doesn't know how to manage up effectively. Should we promote him?"
- "They keep on saying we're good to go, but they don't answer my calls or emails. What could I have done to annoy them?"

dissonance occurs, is just fine and expected. This will stop them from having 'career killing moments' and doing what many less skilled folks might when cognitive dissonance is in play.

Here's what might happen if your client doesn't fully understand the typical response to cognitive dissonance:

In general, when mental conflict boils up inside a person's head, it is relieved by one of several negative defensive maneuvers:

- **Shut down information:** The person rejects incoming information and/or influences. They convince themselves that no issue/problem/conflict really exists. They close themselves off and ignore information that may be important if it doesn't match the world-view they want. They move forward, but they ignore data and insights they should be looking at and folding into their decision-making space.
    - **Suggestion:** Wise leaders take in all information and only discard what isn't truth. Great leaders always keep their mind open to insight, input and other people's opinions.
- **Rationalize:** They rationalize and explain away their behavior; refusing to face the facts. This can happen even when they are faced with compelling and logical information that runs completely counter to their position.
    - **Suggestion:** Prudent leaders weigh incoming information against what they already have proven. They continually check assumptions against facts.
- **Freeze:** They go into state where they are immobilized, or they avoid the new information altogether. Whether this happens because they are in a state of denial, or if they actively refuse

to deal with the situation makes little difference. The bottom line is that they aren't moving forward or reconciling their cognitive dissonance. The longer they freeze, the more people will doubt their leadership abilities. Leaders lead!

- **Suggestion:** Whenever a leader feels the momentum slow, they need to ask themselves why this might be occurring. A leader should always remember that tempo and pace are the foundation for executing goals. It's a leader's responsibility to set the pace – ALWAYS! When there is a 'blip', a stall, a change in cadence, the leader's organization is usually impacted.

On the positive side; people can be open-minded and work toward putting to rights (getting rid of in a positive manner) any uncomfortable feelings that cognitive dissonance might cause. In addition, your coachee could resort to any other defensive means of preserving their current ways of thinking so that their views of the world and of themselves become even further cemented. And that's not good for any coaching engagement!

> Peace is not absence of conflict, it is the ability to handle conflict by peaceful means. -Ronald Reagan

When cognitive dissonance is present there are four options**:**

1. Fight/conflict
2. Flight/Flee
3. Freeze
4. Reconcile/resolve

COGNITIVE DISSONANCE

1. FIGHT/CONFLICT:

Conflict isn't productive or desirable if the parties won't listen or don't try to understand another person's position. If flighting and conflict are the means to resolving cognitive dissonance, then your coachee needs the skills to handle and resolve conflict. Most important: The coachee needs to have skill in recognizing when to use conflict. Not all battles are worth flighting or started, or are winnable. Most times, people can agree to disagree; and still get the job done.

In terms of DISC Factors, the Dominance Factor is the behavioral element that most influences the desire to go into battle. This behavioral component is the forward driver of assertiveness, anger, boldness, decisiveness, forcefulness, and antagonism. The Dominance Factor is often directly in opposition to cooperation.

Let's examine when conflict is:

- Not worth fighting: *There* is a cost/benefit to expending energy, resources and leadership currency. All conflicts need to consider cost/benefit. There are costs in terms of things like political gain or loss, resources (wisely or unwisely deployed), lost opportunity cost, and emotional energy expenditure, just to name a few. Many leaders have gone to battle, only to find out in retrospect that they shouldn't have gone at all. Anyone in a similar position could have seen the cost had they taken the time to look. But in the heat of the moment, the leader didn't step back and first consider the cost. In forgetting to do this, the leader hurts the organization and/or its people.

- Not winnable: A leader's responsibility includes knowing when to engage. Leaders accomplish this by looking at the probability of winning. There's always the possibility of conflict arising, but there is less probability that you'll win every skirmish. If probability of winning is low, it may be wiser to retreat to fight another day. Many a war has been won by retreating from the battle of the day. Likelihood of a fair or favorable outcome should be top of mind as you consider where going into conflict is sensible.

WHEN YOU DECIDE TO CONFRONT CONFLICT

Any functioning workplace will have to deal with varying levels of interpersonal and institutional conflict. Coaching someone to handle conflict better is hard work – on both sides of the coin! Know the benefits of conflict, they'll recognize that it might be best for them to welcome conflict, rather than avoid it. Wouldn't it serve them and their organizations well knowing that the coachee has the tools and skills to harness multiple benefits from engaging with conflict in a healthy way? We already mentioned that the **Dominance Factor** is the primary behavioral component of conflict. But healthy conflict cannot allow the Dominance Factor to roar unchecked. The **Steadiness/Strategy Factor** is the opposite of Dominance Factor. The Steadiness/Strategy Factor controls thoughtfulness, patience, listening, kindness, accuracy, connectedness, and harmony. Logically, a good measure of Steadiness/Strategy Factor should be employed whenever a leader decides that the benefits of conflict outweigh the potential costs.

> Light is meaningful only in relation to darkness, and truth presupposes error. It is these mingled opposites which people our life, which make it pungent, intoxicating. We only exist in terms of this conflict, in the zone where black and white clash. -Louis Aragon

IT'S A LEADER'S RESPONSIBILITY TO ENGAGE IN CONFLICT

Sometimes it seems a leader's primary job is resolving one conflict or another! That said, it may seem like a bit of an oxymoron to have the words 'benefit' and 'conflict' in the same sentence. Conflict including constructive debate, deliberation, disagreement, difference of opinion, concern, complaint, friction, negotiation, or mediation, is not inherently good or bad. It's simply a predestined consequence of human beings connecting with each other. Conflict alone never creates benefits. It is dealing well with conflict that potentially produces benefits. Benefits of conflict stem from understanding another's position, being respectful, communicate effectively, and engaging with a goal of resolving conflict points.

GUIDING PEOPLE THROUGH CONFLICT

When a coachee understands how to guide their people through conflict in a constructive manner, disagreements are not only accepted but seen as an integral component of cooperative problem-solving. For an environment of intellectual stimulation and cooperative problem-solving to exist, people need to feel comfortable getting their opinions and views out on the table. Logically, more ideas from diverse sources generate much better innovative workable solutions. From a purely selfish standpoint, studies show the most promotable leaders acquire these skills. Behavioral maturity leading to promotion is a goal in any Executive Coaching engagement. If your coachee wants to get ahead quicker, they'll have better chances for advancement with this skill in their toolkit.

CONFLICT CAN HAVE BENEFITS LIKE THESE:

Insight & Personal Growth: When people respect each other's opinions, they remain open to insight. When insight occurs, personal growth is the result. Unfortunately, people are prone to become defensive when faced with conflict. Many are unaware of their blind spots. There is nothing better than conflict to bring out passions, feelings, and care-abouts. During conflict when temperatures rise, people are less able to hide their true selves, automatic reactions, and typical reactions. It's not always pretty but gaining self-awareness of how we navigate conflict is the first step to managing oneself better. And if we look and listen to team mates, we can learn a lot about them during conflict! How wonderful would it be to know a person's hot buttons? How respectful might you appear if you took time to understand what makes a coworker hot under the collar and then not add fuel to their fire? The greatest leadership moments come from dealing with adversity.

Improved Productivity and Cognitive diversity: When people feel they can argue the merits of one position or way of doing something over another in an open work environment, they are often motivated to complete their individual and team's goal at a higher level. Cognitive diversity is an important consideration for teamwork. Leaders must ensure that their team is not made up of members whose skill sets, ways of thinking, behavior patterns, and specialties are too similar. If this occurs, there is a lack of cognitive diversity. What this means is that all members of the team will end up reaching similar solutions, and you will not truly be exploring all possible avenues of conflict resolution or of problem solving or innovation. The result is self-supported "groupthink" and the team will not be as effective as had you made allowance for this problem not to rear its ugly head.

Healthier professional Relationships: Commitment and motivation occur best in 'safe' environments. When people feel safe – psychologically and physiologically - they dedicate themselves to goals and teamwork flourishes. When people have a healthy respect for each other and conflict resolution skills are outstanding, relationships thrive.

Contrarians and Optimists have a Voice: The most successful teams have a diversity of backgrounds and approaches. By virtue of their nature, experience, and training, many contrarians act as a team's 'devil's advocate'. They look at planning in terms of what might go wrong, they poke holes in the most robust arguments, discourage innovation because it will destabilize, and they tend to focus on possible negative outcomes, risk, and the apocalypse. Of course, a contrarian is viewed as entirely annoying and frustrating to optimists - the 'Pollyanna's on the team. Optimistic Pollyanna's focus on the best things that can happen, the positive results just down the road, and how wonderful everything will turn out. Pollyanna's and contrarian play an equally vital role in group dynamics, and a leader should make certain both have a voice and that others listen to them. What fun to think of them battling it out! And they will go into conflict – either overtly or covertly. Best to get it out in the open and be done with it. Let it fester at your peril!

Better Problem-Solving: When people debate about how to best satisfy disparate parties interests or 'care-abouts', it often sparks a different, more innovative way of solving problems. Cognitive diversity is the respectful inclusion of different ways of thinking. Many of the best ideas and solutions a group of people can come up with stem from healthy discussions connecting a hodge-podge of perspectives. But high degrees of trust between people require that they think along similar lines, have similar backgrounds and view the world from a prism of mutual understanding. The question is: How can you have different views on life and maintain high trust? It's a conundrum.

> Cognitive diversity is the respectful inclusion of different ways of thinking.

Behavioral study show that the minute people don't have a reference point form their 'experience memory bank', they experience cognitive dissonance. As soon as cognitive dissonance rises, trust goes down. And it happens FAST! That's why recognizing when cognitive dissonance starts to rise – what it feels like, how to deal with it, and how to work through it – is so critically important. No doubt, it's challenging when people don't agree with us, don't understand where we are coming from or won't subscribe to do what we want.

Different positions are exactly what they say they are: Different! Differences, until reconciled, cause friction. If unchecked can escalate to out-and-out conflict. To add to the mix, behavioral tendencies play a role in how people go into and resolve conflict. If you've ever been in a meeting where one or two voices tend to dominate a heated discussion – neither party really listening or giving quarter to the other – you've most likely seen the Dominance Factor in action.

Unfortunately, when the Dominance Factor rises, listening goes down. Inclusiveness goes down. The result is that others are left with little opportunity to express their views or have them heard. The solution is letting the D rise with an equal dose of S. How might this work? The first person uses thoughtfulness (S) before stating their opinion (D). After stating their opinion, they listen (S) and think (S) before they respond with their opinion or suggest a course of action (D). Then the second person does the same. As they continue to seek a mutually beneficial solution, both keep Noble Intent firmly in at the forefront and respectfulness in their demeanor. They realize that there might have to be give and take on both sides or compromise from one quarter or the other. They are willing to put their egos aside for the greater good. This is a vital consideration in conflict resolution.

Timelier issue identification: Workplace conflict can shine a light on deeper problems that need to be addressed. Peeling back the layers of trivial disagreements that reoccur might unearth underlying issues that should be addressed. Thoughtful leaders observe patterns that stem from root causes that need fixing sooner than later. If not brought into the light, these can develop into full-fledged conflict. Additionally, disagreements and respectful debate can identify practices and processes that need to be improved or replaced.

2. FLIGHT/FLEE:

Having a head in the sand approach to cognitive dissonance isn't particularly helpful in the long run, but like conflict, there are some advantages to this. Conflict that is denied, avoided, suppressed or handled ineffectively can harm relationships. But, if people go into conflict too soon, even more harm might occur. Constructive flight/fleeing from an overly-heated debate may be as simple as counting to ten, inhaling and listening without speaking for a minute or two, taking 30 minutes to cool the conversation, or as they do in a courtroom, calling a recess. Destructive flight/fleeing happens when people refuse to communicate. When they avoid the situation and refuse to deal with it in a healthy manner, that's not good at all. It will eventually come to a head if the situation itself can't/won't change. Which brings me to the next piece of advice on Flight/fleeing: It's not necessarily a bad tactic if you know the situation is going to eventually turn your way or be different. Sod if you think it might be useful to consider this approach, ask yourself: Why bother fighting a battle that's unwinnable or not worth it? Rather avoid the discussion until the hand is dealt and the last chip is played. This can go a long way in actually preserving relationships, saving resources, and saving time and energy best spent elsewhere.

3. FREEZE:

Freeze: Often indecision or doing nothing is just as much of a risk as doing the wrong thing. When a leader freezes, they know that something has to change but they haven't yet determined what that must be. Changes in personnel, strategy, resource allocation, communication messages, operations, sales practices, or accounting were warranted, and you know that you have to do something – but you don't. You freeze.

The reasons leaders freeze isn't cut and dried, but cognitive dissonance not being resolved is a common theme. Think back to a time when you knew a leader should have made a move but didn't. How did you view that leader? I'll be it wasn't in a positive light. In most situations, the leader will tell you – in hindsight – that they knew precisely what they needed to do well before they actually put the ball in motion. And most of the time, there were consequences when they froze and didn't take that action in terms of costs, time, energy and often employee morale. Plus, the leader eroded their leadership currency and their Trust Bank. Most leaders don't make decisions for one reason: Fear. They're afraid to let a person go until the replacement is there. They're afraid to change strategy because they might be wrong. They're stuck because they are fearful their team members won't agree with them or that they'll argue with them about the details when the leader hasn't figured it all out yet. All of these have roots in cognitive dissonance – not being able to reconcile where they are with where they need to be. People freeze because they can't clearly see the path forward. They don't like uncertainty. But the mantle of leadership requires walking into the unknown and figuring out the path forward despite the fog. That's the leader's responsibility. A leader must feel the fear, but move forward prudently. Freezing for an inappropriate period of time doesn't gel with this.

The key is to recognize when you are frozen, and be aware that the clock is ticking. Weighing the risk of moving too soon and not fast enough is a delicate balancing act for any leader. But that is precisely what leaders must do. A leader must be ok with the consequences of his decisions, realizing that the risk of no decision and no movement forward may be greater. As long as the leader's choice for forward momentum has followed prudent decision-making guidelines, the probability remains that movement is better than freezing too long.

People view leaders who appear 'frozen' as indecisive and/or weak. A sure-fire way to lose leadership capital in the eyes of your followers and team members is to look like you don't know what to do, where to turn, or how to advance the ball. Ask yourself: Would you follow a frozen leader?

If your coachee ever freezes, and there will be times this occurs, they need to know how to handle this and move prudently forward in the timeframe that the situation calls for. Before we look at how to do this, let's figure out where this freeze response came from. Think back to when humans were roaming the earth hunting and gathering. What's a great response if you see a beast that could do you harm? Run? Nope! Lay low – especially if it hasn't spotted you, is upwind or isn't hunting. The very best survival instinct is to freeze. It's a deep-seated survival reflex. It kept humans out of a lot of trouble. It's also not entirely bad in the business world either. If something unexpected occurs, you shouldn't rush into action. You need to assess the situation and figure out how to keep yourself, your team and the organization safe. Stop (freeze). Think. Then move. The sequence of 'Ready. Fire. Aim.' is there for a reason. It's the best way to hit your target.

4. **RECONCILE THE DIFFERENCE/RESOLVE THE COGNITIVE DISSONANCE AND 'BECOME COMFORTABLE' (TRUST AGAIN) BY UNDERSTANDING FESTINGER'S COGNITIVE DISSONANCE THEORY:**

Almost half a century ago social psychologist Leon Festinger developed the Cognitive Dissonance Theory (Festinger, 1957). The theory is mentioned in most general and social psychology textbooks today, so obviously it's valuable because it stood the test of time. It addresses the persistent human tendency to rationalize and justify.

COGNITIVE DISSONANCE THEORY IS BASED ON THREE FUNDAMENTAL ASSUMPTIONS.

1. People are sensitive to inconsistencies between actions and beliefs. If you hear someone say one thing, but do another, it doesn't sit well. This type of inconsistency breaks trust. It makes people go on guard and they'll question what's actually happening. When inconsistencies pop up, internal bells and whistles go off like alarms. This is an automatic response. **Example**: If you think it's wrong to lie, but you tell a lie to a friend, no matter how small, your mind sends out a signal telling you something's not right with what you're doing. It makes no difference whether it's you or someone else, the alarms will go off when you sense something just isn't right!

2. Awareness of the inconsistency will motivate the person to resolve the cognitive dissonance. They might flee (mentally or physically) and run as far from what's happening (flight/denial) as they can get, fight against what's happening, or force themselves to resolve the issue. The degree to which your beliefs and values conflict with your actions, is the barometer of how much dissonance (uncomfortableness) you'll feel. Also, the greater the dissonance, the more you will be motivated to resolve it.

THE DISSONANCE WILL BE RESOLVED IN ONE OF THREE BASIC WAYS:

1. Change your core values and/or beliefs: If you know you've violated a core principle, you must figure out a reason why and justify it to yourself. Your justification must be stronger than the uncomfortable feeling you're trying to overcome. That might mean you have to change what you believe.

How might trying to change your core values reduce/resolve cognitive dissonance?

Taking the prior example: You know full well that you lied and prior to that moment, it wasn't ok with your values and beliefs. If you change your values or beliefs – you solve the problem. Now you say to yourself: "It was ok to lie." Do this a few times and then you're good with it and can move on. Simply now deciding that lying is o.k. would take care of any dissonance. However, this is by far the hardest for most people because core values and beliefs get locked in early and 'stick'.

2. Change actions: Decide that you'll never lie again and stick to it. This takes a lot of reminding and willpower! You make amends, say you're sorry, try to make things right, and promise that it was a lesson you learned well enough to stop further similar behavior.

How might trying to change your actions reduce/resolve cognitive dissonance?

Joseph was a kind and thoughtful leader. Throughout his career, he prided himself on growing his people, making sure he set them up for success, gave thoughtful feedback and gave people time to change and make the adjustments they needed to make. Joseph got a well-deserved promotion. His new direct superior was a hard-hitting, fast-moving kind of guy. He expected his direct reports to act like he did.

Joseph tried to keep his prior attitude and behavior, but his boss constantly called him out and coached him to be more direct with the feedback he gave as well as timelier. He also insisted he be less sympathetic to team members' complaints and to make decisions based on the bottom line for the good of the company's solvency. To avoid conflict with his boss, Joseph complied. In doing so, he became more and more anxious. He was experiencing high stress due to unresolved cognitive dissonance. His core values were rock solid, and it was going to be impossible to shift his perception, so he had to change his actions.

Joseph had to find a way to act in a manner that balanced he boss' perception of how he should act and align those actions with his core values. He was up for the challenge. We segmented the boss' advice to align actions with expectations.

a. **Timely feedback:** Joseph made sure his boss knew that he was delivering feedback on weekly numbers within 24 hours. This timeframe was acceptable to the boss and worked within Joseph's value system. *He felt it gave him adequate time to provide timely but helpful feedback which solved his initial inner conflict (cognitive dissonance).* Done.

b. **Less sympathetic to team members' complaints:** Joseph realized his boss had a pint. He started to count the number of times people wandered into his office to gripe. It was a lot more than he thought! Each time he found an employee complaining, he started asking what the employee was planning to do about the situation. He focused on the tried-and-true formula of: Situation, Action, Results. Every time he heard a complaint, he steered the employee towards explaining the situation, then coming up with a solution. Rather than allowing the employee to vent but not come up with any actions to reconcile the situation or make it better, this promoted forward positive momentum. He made a call and reported back to his boss and thanked him for the feedback. *Joseph told his boss that the adjustments he was making was actually helping the whole team perform more effectively.* In viewing the actions he took in this way, he kept within his value system.

c. **Make decisions based on the bottom line:** When he thought through the feedback, Joseph admitted that it was true. He didn't think first of the bottom line. In fact, it was an after-thought at best. His boss told him if he wanted to be promoted, he had to adjust this thinking and put actions into place that forced him to create good financial stewardship habits. Upon reflection, Joseph knew that the bottom line was just as important as people. It was logical: If the company didn't turn a profit, it wouldn't be able to keep the workforce well compensated.

In fact, upon reflection, Joseph realized that the year he received his largest bonus was the year the company was most profitable. That was also the year he was promoted and got to hire three new people for his department. They were all still there two years later. Before he was promoted, the woman who had his current position used to go over the department's numbers conscientiously with the entire team on a weekly, monthly and quarterly basis. Joseph thought it might be a good idea to call and get some tips from his prior boss. Angela was more than happy to help Joseph. She said she learned the same way he was, because of similar feedback from her boss. She said that financial discipline was now the key to her new department's success.

As soon as he got back to the office after their talk, Joseph sent an email scheduling weekly and quarterly financial oversight meetings. The focus was sales efficiencies and profitability. Within three months, there was a marked difference across the board. The financial oversight meetings and accountability actions Joseph implemented have changed the way he looks at his department.

His weekly financial reviews have also changed the way he provides feedback on issues. He always comments on the costs and benefits of people's actions and behaviors – positive and negative - to the organization's bottom line. This focus changed the organizational

COGNITIVE DISSONANCE   53

culture to one of shared accountability. As far as his values and cognitive dissonance: As soon as Joseph realized the vital links between financial accountability and his people, he has steadfast in his resolve to make financial oversight a top priority.

3. Change your perception of what you did: To reduce cognitive dissonance, you could reframe what you did in more acceptable terms. Feeling better about something that happened by simply looking at it in a different way can significantly reduce cognitive dissonance. An example: When otherwise honest people fudge the truth, they justify it by saying things like: "I just told them a white lie and didn't really hurt anyone." Or "It's still a lie, but not a big lie, and telling them the truth would have hurt them, so it's ok." By justifying your lies in this way, you think about what you did differently.

Here's the truth of the matter, justification is when you make perception consistent with your actions. Even though you detest liars and don't think of your as one, making it appear ok (because it wasn't a whopper of a lie!) is now acceptable. You line up your past actions with your new way of thinking about what you did.

Reconciliation is 'backward justification. Do it enough times and you become a skilled liar. You look at perception rather than reality, when you didn't typically default to that way of thinking before. The problem is that this is a very slippery slope indeed! If you justify something that you shouldn't have done, next time you're in a similar situation, you'll think it's ok to do it again. And it's NOT! If you reflect on the mental gymnastics you will go through justifying what you shouldn't, you'll instantly recognize why cognitive dissonance training is so vital in Leadership Coaching. But, with any tactic, is there a way that changing perception might actually be the tactic best used?

HOW MIGHT TRYING TO CHANGE PERCEPTION REDUCE/RESOLVE COGNITIVE DISSONANCE?

Susan was promoted from Sales Director to Regional VP of Sales and Marketing. In her new role, she was in charge of pricing and negotiation. In her prior role in sales, Susan's view of the best negotiation tactic was to be fully transparent with prospective customers on pricing and terms. It was easy because she had strict guidelines on what she could or could not promise – all coming from her boss. All sales negotiations were restrictive and the only thing they had latitude on were discounts. The result: Although Susan's team's sales revenues were the best in the country, the discounts they gave made them one of the less profitable. Go figure! If you tell the customer the maximum discount you are allowed to give, they're going to expect it.

As she sat in her brand-new office – newly promoted to the person in charge of revenues - and looked at the numbers across the enterprise, she realized that giving away steep discounts across the enterprise was a sure-fire way to have a short-lived tenure. And boy, did she like her current view! She had to figure out what was going on in her head when she was one level below so that she could coach her Sales Managers not to do what she had done!

In a coaching session, we uncovered the reason for her deep discounting: She knew the manufacturing cost and the company's profit margins. She thought the product was overpriced in relation to what she considered to be a fair price. Fairness and frugality were high level core values that affected her actions. It was unlikely she could shift these. Going with a shift in core values wasn't going to get rid of her cognitive dissonance.

Most of the time, as a Sales Manager, she sanctioned and promoted deep discounts. Her actions were highly consistent, so trying to change her actions was going to be a tough 'sell'. The best tactic was indeed to change Susan's perception of what was fair and reasonable. I did a bit of digging and found out the product took ten years of R&D to bring to market. There were a lot of stops and starts along the way. The founders and the inventor spent tens of millions of dollars in revenue and resources.

I wondered if Susan was fully aware of these sunk costs since she had only been at the firm a couple of years. As luck would have it, Susan had known the extent of these sunk coasts and that the company needed to recoup these. Each product sale wasn't a simple matter of subtracting today's manufacturing costs and operating costs again top line revenue! I asked her: *"How much do you think it what be fair – as a percentage - to be add to each sale to recoup those sunk costs?"* Susan answered: *"It's got to be at least 50%."*

Susan had a lightbulb moment when her perception changed. The switch went on and Susan actually increased pricing the very next quarter. In addition, Susan decreased a Sales Manager's discretion in discounting. They had to write an exception and couldn't do so without Home Office approval. She fielded every call because she wanted each Sales Manager to understand how they were recouping the initial investment for the products. Profits soon ticked up.

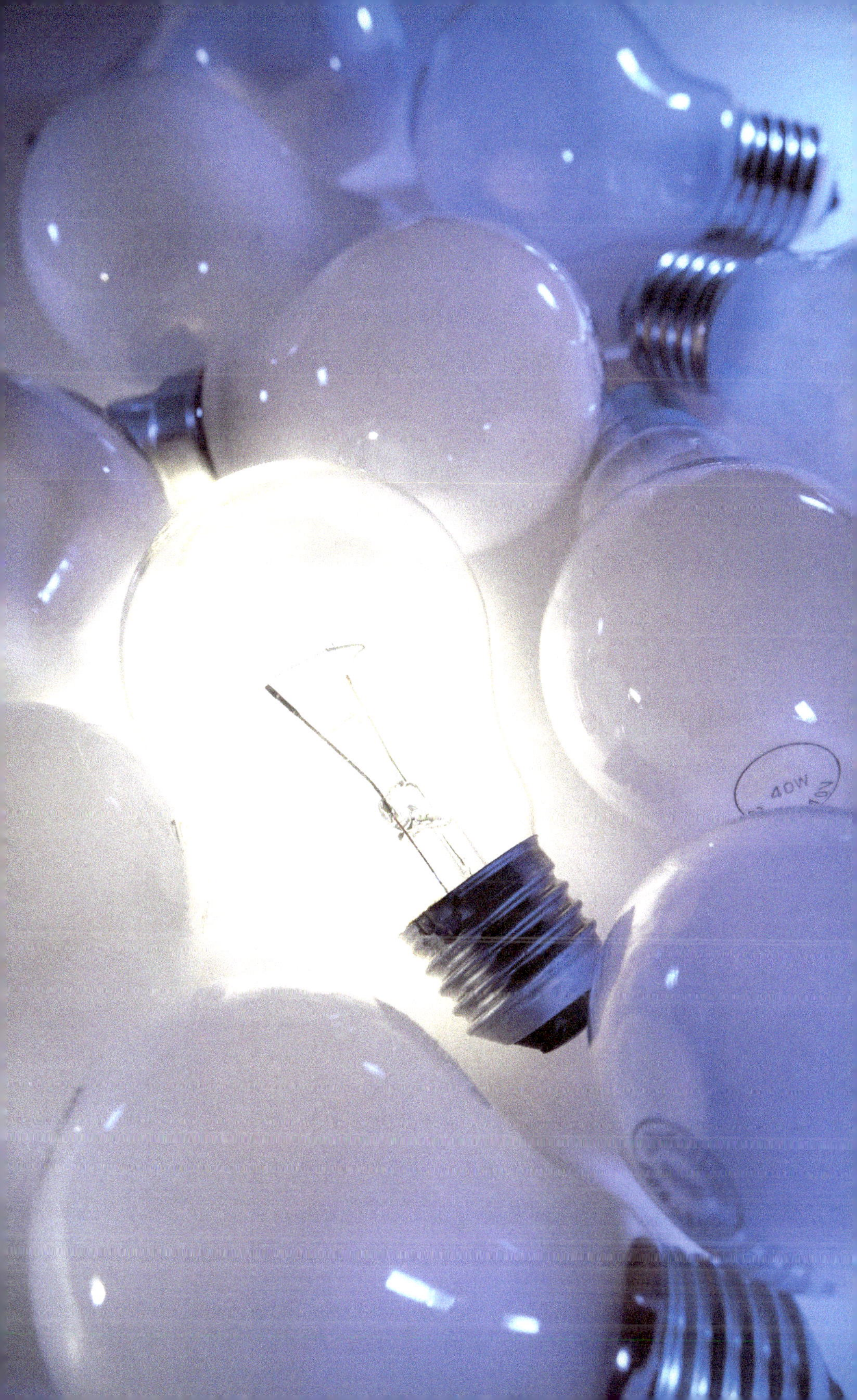
40W

Empower
Enable
LEADER
Encourage
Motivate
Reward
Initiate
Coach

Performance/ Behavior Matrix

As your coachee focuses on the changes they need to make in their behaviors and habits, their objective must be to continue to be a top-notch leader. They should strive to behave in a manner they and others can be proud of. The more success they see in this area, the better they will feel about themselves.

Using the Performance/Behavior Accountability Matrix as a guide, Leadership Behavior Coaching focuses on two key areas:

1. **Enhancing future Performance** for the to drive motivation.
2. **Increasing Behavioral Awareness and Skills** to drive leadership capabilities.

The goal is for the coachee to work towards the upper right-hand box of the model, simultaneously building out their performance (hard) and behavior (soft) skills. This progression is important for their career advancement. The goal is to work toward increasing promotability and leadership maturity in an orderly progression by focusing on KSAs (knowledge, skills, attitude) in both areas.

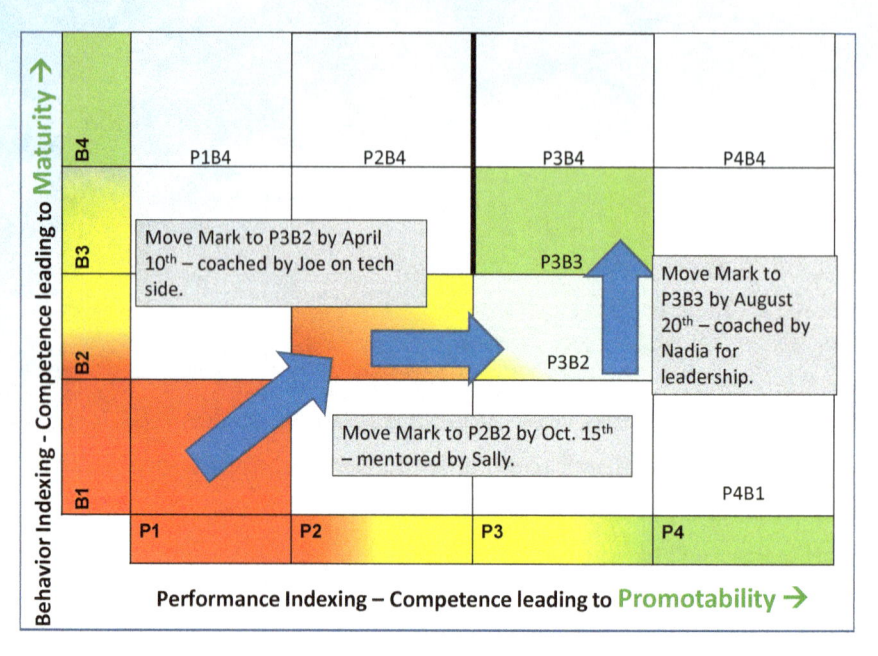

Behavior Indexing - Competence leading to Maturity →

	B4	P1B4	P2B4	P3B4	P4B4
	B3	Move Mark to P3B2 by April 10th – coached by Joe on tech side.		P3B3	Move Mark to P3B3 by August 20th – coached by Nadia for leadership.
	B2			P3B2	
	B1		Move Mark to P2B2 by Oct. 15th – mentored by Sally.		P4B1
		P1	P2	P3	P4

Performance Indexing – Competence leading to Promotability →

Copyright © 2019 by Hellen Davis. All rights reserved.

> Much of a leader's responsibility in creating a positive, high-performance culture is setting the right tone for acceptable behavior and stellar performance. The two – performance and behavior - cannot and should not be separated. Providing feedback on both, doling out rewards and consequences for both, and doing so consistently is what sets a great culture in motion. That day-to-day feedback centered on these - the tenor and tone - really makes the difference. Leadership Behavior requires the leader to set the tone and cadence for feedback on performance and behavior.

Why did we create the model?

The Leadership Behavior Coaching Program created the appropriate processes, models and topic areas for coaching sessions that drive toward growing into a more competent and effective leader.

PERFORMANCE AND BEHAVIOR AS MOTIVATORS AND DRIVERS

By using the Performance/Behavior Accountability Matrix, a Leadership Coach can plot a coachee's progress as they work through their leadership competencies. This proven methodology shows how a coachee can progress systematically through their leadership development goals using performance and behavior as motivators and drivers, building behavioral and functioning skills as they progress.

> A coachee's ability to function in the situations they encounter, as well as the behaviors they exhibit as they face these, affect promotability (knowing WHAT to do) and behavioral maturity (knowing HOW to do it). Lack of appropriate leadership skills causes stress for the coachee and team members. Inappropriate behavior makes coachees think they aren't ready for the role or that they don't/can't 'fit in'. This is an illusion that the many coachees often operate under. This may lead to self-defeating prophesies becoming reality. A leader's lack of self-confidence does play a

role in their effectiveness. Second-guessing, being tentative, and seeming unsure of how to make decisions or take action can stem from a lack of self-confidence. Building appropriate technical, leadership, performance, operational, and behavioral skills that lead to better leadership habits increases confidence and competence.

The eLearning process outlines the consequences of staying in one of the Performance/Behavior Matrix boxes without making progress. It demonstrates how a coachee **without proper behavioral skills, habits, and awareness can be just as damaging to themselves and those around them as a highly mature** person with little awareness of what the 'performance expectations' of themselves and/or group are. More important, the Performance/Behavior Matrix underscores the necessity of working simultaneously on behavior and performance capabilities.

Executive Coaching and Leadership Behavior Coaching success is noticeable when the coachee strives to possess strong performance skills, is engaged in the education process, and wants to achieve a level of behavioral knowledge whereby the coachee becomes a trusted and respected leader. Please remember that a coach's success is not necessarily tied to the coachee's actions. An old saying comes to mind: "You can lead a horse to water, but you can't make them drink."

COACHEES WILL ACHIEVE A HIGH LEVEL OF SUCCESS IN THEIR LEADERSHIP EFFORTS WHEN THEY ARE WILLING TO:

- Examine themselves and look at what actions and habits they want.
- Assess other people's reasonable expectations of them.
- Put their ego and emotions aside (be objective).
- Take in feedback.
- Make necessary changes.
- Help others who are struggling, and ultimately
- Teach others what they've learned and give back.

Assessing Where the Coachee is on the Performance/Behavior Matrix

When using the Performance/Behavior Matrix with coaching coachees, **it is important to be honest in your assessment of the** coachee's current Performance and Behavior skills on separate scales. Once you have independently assessed each level, refer back to the Performance/Behavior Matrix to see where they are, and how they can improve. Behavior skills (from the bottom to the top of the chart B1-B4), relate to how employees become much easier to work with as they achieve maturity in their current role. As they advance through the stages of performance (from the left to the right of the chart P1-P4), they are more likely to be viewed as a go-to person and as an expert in their field. In order to become that invaluable and irreplaceable stellar role model, you must have highly advanced skills in both categories.

As your coachee enhances their performance and successfully changes habits and behaviors, they will achieve *Transformational Results*. As an example of why this is important: A highly technically skilled IT leader **without proper behavioral skills and awareness can be just as damaging to a team as a highly mature employee/teammate with no technical skills at all!** Employees will not go the extra mile for either. One of the keys to leadership success in an IT department is to possess strong technical skills and achieve a level of behavioral intelligence to become a trusted and respected team leader or executive. When a technically skilled individual learns to put ego aside, help others who are struggling (rather than *throw them under the bus*), and ultimately teach others to do their job… they will achieve success within their organization and rise in their career.

WHY BEHAVIOR MATTERS

When a coachee acts in ways that are more consistent with their desired core values, their self-confidence as a leader increases. **Appropriate behavior drives leadership qualities and build leadership currency.**

Behavior plays a key role in leadership efforts, but it is rarely formally taught until the coachee reaches a certain level. Because of this, people in the leadership positions might have developed behavioral issues when it comes to situational awareness, flexibility, communication, providing direction or feedback, and/or self-awareness. As many employees, bosses, and Leadership Coaches know, this can be problematic! In fact, if asked what keeps them up at night; coaches will tell you it's issues around coachee behavior! Ask the same question of employees and bosses, and you'll get the same response. It's behavior that gives them indigestion and sleepless nights! Looking at the Behavior Indexing chart, you can easily assess where you think the coachee is with their leadership efforts because there are clear delineations between the levels (guidelines below) The eLearning and Leadership Report will help lead the coachee through behavioral models and education they probably haven't concentrated enough on.

Behavior Indexing

INDABA
GLOBAL

Level	Four Levels to Satisfy Your <u>Current</u> Job Requirements
B4	**Have Passion and Encourage Others** (Service-minded): Be a Team Player who is fully willing and able to support peers, employees, and leaders. Walk the walk; talk the talk.
B3	**Set Ego Aside** (Releasing Control) - Take others into consideration. Use this critical knowledge to adjust your behavior if necessary. Make a conscious effort to fit your behavior to every situation; and/or work on habits ('morphing' over the long term). Work diligently to interact and communicate more effectively, with greater confidence, yielding better overall leadership results.
B2	**Understand Your Impact on Others** (3rd Party Perception): EXACTLY how their peers view you. Adapting your behavior is the key to success. Many people see themselves one way, while their peers may see them in an entirely different way. This difference in perception is the root cause of conflict, misunderstandings, mistrust, loss of leadership currency, and ultimately can cause an abundance of problems.
B1	**Understand How Self-Perception Affects Us** (Self-Awareness): We judge ourselves (good and bad). Take measure of yourself objectively. **The first step is to complete your DISCflex assessment.** Willing to take a measure of who you are, based on things you value and your expectations of how you should behave as a leader. This process culminates in self-perception. Self-judgment and judgment of others cannot be easily stopped; and our actions, communication, and attitude are determined and influenced by it.

WHY BEING ABLE TO PERFORM MATTERS

When a coachee is able to perform according to expectations (theirs and others) their uncertainty, tentativeness, and disappointment decreases. Frustration decreases, pride and self-confidence increase. **Performing well drives meaningfulness, purpose and defines their role as a member of society.** Looking at the Performing Indexing chart, you can easily assess where you think the coachee is with their leadership efforts because there are clear delineations between the levels. The activities in the eLearning and the DISCflex Leadership Behavior Report help build the coachee's performing capacity by teaching them core principles.

Performance Indexing

Level	Four Levels to Satisfy Your Current Job Requirements
P4	**Teach Someone Else to Do Your Job and Support Leadership Efforts** – Teaching someone what you've learned is important. Sharing knowledge with team members is the mark of a leader.
P3	**Implement Plan and Measure Progress** (Accountability) – Setting proper benchmarks, accountability guidelines, and analyzing results is essential to building your job and/or leadership competencies.
P2	**Set Goals** – You must set performance goals before you can gain an understanding of where performance and knowledge gaps exist.
P1	**Uncover Expectations** – Be willing to start leadership efforts. The first thing is to identify responsibilities and expectations, and complete your personal SWOT analysis. This will increase awareness of how your leadership efforts will benefit yourself and others on the team.

NAVIGATING BEHAVIOR

Behavior is often difficult for employees, managers and leadership to talk about because most people don't understand precisely how behaviors work and habits 'stick'. The DISCflex Leadership Behavior Report and recommended eLearning help coachees move through the Performance/Behavior Matrix because it is a roadmap for leadership efforts. When you explain the Performance/Behavior Matrix to coachees, they'll understand it is a distinct process to assessing behavior and their skills and performing abilities in a methodical way.

Behavior Indexing - Competence leading to Maturity →

	P1	P2	P3	P4
B4	**Enthusiastic, Motivated Team Member** (much like a bounding puppy! Wants to please, coachable, and with guidance can become competent)*	Understands expectations and impact on those around them, willing to learn and be groomed.	Adaptable, Reliable, Trustworthy 1. Competent Manager* 2. Technical Lead/Program Manager	**Stellar Role Model** 1. Level 5 Leader* 2. Customer focused Technical Expert* 3. Highly Respected Manager 4. Employee Role Model
B3	Willing to learn, prepared to work.	Have the general ability to cope with the demands of the job, but there is nothing spectacular about their performance.	Coming into their own, building the respect of their peers, and consistently banks their leadership currency. Operates with Noble Intent.	The typical 'go to' person and resource for tasks and deliverables.
B2	Not as motivated as they should be, not viewed as an invaluable employee. Managers often describe them as permission askers.	Just enough to get by, but not someone who other employees typically 'go to'.	Will get their work done, and they appear comfortable. But they will rarely if ever go above and beyond, or step outside their comfort zone.	Great ability, wonderful potential, but just frustrates the heck out of their managers! They need recognition, reminders, and tender loving care (all the time!)
B1	**Typical Entry Level Employee** Don't know what they don't know, but they beat out 450 candidates for the job!	Just enough knowledge to get themselves and the organization in trouble! Sometimes they are described as permission takers without adequate skills or understanding.	Core competencies acceptable, social skills not so much! Not the person you want taking the client out to dinner... Operates from a little bit of fear for their job, so their arrogance is curbed.	**Prima Donna** Highly Capable Individual (and do they know it!) Can be viewed as arrogant, exceptionally competent*

Performance Indexing – Competence leading to Promotability →

When you look at the Performance/Behavior Matrix charts in this section, you'll see why this Performance/Behavior Matrix Process is so important! If a coachee looks like they are at the B1 and B2 level, you can ascertain whether they are able to start to focus on setting their ego aside and take others into consideration (B3). The DISCflex Leadership Behavior Report and recommended eLearning help teach the coachee about their behavior, pattern, style, strengths, weaknesses, decision making style, and ways of looking at their situation. It details how their communication might affect others' opinions about them (B1). Coachees will also be able to invite others to take a 3rd Party Assessment about their behaviors to find out how others perceive them (B2). Using the self-perception hand-in-hand with the 3rd party assessment results, a coachee can get a better understanding of where they are today versus where they want to be tomorrow.

Performance/Behavior Matrix Case Study

OVERVIEW

Leadership Coaches often look for the quickest and most effective way to point a coachee in the 'right' direction for developing their leadership capabilities. With the limited amount of time, budget, and resources available, ramping the skills and capabilities of someone new to their leadership role is often a difficult task. Both the coachee and Leadership Coach recognize the importance of pulling up behavior and performing skills, and ideally the coachee is open to finding a solution most suitable to incorporating both of those concepts into their leadership arsenal and welcomes the input and feedback from the coaching sessions.

Looking at the Performance/Behavior Matrix, the Leadership Coach knows they have to motivate their coachee to two different points in the matrix (boxes) to grow their leadership acumen. As the coaching sessions progress, the Leadership Coach has to figure out how to leverage both the performing skills and behaviors of their coachee at appropriate points in their coachee's development. In particular, the Leadership Coach needs to track the coachee's development.

The Leadership Coach has to be systematic in their approach as they motivate their coachee toward the next level of leadership knowledge and growth. By using the Performance/Behavior Matrix as their guideline, the Leadership Coach can make an assessment, formulate a coaching plan, and track their coachee's progress. The goal is to have a series of orderly behavior and skills development moments that progress the coachee through the Performance/Behavior Matrix working towards the upper right-hand quadrant of the model. By incorporating the appropriate aspects of performing/skills and behavior, the Leadership Coach can track coachee's progress as they move farther up and to the right on the Performance/Behavior Matrix.

PROBLEM

In Leadership Behavior Coaching, the Leadership Coach consistently encounters four overarching difficulties while running their practice. It is best to try to overcome these so that you can run effective coaching sessions:

1. A lack of knowledge or training in behavior and skills.
2. Pricing and marketing skills and the time management skills to accomplish these.

3. Know-how in fleshing out coachee expectations incorporating a format for continued follow-up including checking accountability metrics.
4. Onboarding/starting new coachees with various start dates and different coaching needs.

Also, a Leadership Coach needs to plot where they want their coachees to be on the chart based on the coachee's willingness, skills, current behavior, and experience. Then, the Leadership Coach needs to plot where their coachees need to be in the appropriate time periods.

THE LEADERSHIP COACH HAS TO DECIDE:

- Should they work on adjusting coachee's behaviors first and then ramp up the performing aspect? Or vice versa?
- Is it actually possible to do both at the same time? Would the time be best spent working on both simultaneously?
- What are the pros/cons of each approach?
- Would you use the same coach/mentor, or can you ask for assistance from another source and/or require additional reading materials, a rotation, attending classes, etc. to supplement leadership efforts?
- What are your options?
- What are the appropriate timelines? How can we best track skills progress and behavioral progress (or lack thereof) against timeline expectations?

SOLVE

1. Based on your experience, what should the Leadership Coaching schedule look like to move the coachee to the top right corner of the Performance/Behavior Matrix?

2. What are some specifics that you could suggest moving a new coachee from P1B1 to P3B2 within one month of beginning the Coaching Program?

3. What are the consequences of moving a coachee to P4B1? To their supporter network, self, and peers they are friends with and/or working within their leadership efforts?

4. Using the Performance/Behavior Matrix, what suggestions could you make that might solve the cost, time, and knowledge gaps to fit a typical coachee's requirements?

_____

_____

> **Leadership is not about a title or a designation. It's about impact, influence and inspiration. Impact involves getting results, influence is about spreading the passion you have for your work, and you have to inspire team-mates and customers. -Robin S. Sharma**

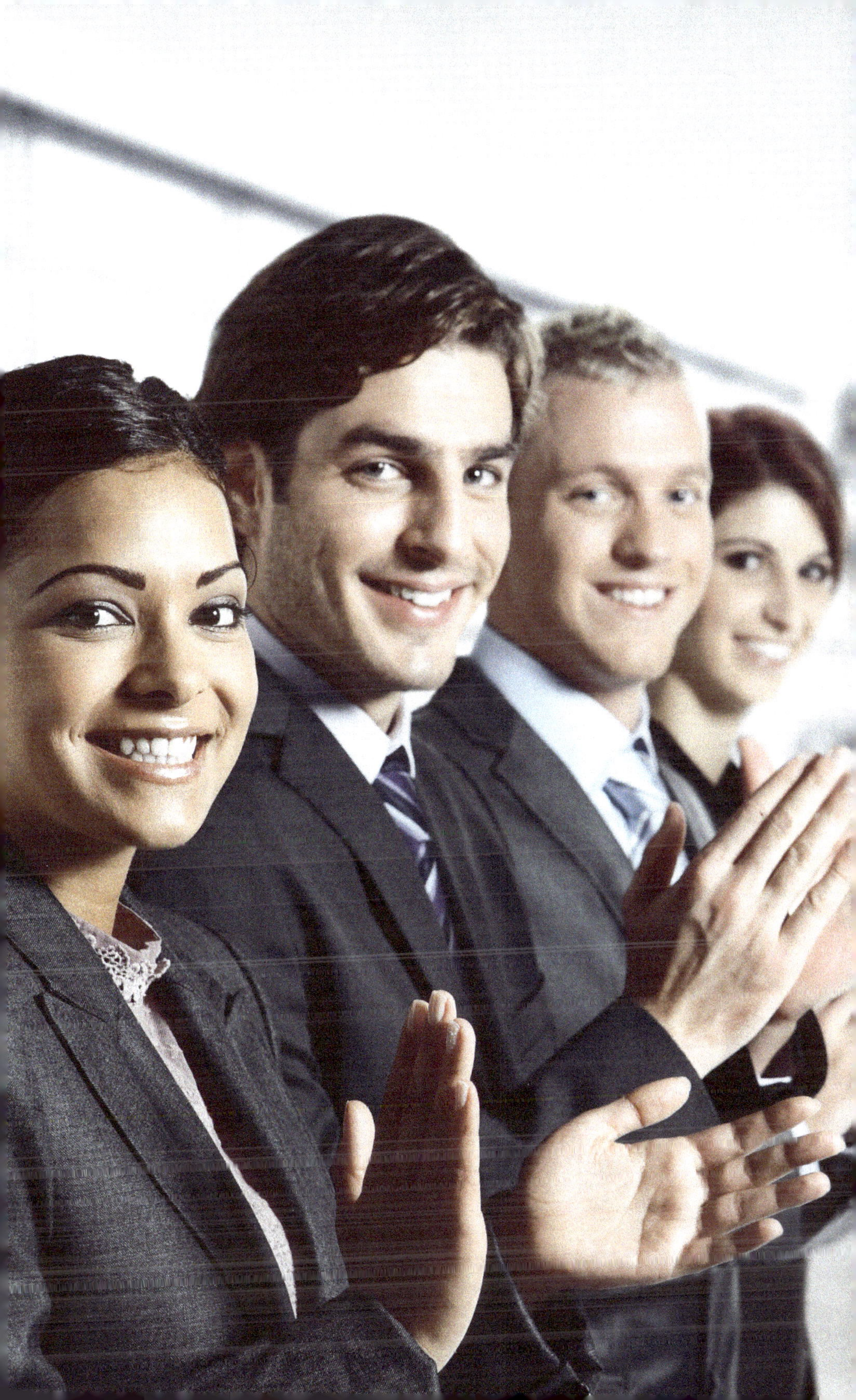

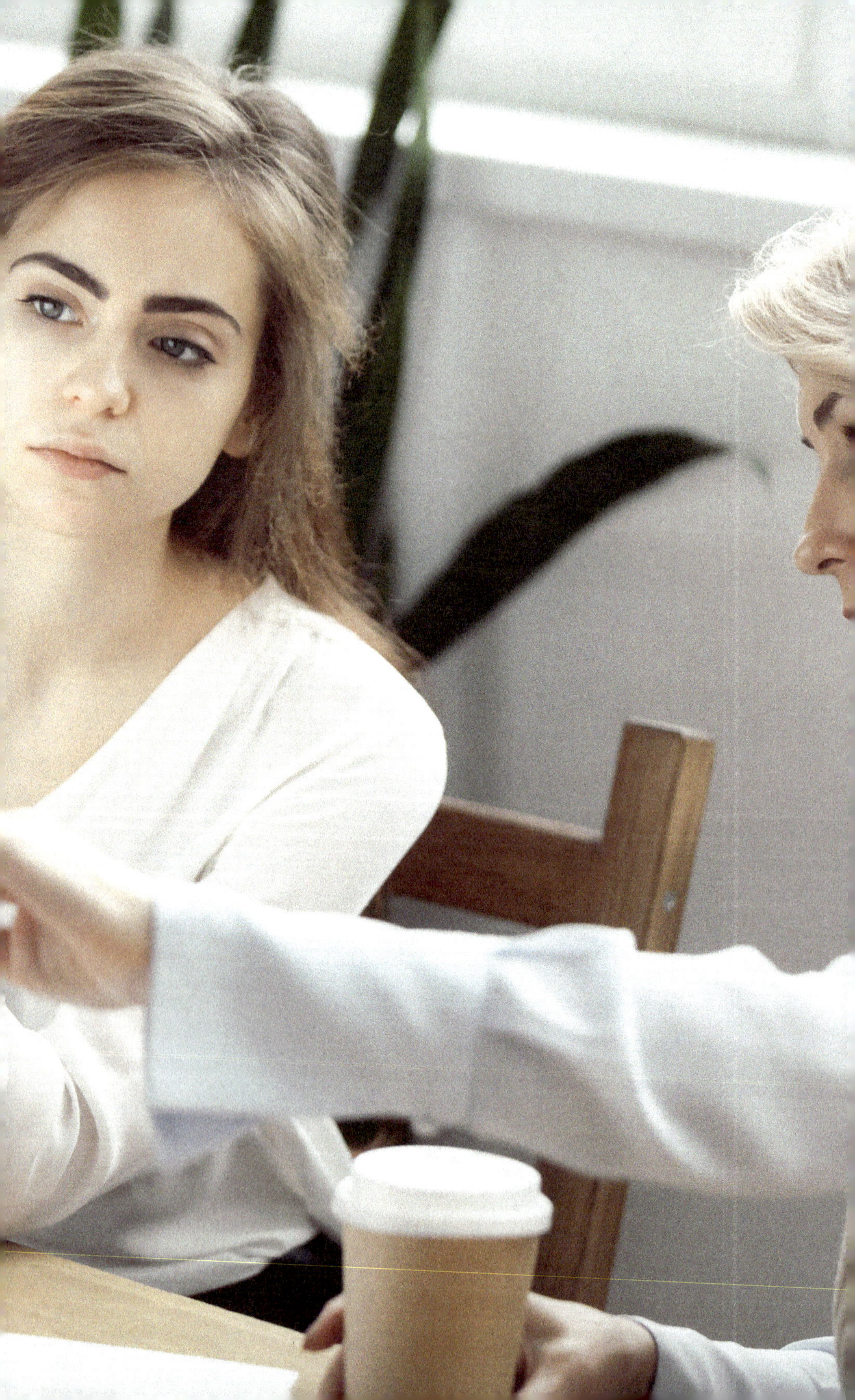

Communication During Leadership Behavior Coaching Sessions

Setting Up Great Communication

In the next segments, we will go over the communication skills required to be an effective coach include the capability to:

1. Pose effective questions.
2. Actively listen without judgment.
3. Provide feedback effectively that provokes thoughtful responses
4. Help the coachee work through meaningful goals leading to desired outcomes.
5. Hold the coachee accountable to their goals and promises

A few well-chosen or poorly-chosen words or posing the right question at just the right moment in a person's life, can transform their views, beliefs, goals and outcomes for the rest of their life.

During your coaching sessions, the roles of sender and receiver constantly shift. As soon as you send a message to your coachee, your expectation is that they will respond to you. The same happens when they speak. What is often misunderstood about the sender/receiver relationship is that there are no cut-and-dried lines of distinction between when you stop sending and begin receiving; and vice versa. In fact, you continue receiving communication from others even when you are sending out messages. Your senses are constantly picking up signals sent – body language, interruptions, etc. - even while you are speaking. When you are listening, you often can't help that your body signals responses through conscious or unconscious body language. Plus, when people interrupt each other, the lines between sender and receiver are blurred even further.

SO, WHAT DOES ALL THIS MEAN TO YOU AND THE PEOPLE TO COMMUNICATE WITH?

If you are sending or receiving a message during a coaching session, you need to make sure that your body language is supporting your intended communication.

It also means that your non-verbal communication can stand in the way of effective communication. You may be clear verbally about something, however, the coachee may not have accurately received the message. Why? Your body language (accompanying the verbal message) didn't lined up with your intent. Example: Delivering a tough message when you are slouching isn't desirable! Stand up straight and/or look serious-minded when you speak about thoughtful issues. The other person will see that you mean business!

This tells you that it is not just WHAT you say, but HOW you say it (our verbal inflection) that can make a huge difference when you communicate.

Coachee Perception Overrides Reality

Perception is how a person filters reality through their senses. In much communication, perception overrides reality. A coachee's experiences, beliefs and values provide the building blocks of their specific perception. Their stress level when they hear a message plays a part in how they interpret that communication. Sometimes, you'll shake your head, thinking: *"How could they possibly think that?"* The answer is either:

- They filtered your message through their perception; or
- Your filter and delivery skewed your intent. You thought you said something clearly but because of your filter, something went haywire.

Perception is how a person filters reality through their senses. In most communication, perception overrides reality.

During coaching sessions, it is extremely important to pay attention to the coachee - what they are *saying and doing* - and to have clarity on the context of the conversation and to assess what they are thinking. In relating to the coachee, you will be able to prepare what to say or do next. Whatever they think of your message, the other person will in turn respond to it - either in a positive or negative fashion. Keeping your antenna up, being vigilant about trying to see things from their perspective and trying to communicate as clearly as possible will go a long way in keeping communication lines open.

ASK THE RIGHT QUESTIONS

The Art of Asking Purposeful Questions

Pose Effective Questions

> What's been lost is expecting communication – especially questions - to be artful, playful, to have ambiguity, to have form, to be contemplative, to wish them to be profoundly and artfully crafted. Questions need to drill to the heart of the matter – with intention – with a result in mind. If a Leader or Leadership Coach wants people to remember their questions and come up with the proper responses, they'll have to understand that the questions they pose need to transcend the norm. Those important questions need to prod, inspire, motivate, discover truth and uncover thinking. When they do so, yes, they are ARTFULLY POSED! -Hellen Davis

WHY ASK QUESTIONS DURING COACHING SESSIONS?

> If you ask questions when trust is low and/or emotions are high, conversations can go badly.

Much of what a Leadership Coach does is observational. We watch and listen to coachee's signals. Much of this observation comes because of asking questions. Gathering information is a basic human activity. People use information to learn, help solve problems, assist in decision making, and to understand each other better. Questioning is the key to gaining more information and confirming what we already know.

The bottom line: Without effective questioning techniques, your coaching sessions are bound to be a lot less effective. We already know that if you ask questions when trust is low and/or emotions are high, conversations can go badly.

What is the purpose... Ask Questions to:

- **Maintain control of a conversation:** The person asking the questions is typically in control of the conversation. They set the pace, determine the direction, and bring up the topics under examination.
    - "How old were you when you first realized you had leadership qualities?"
    - "What type of friends/business people do you hang out with in your off-hours? Why did you gravitate to them? What do those different relationships provide?"

- "How is your relationship with each of your team members since you've made that announcement?"
- Explore the person's emotional state: It's often necessary to make the person aware of their emotional state. Bringing awareness through questions is a softer, and highly effective way of broaching the 'emotions' subject.
- "I noticed that when you told me about what Betty said, that your demeanor changed. What happened?"
- "Your stress level has elevated. What upset you in the last five minutes?"
- "How are you doing today, after the past few weeks of hyper-activity?"
- "What have you been working on behavior-wise since our last conversation? I know this was setting up to be an emotion-filled week for a few of your employees."

- **Obtain Information:** Gathering information provides a window into the coachee's thinking on a subject. It can tell you what path they're heading down, if they've put adequate (or appropriate) thought into something, or if they are ready to explore other options.
  - "Do you have a strategy to talk to David about his performance and the customer's feedback about his team? You said it was important to get your feedback right so that he doesn't get so upset that he'll leave, correct? You mentioned that every time you've given him this type of feedback, within four weeks he's in your office saying he's interviewing either internally or with

another company. You said you wanted to address his sensitivity about receiving objective feedback and were going to rehearse before you delivered. Are you ready?"
- "When did you first realize you might be in trouble with this project?"

- **Seek clarification and/or reduce misunderstandings:** Perception and filtering skew understanding. Asking clarifying questions is vital to get people on the same page.
    - "Could I take a moment to ask you what you meant when you said that you had never seen a team member put in as much time and effort but fail at delivering what you asked for? Can we take a few moments to step through what might have happened?"
    - "I thought I heard you say that you were feeling badly that you hadn't spoken to John. Isn't John the guy you were thinking about promoting? Isn't he your high potential project lead who is in NYC? What is going through your head about wanting to talk to him but not actually taking the time to call him?"

- **Express an interest:** You can open up further conversations about a subject if you show interest by asking a follow-up question.
    - "That's interesting. Can you tell me more about it?"
    - "So, you enjoyed working through your annual review and next year's strategy deck? You said it gave you some kind of mental release. Can you tell me more about why you enjoyed this so much?"

- **Assist someone:** Many people never ask for help, but if asked if they'd accept it, they will.
    - "Can I help you work through that activity/thinking?"
    - "Can I provide a bit of insight into what might be going on here?"
    - "Can I help out by walking you through some steps that might clarify things?"
    - "Would it relieve your burden a bit if I just sat and listened?
    - "Can I ease your mind by saying that it's ok? Lots of people go through things like this"
    - "Does it make you feel any better knowing that you're not alone in this?"
    - "What might improve your state of mind or stress levels and how can other people help you?"

- **Encourage Participation:** Coaching sessions can be stressful, and some coachees shut down. Questions can help a coachee open up. Take care to monitor the coachee's stress level when posing questions. Many find answering questions about themselves very stressful. Make certain to watch for signs that the coachee isn't feeling too uncomfortable, embarrassed, frustrated, or awkward. You might find that sometimes leaders don't like to get called out or held accountable for doing what they agreed to do in coaching sessions. As your coaching sessions progress and trust goes up, these emotions will most likely lessen.
    - "What about taking a facilitator role in your next leadership offsite? I think this will be a good way to work on your communication goals. What do you think?"
    - "I've noticed that you shut down whenever I ask about

what happened with your boss. I realize your relationship with her hasn't been great because your team's numbers are way down. I know this is stressful. But this is a safe place for those discussions. Do you know that sometimes, by just starting to get things out in the open, they don't seem quite as bad? How can we start the ball rolling on getting this out on the table and coming up with some options to fix this situation or at least open up the communication between you and her?"

- **Gain trust or Build Rapport:** People love to have something in common with those they confide in. Asking questions to establish common interests, experiences, work-life, habits, ways of looking at life, locations, or linkages in interests might be an effective gateway to building these.
    - "I didn't know you were from Buffalo, too. When did you leave there? Where did you go to school? Did you start work there? Are your family members still in the area?"
    - "I was in the IT department, too! Who was heading it up while you were there? What big projects did you help with?"
    - "I like history, too. What kind of history do you find most fascinating?"
    - "My right-hand, Jill, loves putting sales and marketing materials together. I've always admired creative minds. I saw the slide deck your team put together for the annual conference. I asked Susan who was behind it and she said it was all your inspiration. Where do you think you got your creative talent from? How did you learn to get complex ideas across to everyone so well?"

- **Test knowledge**: Quizzes, examinations, and pointed questions about the grasp a coachee has on subject matter knowledge is a fundamental in coaching sessions. You cannot effectively move forward in a coaching discussion if you aren't on the same page with a concept, model or theory.
    - "Are you familiar with Perceptual Prisms?"
    - "Do you know much about Maslow's Pyramid of Motivation?"
    - "Have you looked at how your project manager is running his operation in terms of the Decision-Making Matrix? You keep saying that he seems like a fire fighter, always high energy and gets the job done, but burning out his team. Do you think it might be because he isn't proactive enough in making decisions ahead of the curve?"
    - "Have you ever heard of the Performance/Behavior Matrix?"

- **Inspire deeper thought:** A question may be posed to encourage a coachee to think about something at a deeper level or to have them contemplate a topic in a new way.
    - "Learning more about decision making actually makes you better at making decisions. Studies show that reading one or two articles on that particular subject is often enough to change thought processes. Isn't that fascinating?"
    - "Why do you think it important to stop traveling so much and letting your direct reports step up in this area? Besides having them forge stronger relationships with their coachees, have you thought about the secondary and tertiary benefits to them and the coachees? There's some interesting links between seeing people in person,

breaking bread over a business discussion and coachee retention numbers for teams. I wonder if it might be beneficial to track retention and also add on business? I would think that a comparison to last year's numbers, when your folks were not 'meeting and greeting', when it was only you on the road with coachee meetings – that might be very interesting."

- **Get the coachee 'out of the weeds':** People can get wrapped around the axel and stuck in the weeds if they can't rise above any inconsequential trifling matters, minutia, or get away from the details.
    - "Have you looked at the Urgent versus Important Model? From what you are saying, you're seemingly still mired in a lot of the details of running your department. Has anyone ever accused you of micromanaging?"

LEADERS AND COACHES AREN'T PERFECT, AND BOTH CAN JUMP TO CONCLUSIONS

Before we continue, it's important to consider that leaders and coaches are human and therefore, are not perfect. We have to allow for people's inclination to naturally jump to conclusions. Conclusions are like butterflies escaping from your subconscious.

We have to consider that we may be prone to letting assumptions cloud our thinking; no matter how hard we try not to. *How do we steer clear of doing this? How do we contain the butterflies before they take flight?* Instead of closing off dialog, which may prevent important information from surfacing, we can ask more questions that are designed to uncover facts and discover intentions. Equally important, we can learn what types of biases tend to make people jump to conclusions and try to recognize when these might be in play.

CONFIRMATION BIAS

One of the prejudices that comes into play when you jump to conclusions is a **cognitive bias** called Confirmation Bias. Confirmation Bias is the tendency for you to search for or interpret information in a way that **confirms your preconceptions, deductions, reasonings,**

guesses, logical interpretations, and ways you think things should happen. Confirmation Bias results in behaviors where people seek substantiation for the things they believe (or want to believe).

Confirmation bias is as old as man. Looking back to when people thought the world was flat: If you think the world is flat, you won't send your ships too far west or east past where you know is safe. You'll argue your point with the fact that many ships that ventured too far never returned. Every time you hear of a ship long past due, you'll think it fell of the Earth into the abyss. A more modern example: If you think you'll die on an airplane, you won't fly. You'll point to every plane crash as proof that this form of travel is unsafe.

As a leader, you may form a notion about why something keeps happening on your team. Imagine that people are consistently non-cooperative. You've commented that people aren't sharing resources, information or playing nicely in the sandbox. You've decided it is because you have the wrong leaders in place. If confirmation bias is in play inside your head, you'll seek evidence that confirms your suspicions about certain people, while ignoring data or other inputs that contrary to your view. You may point to a three-question survey that shows morale is down 3 points, blaming this slump on your leaders, ignoring that fact that your firm recently lost its largest customer, decreasing revenues by 6%. If you ignore the effects of your confirmation bias, you may incorrectly attribute root cause. The consequence: You'll address issues and attempt to fix things using methods that aren't on point.

DIFFICULT TO DETECT

Confirmation bias is difficult to detect if you're not on guard looking for its presence. Even if you don't actively seek this type of confirming evidence out, your ears will perk up or you'll get excited when something pops up to confirm your thoughts or suspicions. Or you might give more weight or credence to input than you should if that input checks a box you wanted to check. If you are a leader who does this, team members will recognize it, and will please you by bringing you things that you want to see or hear, and they'll keep information away from you that displeases you. This pleasing of the leader might not be malicious or happen on the conscious level. Many don't realize this behavior can happen at the subconscious level, when people are in sync or have a high level of trust.

When Confirmation Bias is in play in a team setting, an individual will seek ways to put proof of their views in front of those they are trying to influence. This is dangerous for the leader if a team member is skewing inputs or giving too much weight to assumptions because of their confirmation bias. Their goal is that this proof (or information) they are providing will sway others toward their way of thinking. Unfortunately, the dark side of Confirmation Bias requires agreement from others to proceed in the direction of that influencer's goals. It doesn't do any good for the individual if nobody else agrees with them or confirms their views. The risk here is that the person using Confirmation Bias will only provide the facts that substantiate their views. The consequences can be quite interesting and costly. Here are some examples of what might occur:

- The person might steer people away from opportunities that are in actual fact best by swaying decision makers' perceptions. How? They only provide information to discount that opportunity. They skew the numbers away from the best opportunity. If successful in to what they believe is the course of action to be followed, the firm will have substantial lost opportunity costs. Unfortunately, these are rarely taken into consideration in an after-action review. You should never make this mistake!

- They might endorse hires or discount great candidates by voicing invalid concerns.

- The influencer may ignore other's inputs or ideas, shouting them down whenever they run contrary to their thinking. The long-term costs of this behavior are dire. People just give up talking if they are faced with going up against this person in the future.

- By controlling the agenda, they may not even let those inputs be heard at all. By presenting information in a Confirmation Biased state, they might be able to stop forward progress on current initiatives.

LEADERSHIP CONFIRMATION BIAS

Equally dangerous is when a leader ignores or discounts inputs that fly in the face of what that leader currently thinks. When you ignore or disregard information because of confirmation bias, you run the risk of that information coming to light later. If someone who is holding you accountable up the chain of command discovers this, they will call your judgment into question. If you discount contrary information, giving more weight to things that buoy up your position, how will that look? Leader-like? Opinionated? Ill-informed? Stubborn? Inflexible?

Confirmation bias in a leader or leadership team is particularly threatening to team dynamics. If the leader only respects information that corroborates their views, that is precisely what team members will give them. Providing anything that runs counter to this might be viewed as politically risky or as a career-killing move. Think about it from the person's viewpoint who doesn't agree: Why tell the Emperor he has no clothes when the risks far outweigh the rewards? But any leader worth their weight knows that hidden information and facts and data are going to surface. It's just a matter of time! If decisions are made on 'bad' information, it's the leader's fault for not checking against assumptions, facts, and biases. The risks of confirmation bias fall squarely at the feet of the leader.

THE CURE OF CONFIRMATION BIAS

- Question why you might become excited or pleased with certain information popping up.
- Ask why people are holding back certain data.
- Enquire about the depth and breadth of information people are feeding you.
- Request that an unbiased third-party weigh in or review the inputs.
- Mandate that several sources validate any critical information.
- Review the assumptions matrix before finalizing decisions.
- Demand that information, no matter how bad, be brought to you in a timely fashion.

Side Effects of Not Asking Enough Questions

As leaders and coaches, we always have to remember that a side effect of not asking enough questions is a breakdown of process. When this occurs, it means flawed thinking can enter the coaching sessions. Too few questions being asked might mean there's incomplete analysis. This may result in less than desirable decision-making. With decision making that is questionable, actions and deliverables aren't lined up. Why did this happen? Because people jumped to judgment, leapt to conclusions too fast, or didn't think to probe just a little bit more. If you are coming at this from a leadership perspective: Targeted intention-based questions are vitally important to the integrity of the organization. From a coaching perspective: Your responsibility is to probe, ask, uncover, examine, and question.

Great leaders and awesome coaches take the time to figure out how to ask better questions. They are purposeful and respectful simultaneously. They slow down and listen. Then they ask follow-up questions for clarification. In this way, the coachee can learn how to come to better conclusions.

JUST AS IMPORTANT, QUESTIONS SAVE TIME. THEY HELP TO LESSEN CONFLICT.

If you haven't asked the appropriate questions in a timely manner, you'll only have to circle back to them later. If you've launched into action without probing about the deliverables, resources, team members, and/or processes you most likely are going to force yourself into conflict. To some it seems counterintuitive to ask more questions up front, potential surfacing unpleasantness, disagreements, and the like (e.g. at the beginning of a project) when everyone is excited and motivated. But the reason is probably that they don't like asking questions. Period!

> One thing is for sure, when things go bad, if you don't talk about things up front, the discussions won't nearly be as pleasant. Another thing is just about guaranteed: Tensions are going to be higher than had you proactively asked relevant questions.

Knowing this, wouldn't it make sense to poke at plans before anyone starts them?

Doesn't it make sense to question the direction, make sure that everything is in sync and that things have been properly vetted and thought through? Wouldn't this be wise? Wouldn't it save some careers? Wouldn't it be better to lend some advice, offer suggestions or speak bluntly about the consequences you might see before people get themselves in trouble? Mightn't some great questions posed upfront surface concerns that might save someone a bit of embarrassment? And possibly a tone of wasted efforts? As far as the bottom line: Wouldn't this save money, too?

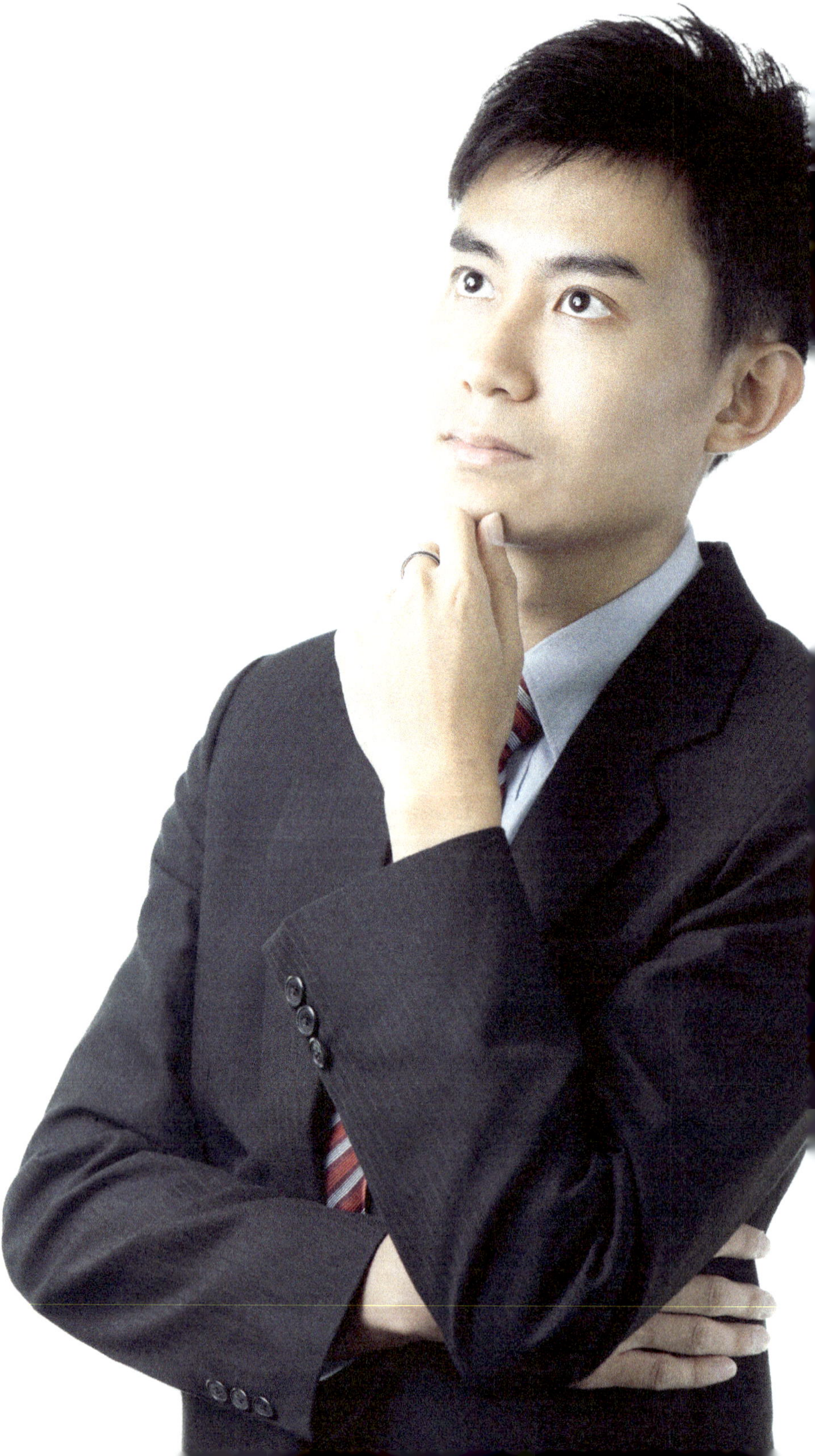

Responses to Questions

> I question everything. I even question why I am considering asking the question. I think about the response I might be provoking from the other person. When I respond, I think not only about my response, but of the intention of the questioner and their reaction. That's when communication starts to be truly effective.

There are a variety of questioning techniques. It stands to reason there must also be a number of ways a coachee can respond. One of the first discussions we recommend you have with coachees is to go over the concept of how people respond to questions. We suggest that you go over each point, then discuss the various responses and their pros and cons in detail. Specifically view the consequences in the light of leadership efforts, enhancing and/or damaging relationships, and impact the various responses have on the coachee's Self-Talk and decision making.

A COACHEE CAN PROVIDE A RESPONSE THAT IS A/AN:

- **Honest and direct response:** The truth is the Ideal answer, especially during coaching sessions.

- **Partially Answering:** Coachees may give an incomplete, limited, biased, one-sided, or be selective about which questions or parts of questions they prefer to respond to. Perhaps the coachee does this to appear 'better' than they think others views them. Maybe this is a pattern of behavior. Possibly the coachee is guilty but they could very well be embarrassed, ill at ease, proud, humiliated, shy, uncomfortable, nervous, or self-conscious and that is the reason they feel they cannot disclose everything. Whatever the case, a Leadership Coach must probe and get to the bottom of the issue. Full, honest, forthright answers are the goal. Any of the reasons previously listed run counter to leadership efforts. Authentic responses require that the coachee move forward through their discomfort. In all instances, it requires being:
  - Trustworthy
  - Genuine
  - Realistic
  - Accurate
  - Dependable
  - Reliable
  - Authentic
  - Truthful

- **Stalling:** Although similar to avoiding answering a question, coachees can use stalling when they don't want to respond right now. They'll also use stalling tactics when they need a bit more time to put together an acceptable answer. This isn't always a negative. Sometimes a coach has to allow for this.

- **Misunderstanding/Out of context:** The coachee may not understand the intent or context of the question. As such, they may respond with words that are disconnected or irrelevant to the question. It may be appropriate to rephrase your question or come at the topic in another way in these cases.

- **Skewing by Using the Numbers:** Using statistical evidence to inflate, skew, sensationalize, confuse, or diminish isn't new. But the ways data can be sliced and diced in many ways to 'tell the story'. Statistics can lead people to lose insight rather than gain it. "A well-wrapped statistic can mislead, but it can rarely be pinned on the person using the data."

- **Refusal:** The coachee can refuse to answer, either by remaining silent or by saying, 'I am not answering'.
    - "I'd rather not talk about that."
    - "Reliving what's happened is too painful."
    - "Can we move on to something else now?"
    - "Why do we have to go there? I'm really not going to tell you that stuff because I promised someone I wouldn't."

- **Lies that are Technically Truths:** Two forms of lying that most often occur in corporate settings and in coaching sessions are 1. willful omission and 2. paltering (skew perception in their favor). Some people use these as a self-preservation strategy because in their minds, they're telling the truth (allowing distorted perception) or not actually lying because they aren't saying something untruthful (willful omission). So, they think they're being honest. Make no mistake, it's all about intention to deceive to make something happen in their favor. People who do this might need an immediate reminder about what it feels like to be on the other side of a lie of omission or paltering. Anyone deceived in this manner will simply think the other person is being just as dishonest as if they lied outright to their faces.

- **Willful Omission:** Lying by omission happens when a person purposefully leaves out important information or fails to correct a misconception in order to hide the truth. Their rationale: "But I didn't lie. I just didn't tell you." Coaching discussion: "Leon, I thought you discussed this matter with your team leader, Joseph, last week. I assumed you and the others were ok with meeting on Thursday just after lunchtime. You said you liked that time. I just got a text from Joseph asking why I am insisting our meeting happen then. And they're asking why the meeting can't happen either early morning or late in the afternoon because it's smack dab in the middle of the work day and they think it's pain to get over here just because it's my meeting. They also wanted to know if I can't switch the time, since it's only me from this side, can I go to your offices? The truth is, I blocked off time and rescheduled a few other meetings to accommodate your request. It wasn't my requirement to meet when you wanted. Why would both of us be wondering what happened here?" Leon responds: "Well, I didn't tell Joseph that you made the schedule. When I told him the meeting time and venue, he just assumed. And I didn't tell you that I couldn't meet at any other times, I just said I liked meeting right after lunch. I didn't lie about it at all!" Coaching discussion: "Ok, Leon, that's technically true, but you weren't forthcoming either. The result is that Joseph thinks my scheduling and my demands are upsetting their work scheduling. They all now think I'm being unreasonable. You gave them that impression about me, when it's really you. Do you understand how that might happen when you didn't let either of us into the picture? I think you just wanted to leave work for a break midday. I know so many hours at that pace haven't been good for your stress levels. I get it, but de-facto lying by omission to get something only you wanted isn't good for the team. We agreed on honesty and transparency. Weren't you worried one of us would question this? What are your actions to fix this misunderstanding and get us back on track? It's not really my job to fix this, but I can assure you that I'll make sure that everything is cleared up as much as it can for my reputation."

- **Paltering:** Paltering is a form of deception that happens when a person makes statements that are technically true but are purposely uttered to skew perception or to mislead. When a coachee is paltering, they know they're giving a false or distorted impression, even if they're telling the truth. "Leon, how far did you get on that report for the accounting department?" Leon palters: "I actually enjoyed setting everything up and reading the budget section on Forward Strategies (which he knows is towards the end of the reading materials). I think the timelines are short for getting it out the door, but very doable." In this instance, Leon has only skimmed through the materials and has not yet started on the meat of the report! But he is technically not lying. If you find this occurring, ask for verification.

- **Distortion and exaggeration:** Coachees may give distorted answers to questions based on their perceptions of social norms, stereotypes, the culture they grew up in, the influences of other people in their life, their experiences, to make themselves look good, to avoid situations, and/or other forms of slanted decision making, prejudices, or biases. Distortion is a bit unlike outright lying because coachees may not realize their answers are influenced by thought patterns that are skewed or biased. As an example, coachees might not realize they are exaggerating. Exaggeration is a form of distortion. When coachees use exaggeration, they are trying to skew perception of who they are, what they've accomplished/done, or where they came from. One of the more common is to inflate resumes or accomplishments. Whether the person exaggerates or distorts perception to come across as more 'normal' or successful is irrelevant. What is relevant is that they are not being forthright, honest, or authentic. The reasons they are using distortion or exaggerating should be a topic of discussion.

- **Untruth or Lie:** No one enjoys calling people out for lying. Being called a liar is one of the most insulting things you can say to another. But studies show that lying is a normal and fairly regular behavior. People lie for a variety of reasons. It would be so simple if there was only one reason for lying! To compound the complexity of dealing with lies, most of us receive conflicting messages about lying. On one hand, we're told that it's always better to tell the truth, in reality society often encourages and even rewards deception. Show up late for an early morning meeting at work? It's best not to admit to your boss that you were out partying the night before and overslept. So, you'll lie, saying you were stuck in traffic – a bold-faced lie. Unfortunately, deception and lying is essential to many occupations. Lawyers construct barely plausible theories on behalf of their coachees. Police say things that might not be revealing to suspects to get at the truth. Reporters and bail bondsmen misrepresent themselves to gain access. Negotiators don't provide facts they know might result in better outcomes for the other side. A Leadership Coach must anticipate this. The best way to uncover the truth and discover lies is to ask probing questions and maintain a safe and trust-filled environment for your coaching sessions.

- **Avoiding the answer:** When asked a 'difficult or tough question' which probably has an answer that would shed a potential negative on the coachee, they choose to wiggle out of answering. They make the choice to evade or sidestep the request for truthful information rather than being frank, open, straightforward, forthcoming, or authentic. A word of warning is important: When subordinates are questioned by people in authority, strange things happen in a person's mind… Some are more honest, some hide things more. When coachees try to avoid answering, a Leadership Coach has to probe why. Avoiding asking the tough questions and appropriate follow-ups is a recipe for failing in your leadership efforts.

Discovery or Confirmation – What's the purpose of your question?

The first consideration when you ask questions is to decide if your question's purpose is to:

1. discover new information
2. confirm or disprove your assumptions or what you suspected.

Regardless of whether you are using questioning for discovery or confirmation, the knowledge you get from the coachee's response is telling. In this you are somewhat of a Leadership Coach detective.

IT IS BEST TO CONSIDER THESE STEPS TO MAKE SURE YOU STAY ON TRACK:

1. Review new information to effectively deduce value and meaning. Get supplemental insight from as many sources as possible.
2. Reference existing and supplementary facts if available.
3. Establish significance and relevance of new information.
4. Determine how the context of this information changes any prior understandings, promises, or undertakings. *Ask:* "Does this new input change the intentions, meaning or situations?"
5. Derive new ways of thinking/different approaches from the information. Figure out the consequences and impacts (if any).
6. Have the coachee determine if any decisions need to be adjusted or made. Have the coachee offer suggestions or recommendations from the resulting knowledge.

NEW INFORMATION

When your coachee provides you with additional knowledge, you have to allow for this information to meld (assimilate) with what you already know. But before you do that, you should confirm the new information is factual, has merit, or is relevant. During coaching sessions, the purpose of any information is to turn what you know into something useful. **This is called actionable intelligence.**

NEW INFORMATION CRITERIA

New information should be viewed as useful for **three general purposes**:

1. Leads to an increase in understanding.
2. Steers toward a decrease in uncertainty.
3. Can be used for better decision making.

The **litmus test** for new information should be that it is:

1. Accurate and timely,
2. Specific and organized for a purpose,
3. Presented within a context that gives it meaning and relevance.

Information is valuable because it can affect behavior, a decision, or an outcome. A piece of information is considered valueless if, after receiving it, things remain unchanged. The intelligence did not produce *action*.

Example: If a coachee learns that her company's net profit decreased in the past month, she may use this information as a reason to become anxious about their future financial stability. But because the woman took no action to address the problem, the information was tantamount to value-less. New information without positive change is a tad above useless. In this example, if she does nothing, her anxiety will most certainly increase until newer information enters.

Deciding that worrying isn't proactive, the woman might decide to spruce up the company's brand identity, increase marketing efforts, look at the monthly departmental spending, and/or just instruct a team member to keep their finger in the wind looking for other financial changes in the company before she does her final decision making. In this way, she's made progress because she used the information to take corrective action. She's keeping ahead of the game and keeping her stress in check.

The new information in this example propels positive action. But be warned, not all action is necessarily good nor will lead to a positive outcome. Using intelligence to inform great decision making is important.

> Prudent decision making most often leads to positive outcomes.

NEW INFORMATION AND UNCERTAINTY

New Information can resolve uncertainty. This is a powerful concept in coaching. If your coachee is displaying signs of anxiety, new targeted information can lessen their angst. Information is powerful because when people feel confident, they'll tend to act on information sooner than if they are unsure of the facts.

On the flip side, getting new information means that you might uncover something that initially increases worry. But as a leader, having knowledge is typically better than being blindsided. The best thing to decrease stress and worry is to put together a strategy and execute with discipline. Use the information to drive action and behavior.

EXAMPLES OF NEW INFORMATION QUESTIONS:

"Joe, do you think it might be good to check on whether what you're thinking is going to happen, is actually true? You appear to be wondering if one or another of the Executive Team will be at the awards dinner. Why don't you just ask if they will. It's not very productive to spend your time wringing your hands over whether they'll be there or not. If they won't be there, you can rest easy. If they will be there, let's talk through a strategy to get you through the presentation you and your team will put together. Perhaps it might help to put a different spin on this: You did say you wanted to get more exposure. This might be the perfect opportunity, even though you might think it's too soon because the product still has bugs. You can use this opportunity to address the issues head-on and speak to how these painful fixes will positively impact the future of the organization. Everyone in your sector has faced the exact same issues, and you're ahead of them in the marketplace. You can certainly highlight this. How does that sound? Like a logical thing for you to do?"

SEEKING OUT NEW INFORMATION

In the example of a decrease in company profits, if the company posted profits the following month, the information provides the answer to the questions that may have been bouncing around in the coachee's head about the future. Technically, the uncertainty of any event is measured by its probability of occurrence. The more information a person has about that probability, the better able they are to assess the risk – to themselves and others. The more uncertain an event, the more information is required to resolve uncertainty of that event.

In terms of DISC Factors, behavior plays an impressive role in how people handle uncertainty. For example:

- The higher the Dominance Factor, the quicker people will react.
- The higher the Influence Factor, the more team members will tend to want to have meetings to talk things through.
- The higher a person's natural Steadiness/Strategy Factor, the more certainty (or contingency strategies) they'll require to remain stress-free.
- The higher the Compliance Factor, the more people will look at planning impacts.

EXAMPLES OF NEW INFORMATION QUESTIONS:

Dana, based on what's come to light, what changes do you think you need to make this week in your communication with your technical lead?

Alex, now that you know who'll be at the presentation, how do you think you should dress? How do you think you should act? What do you think are some things you should say to help your leadership view you and your team in the best possible light? What are some things you should do or say in the presentation to find out what the CIO thinks of your efforts thus far?

Facts versus Assumptions: Confirm or Disprove What You Thought

One of the characteristics of a great Leadership Coach is their skill in distinguishing between facts and assumptions. Another is being able to educate their coachees about how assumptions impact them and their organizations.

FACTS

Facts are something known or proven to be true. Facts are confirmation of things that actually occurred.

ASSUMPTIONS

An assumption is what a person *thinks is correct* or *anticipates* being correct in the future. You can make an assumption expecting proof, or not. An example: People might make the assumption that you're a nerd if you wear glasses, even though that's not true. You might make the assumption that an employee will tell the truth. People make assumptions that others will deal with them in good faith. Assumptions are the basis of trust. **Warning:** In Leadership Coaching sessions, assumptions need confirmation before decisions are locked down.

Assumptions aren't bad in and of themselves. It's a Leadership Coach's or coachee's reliance on them that cause problems. Let's face it. There is no way we can possibly know everything about our coachees, nor can they know everything about the people they work with either. We actually spend very little time with others in relation to their entire life. **Therefore, Leadership Coaches and their coachees have to make assumptions.**

Making assumptions and figuring out if they are accurate is a natural process of being human and of decision making. The better you are at asking questions, they better you'll be at deciphering assumption versus fact. Because people like certainty, your mind will spin as it continually checks assumptions against facts and data getting to a place it feels comfortable with the assumptions you are making. If you or the people you are dealing with are too uncomfortable to ask the appropriate questions to reveal facts versus assumptions, or they are unwilling to do so, you'll have a big problem here. Sometimes it takes tough questions and courage to complete the information gathering about assumptions. Furthermore, your personal satisfaction level is key. Some people are natural doubters. They'll require a lot of certainty and more facts and verification before they make decisions, much less act on assumptions. Others act on their hunches routinely without doing much checking at all. The best leaders understand this and monitor the level of assumption making they'll do in various situations.

What is the barometer of appropriate assumptions for individuals?

- Tolerance for risk (personal and for their team/organization).
- Value or importance they place on the decision and/or outcome (important versus non-important).

- Timeliness of the decision they must make (urgent versus non-urgent).

HOW DO ASSUMPTIONS BEGIN?

It's normal to make assumptions. People have to make assumptions. Why? Because you'll rarely have a complete set of facts and data. In the absence of complete information, you have to fill in the blanks yourself to:

- Make sense of the situation,
- Make educated guesses about what might happen, and/or
- Make the best decision you can, given what you currently know.

Your perception plays a huge part in how you make assumptions. As you know, perception comes from what you are sensing is happening, combined with what your Self-Talk is saying. Your Self-Talk filters through the prism of your rational brain as well as your emotional self. It looks at past experience as a guide to what will happen. It looks for common ground and similar events to forecast what will happen. If a conversation with team members typically go well, that's what you'll expect this time: Good discussions and respectful interacts. If they didn't, you won't.

> The worst thing about making assumptions is that it can become a bad habit. The more you make assumptions, the easier it is to continue making them.

ASSUMPTIONS CAN BE WRONG.

Rationally, we are warned that the past doesn't necessarily predict the future, but we need patterns and consistency to process events and make decisions about how to behave. When we lack all the information, we look back to move forward. We rely on the assumption that what happened before is likely to repeat. Make no mistake, assumptions keep you stuck in the past. Assumptions rely on old information to fill in blanks and connect dots. Instead of expanding your horizons, you take sanctuary in the past. You go with the path of least resistance thinking this is the safer bet, but in reality, this strategy kills innovation and limits your choices.

MAKING ASSUMPTIONS IS LAZY BEHAVIOR.

When your mind doesn't have enough information, you connect the dots. You fill in the blanks. Your mind will do this regardless of you instructing that it shouldn't. You essentially have to make assumptions to run through 'what ifs'. Contingency planning requires that you look at different scenarios based on various assumptions. However, if rather than asking questions to get the information you need or digging to verify your suppositions, you let the assumptions continue until forced to make decisions; this will eventually get you in trouble, no matter how great your leadership or decision-making track record.

Additionally, if you jump to conclusions right away, or 'going with your gut'; skipping the whole cumbersome 'verifying thing'; this is also problematic. In the best-case scenario, your assumptions bear out. In the worst case, you'll jump to conclusions that are completely incorrect, with no basis in facts and data and absolutely no bearing on the reality of the situation. You can easily see why you should think very carefully about the risks versus rewards whenever you use an unconfirmed assumption to make a decision. This is something that any leader should be disciplined in doing.

LEADERSHIP BEHAVIOR COACHING REQUIRES LOOKING AT ASSUMPTIONS VERSUS FACTS AND DATA.

As a Leadership Coach, when you start to figure out who the coachee is, where they came from, what experiences they had, how best to help them in their leadership efforts, you're on the road to simultaneously making assumptions and trying to figure out the truth and facts. It is what it is. Make two columns in your head when putting the pieces together: One for facts and data you've verified, the other for assumptions. Your mantra must be: Assume, then Confirm!

> Always assume that the basis of your actions and decision making will have to withstand an after-action review. If you keep this in the back of your mind, you'll look at the assumptions you're making a bit more. Therefore, you'll be willing to ask the tough questions required.

RECOGNIZING ASSUMPTIONS

Once you label something as an assumption, you have a discussion to determine its impact on your coachee's ability to work the process and follow through with their responsibilities and commitments. If you are not sure if something is a fact, it's an assumption until you prove it otherwise. You must ask questions to resolve assumption versus facts. This is often a very tough thing to do. It may take a while and there might be some uncomfortable moments. It might take some digging. But it must be done. Go back to the list entitled: Why Ask Questions During Coaching Sessions? With this list in hand, view it through the lens of confirming assumptions.

A word of warning: If you don't realize something is an assumption, it will not cross your mind to confirm it. This is dangerous! New and experienced coaches and leaders alike will make this mistake until they realize how critical this concept is. But the reasons may be different. New coaches may not know enough to have a thorough understanding of the organization's environment or a significant understanding of situations their coachees might be dealing with. This is also difficult for experienced Leadership Coaches because, "Hey, I've seen it all. I know exactly what this coachee needs. Been there, done that!"

How to best guard against assumptions clouding your coaching sessions?

Assume everything you know is an assumption! Then, test your assumptions by asking questions to verify information. Continually check yourself.

ASK YOURSELF:

- "How do I know this?"
- "How have I verified this?"
- "Where is the source of this information?"
- "Has anything changed since I first uncovered these facts?"

Learn to question with Broad-based Questions, then drill down with Detail-based Questions until the assumptions are confirmed. This leads you to ask better and more meaningful questions as your coaching relationship matures. The more you practice this the better you will become. Remember, the hardest part about unearthing the facts versus what you are guessing to be true, is recognizing what assumptions you are making. You cannot make suggestions, walk the coachee through the process of formulating a strategy or plan, or the like, based on guesses. *Guesses (hopefully educated!) are precisely what most assumptions are.*

HOW DO YOU STOP MAKING ASSUMPTIONS?

If you start to assume something, recognize you are doing so. Knowing that assumptions are a natural part of business life, embrace that. However, you have to check assumptions, especially ones that involve substantial decision-making risk. Your job is to ask questions. Lots of them. Before making any decision, check the veracity of any assumptions. Even if this means finding out a truth that might be painful to hear.

NIP THE UNCONSCIOUS HABIT OF MAKING ASSUMPTIONS IN THE BUD.

If you think you're not that bad, that you don't make many assumptions, test yourself for three days. Get a piece of paper and make a tally mark for every assumption you make. Add 50% for the ones you simply didn't notice or didn't tally. Humor us. We'll guarantee you'll be surprised by the result.

Bottom line: If you start asking questions and stopped making so many assumptions, you'll be a better Leadership Coach and a better leader.

AFTER ACTION REVIEW HELPS STOP ASSUMPTIONS NEXT TIME

As a final step, review every coachee coaching sessions and encounter. To grow as coaches, we must assess our effectiveness. I know this is true: If you rethink your assumptions, if you review your assumptions in terms of how they might have affected coaching outcomes, you'll be all the better for it. None of us like to do this, but it's vital for your growth as a professional. Ask yourself: What assumptions did you base your approach on that were inaccurate or flawed? What could you have done to confirm you have a thorough understanding next time? How will you recognize that type of assumption in the future? Your best defense against assumptions is to be prepared to look at everything you believe to be true in the light of confirmation.

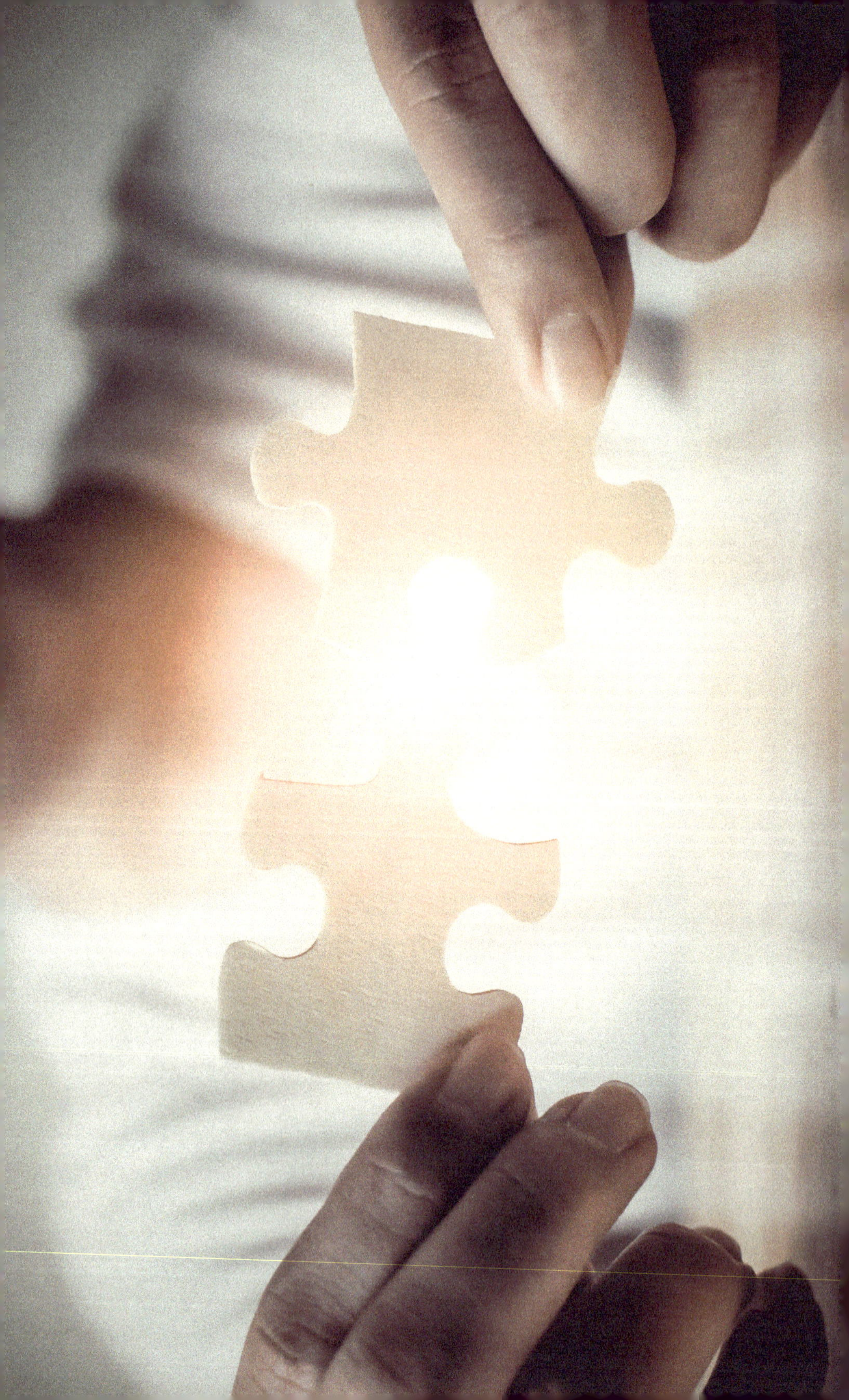

Timing Questions and Responses

> Timing is like putting the pieces of a puzzle together. When it fits, it works.

Coaches might not consider the importance of timing and timeliness in asking questions. Timing is like putting the pieces of a puzzle together. When it fits, it works. You can pose questions with a 'timing element' to either:

- Promote patience and thoughtfulness or
- Propel action and a sense of urgency.

Speed of Response Time – Slower or Quicker

You can stimulate a quicker or slower response time from your coachee by posing the right type of question and by adjusting your body language, tone, word choice, and/or gestures.

THOUGHTFUL QUESTIONS REQUIRE PATIENT LISTENING

When asking questions designed to make the coachee think a bit deeper, you have to take on the persona of 'patience and openness'. People often have a habit of answering too quickly, without adequate thoughtfulness. If you want a more thoughtful answer, slow down the pace of your questions and use tactics to slow down the responder's answer. The worst thing you can do when asking a coachee thoughtful questions is to instill a sense of urgency. Asking questions requires a certain amount of finesse in order to allow the coachee to feel that being vulnerable is ok, and that not having the perfect answer is fine. More important, allowing time and being thoughtful will allow the coachee to give you a truthful answer, rather than the one they think you want to hear.

SLOWING DOWN THE PACE OF RESPONSES

If the coach doesn't allow the coachee the appropriate amount of time to provide a thoughtful response, the coach won't get the response that might be most helpful or one that has the depth of thinking necessary. You may fuel a quicker response than is prudent by looking impatient, leaning forward in anticipation of a response, tapping or fidgeting. If your demeanor isn't patient or calm, they coachee will feel they need to hurry to reply.

- Quiet your breathing and slow down the pace of your words.
- Pause longer between statements and questions.
- Do not interrupt.
- Be patient.
- Compose yourself, listen intently, and be understanding.

- Do not prompt, disturb the flow or intrude if the coachee is thinking out loud.
- Do not suggest solutions or build on the coachee's ideas.
- Ask for clarity on points.
- Choose words that prompt thoughtfulness and patience.
    - "John, take your time with this."
    - "Mull it over before you answer."
    - "Consider your response carefully."
    - "Chew over the consequences of each for a while. Then give me your best guess."
    "Don't give me the first thing that pops into your head. It's ok to ponder this one over and get back to me in a little while."
    - "Let me give you a head's up that this is a brain-teaser and I know that there are several ways we can go. I really want some hard thought to go into this."
    - "Betty, there's nothing wrong with brainstorming on this and trying to figure this out together. I don't expect you to leap into action. I'd prefer a more measured approach on this one."

In order to slow things to the appropriate pace, you might ask:

- "Jessie, if you think about this decision a little more, what are some of the things you need to consider that you haven't already thought about?"
- "Why don't you take an additional five minutes to consider your answer before you throw one out there?"

QUICKENING THE PACE OF RESPONSES

ACTION-BASED QUESTIONS SHOULD PROPEL MOTIVATION

Action-based and decision-making questions stimulate the coachee to make choices about what to do. These should propel the coachee forward and instill a sense of urgency and/or motivation. If you want to help your coachee make the right decisions, you need to study how the timing of your line of questioning people affects leadership efforts. In your coaching sessions, you must ask the questions that really matter to stimulate timely responses and actions.

If the questions don't promote subsequent action-based thinking, the coachee's leadership efforts may stall. A Leadership Coach might not be providing an adequate sense of urgency if they look too relaxed, allow the coachee to mull over things that have already been decided against, let the coachee whine and complain rather than answer the direct question, or display body language that is overly tolerant, extremely easy-going, too friendly, extremely good-natured, or exceedingly unflappable.

- Take on the posture of action.
- Speed up the words.
- Ask two or more questions immediately after one another, then circle back to the first.
- Use gestures to prompt a response.
- Lean forward.
- Raise your eyebrows with excitement.
- Show enthusiasm.
- Call a halt if the coachee 'goes down a rabbit hole'.

- Respectfully interrupt any whining or complaining.
- Take non-issues off the discussion list. Wrap boundaries around 'no go' time-wasting topics.
- Put non-important/non-urgent issue on the back burner.
- Choose words that prompt action, drive urgency, and propel the need for a speedy response (even it isn't perfect). Notice the difference between these sentences and the prior examples to slow down response times.
    - "John, I have to get your first impression or gut response on this one. Unfortunately, we can't take our time with this matter."
    - "I would prefer your to 'blink' this one, and just get it done. Then when we have time to circle back, we might have time to mull over if we got it right. But next time, I want to be more proactive, so we don't jam ourselves up against a wall like we're doing on this one. Not optimal at all!"
    - "Consider your response a gut instinct call. I trust your intuition and judgment. You've done things like this a thousand times and I'll bet you can make the call in your sleep!"
    - "I realize there are costs in moving quickly, but the benefits of speed to market far outweigh any of these. Our Sales Team has to get out there and bring in the revenue for this product starting in two weeks. I suggest your Marketing Team stop chewing over the consequences and stop fixing every single feature and benefit on every webpage and just give us something to launch that the customer will be intrigued by. Our guys know this product inside and out and are chomping at the bit to sell, sell, sell. What can we do to get this out there in time? Give me your

best guess as to what we can expect. I am not slowing down sale efforts."
- "Just give me the first thing that pops into your head. It's ok to blurt something out. I'd rather you did that and get the ball rolling with ideas. I want us to push the envelope on this one!"
- "Let me give you a head's up that I know this has been a brain-teaser. I fully realize that there are several ways we can go. But I really want some action on this and need some answers, even if you consider them half-baked by close of business today. There's a time for thinking and a time for action, and I think it's time we go with the latter."
- "Betty, there's nothing wrong with brainstorming on this and trying to figure this out together as a team. I didn't expect you to leap into action. Two weeks ago, I said I'd prefer a more measured approach on this one. Tell me what you've come up with and when you are going from planning into execution mode. Also, what's the delivery date and what are milestones we'll be tracking?"

To speed decision making and propel action, a Leadership Coach might ask:

- "Jessie, we talked about what decisions you need to make and what actions you should make sure happen before our next coaching session. They look like they were on the tip of your tongue, just ready to come pouring out. What did you decide was the right timing for actually taking action and getting these things off your plate?"

- "Why don't you just blurt out the first thing that you're thinking about doing? What's right in front of you – inside your head – right now? I know you've been thinking of this for a long time."

Big Picture versus Details Questioning

The questioner should always try to figure out where the coachee is on the Bull's Eye of Motivation. You might remember that this model relies on the fact that the coachee will be more motivated and/or feel more emotional involvement the closer to the center of the bull's eye (where you exist). The further away from the center their view is (the outer rings), the less emotional involvement, drive and/or motivation a person will typically feel. The outer rings are the 'Bigger Picture'. The questions that address the inner ring topics typically have detail and impact more relevant to the coachee. The lens that you view a situation through often changes the person's level of emotional involvement, commitment, enthusiasm, connection, engagement, interest, stress levels, detachment and drive. That same lens can impact the stress a coachee feels during coaching sessions.

Using the Bull's Eye of Motivation in your line of questioning, you can help steer the coachee toward a more appropriate viewpoint for the conversation or for the goals under consideration, either propelling more emotional involvement or less, a wider view of the organization or focused on a smaller team. Knowing that the questions you pose could very well determine the person's view, it makes sense to think about this model and plan for a setup that helps the coachee think things through. Perhaps you think a close-up more 'me-centered' view is the place for the coachee to start talking things through. Maybe starting at the center where the coachee is the focal point isn't appropriate and a more organization-centric view will drive better results.

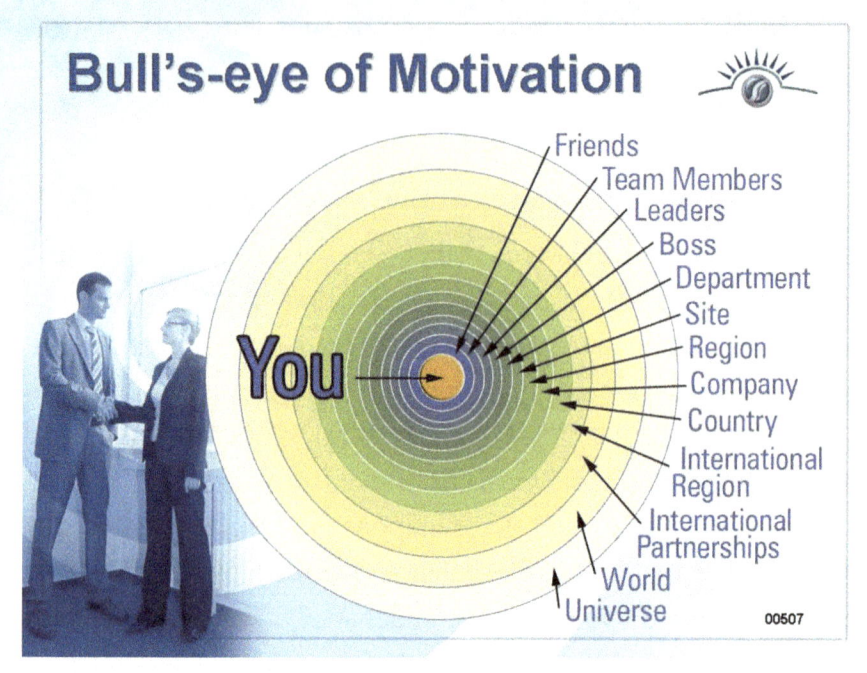

Bull's-eye of Motivation

Friends
Team Members
Leaders
Boss
Department
Site
Region
Company
Country
International Region
International Partnerships
World
Universe

You

00507

SEGMENTING YOUR FOCUS CAN ENCOURAGE THE RESPONSES YOU NEED

Posing questions with a viewpoint in mind gives you the power to solicit employees' views of various inter- or intra-depart initiatives:

- What process can you think of to fix in your team within the next 30 days that might save time or resources?
- What three people on your team can we tap for this pilot?
- If you think back to between six and nine months ago, what do you think we could have done better to avoid what we're facing today?
- I want you to look at this through the lens of your peers in the

finance department. Can you come up with a better way to communicate with them next time... without the same level of stress for either party?
- I'm not suggesting that you to adjust your dress every day, but when you present in front of the Executive Team, it's best to put your best foot forward. That means you should look and act the art of someone who is poised for promotion. I choose to always wear a jacket and tie. I want to make sure they remember you in the best possible light.

ASKING A SERIES OF EXPANSION-VIEW QUESTIONS CAN SPARK INNOVATION:

Inviting people to respond in the appropriate viewpoint can help avoid rework, fire-drills, and help drive process improvement:

Conjuring up the appropriate lens can help employees be less team-centric and more cooperative and collaborative:

Big Broad Narrow Detail Model

BIG BROAD NARROW DETAIL MODEL

Asking questions requires a certain discipline of thinking. To structure the right questions, it is important to determine what type of response you are looking for. The goal of the Big Broad Narrow Detail Model is to provide an easy way to remember to be disciplined and purposeful in posing questions. Misunderstandings, irritation, impatience, and frustration between asker and responder usually occur because people aren't on the same page. The intention and/or purpose of

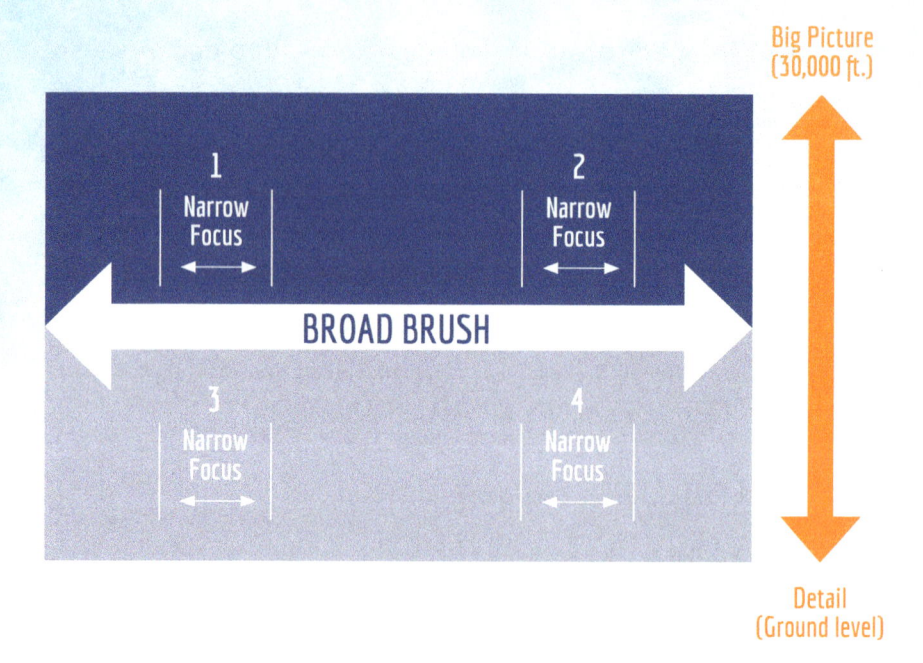

[Diagram: A rectangle divided into four quadrants labeled 1, 2, 3, 4, each marked "Narrow Focus" with horizontal double-arrows. A horizontal double-arrow labeled "BROAD BRUSH" spans across the middle. A vertical double-arrow on the right ranges from "Big Picture (30,000 ft.)" at the top to "Detail (Ground level)" at the bottom.]

the question should be clear to both parties. Getting on the same page saves time and is highly efficient. It keeps stress levels lower.

The best way to do this is to think about the response you are looking for then segment your line of questioning into the appropriate focus. When you segment, slice, or separate the focus of your questions, people can more easily understand what their response should be. They understand what you are looking for. The Big Broad Narrow Detail Model can help you remember to segment your focus into four different areas. This is tremendously valuable to decision making.

BENEFITS:

This model can:

- Bring discipline to your thinking as you pose questions.
- Analyze whether the person's response matches the focal intent you are looking for.
- Match your intent with their response, so you can easily see if any misunderstandings are occurring.

HERE ARE THE FOUR FOCUS AREAS:

1. BIG PICTURE (30,000-FOOT LEVEL) VERSUS DETAILS

Big Picture versus Detail question are actually polar opposites – just as the behaviors of Dominance Factor and Steadiness/Strategy Factor oppose each other. If you look at the picture of the model, you'll see the 30,000-foot level Big Picture is high above the details. It's more strategic like the Steadiness/Strategy Factor. In contrast, ticking off things on a detailed 'to do' list is more Dominance Factor types of behavior. (Compiling that 'to do' list is a Compliance Factor skill, but going through the list and getting things accomplished is definitely a Dominance Factor behavioral tendency!) Being able to differentiate between these two levels of focus is important because they require a different KIND of thinking. The Big Picture is more conceptual, theoretical, and/or abstract. Diving into the details is more concrete, specific, distinct, and/or definite in nature. Responders often find it difficult to flip between these two different ways of thinking. In addition, the asker the responder – in flipping between these two – will often be out of sync going back and forth. AS you can imagine, this can be extremely frustrating. One or the other has to recalibrate the level and a push-me-pull-me is the result.

a. Are you looking for answers that are at the 30,000-foot level? Do you want the responder to focus on the Big Picture?
b. Do you want the answerer to concentrate on the details?

2. **BROAD BRUSH VERSUS NARROW FOCUS**

Broad brush focus paints a swath across a topic, area, or timeframe. Narrow focus pinpoints a topic, area, or timeframe. As with Big Picture and Detail thinking, the mind mulls over these two in a distinctly different manner. Broad brush thinking speaks to general terms. It is typically expansive in nature and goes across-the-board. If you are posing questions in a Broad-Brush manner, you should expect responses that are more sweeping, wide-ranging, far-reaching and universal. Contrary to Broad Brush, Narrow Focus expects the responder to address the question in terms of the boundaries and limits the asker set. The answers will tend to be*In-depth Limited Restricted*

c. Are you most interested in an overview; brushing broadly over the scope, entire timeline, or topic?
d. Do you want to discuss issues, topics, or subject matter that falls into a narrow band or only covers a narrow focus?

BIG PICTURE (30,000-FOOT LEVEL) QUESTIONS

These Big Picture-type questions elevate coaching session discussions to a higher level whereby you can look at the interconnectedness of behaviors, habits, decision making, relationships, etc. The goal is to best examine the connections between individual problems. Big Picture Questions are designed to look at things from the 30,000-foot level. Asking them helps the coachee 'zoom out'.

- "Taking a step back, what are the larger issues for your leadership efforts'?"
- "Are we even addressing the right question with this issue? Shouldn't we step back and look at it from a higher level before making any important decisions?"

Being too immersed in an immediate problem or issue often makes it harder to see the overall context behind it.

- "Instead of talking about these issues separately, what are the larger trends we should be concerned with regarding your management style?"
- "How does the bigger issue of losing your temper three times in the past month tie in with being dismissive, not listening, and cursing to yourself constantly all tie together with how angry you get with your team? Could the root cause of your explosions be a series of escalating negative behaviors?"

DETAIL QUESTIONS: DETAILED, ACTION OR 'HOW TO' QUESTION

Asking Detail, Action or 'How To' Questions will allow you to do a deep dive into critical areas where people are performing (doing). Without asking detailed questions, the coachee may never address the unique behaviors that have:

a. held them back and/or
b. will propel them forward.

Prudent decision making requires rigor and discipline. Rigor, efficiency, and/or disciplined performance requires detail. It's that simple. The thing to be aware of is that many coachees don't like going into detail about what they need to do for a number of reasons. They might not have thought things through. They might not know what they should have known. They might have let things slide and now they're in trouble. They don't want you to know how bad it is. These don't help solve anything.

> Your job is to 'go there'. You have to dig in and ask questions that lead where they don't want to go.

It's uncomfortable to keep digging, poking and uncovering 'stuff'. Coachees typically don't like it when you discover that they haven't figured it all out yet or that what they did didn't work out as expected. Ok. Own this: Your job is to 'go there'. You have to dig in and ask questions that lead where they don't want to go, have avoided discussing in the past, is too painful, is too hard, will hold them accountable, etc. By asking detailed questions, they can think through what's happened and drill down to what they need to do. That's your responsibility as a Leadership Coach.

Detail Questions: "Now that we've had a look from the 30,000-foot level, we can start to drill down to some of the things that you talked about changing. Let's begin with stimulation that is holding you back from sleeping at night and what's making you edgy. Then we'll talk about the consequences to your leadership currency – short and long term – of fatigue and staying up too late. Let's break it down: What specifically is it that could be causing you to stay awake until the wee hours of the morning?"

Response: I used to drink coffee in the late afternoon not get through those after lunch meetings, but it didn't affect me like it does now. I guess it's because at night I'd drink a glass of wine to relax. Now that I'm not drinking any alcohol, I think my system is overly stimulated by the caffeine. There's nothing bringing me down anymore."

Detail Questions: "Ok, I get that. What do you think you can do to avoid caffeine late in the day or do something else to counterbalance its effects besides drinking alcohol?"

Response: "Well, I can stop caffeine after 4 pm. That's got to help! Also, I can drink lots more water to dilute it if I do take a cup later in the day. Those two things should help a bit. Also, I can go for a walk or workout to get my juices flowing so that I'll be physically tired in the evening. That should also help to work the caffeine and stress out of my system."

Close out for accountability: "Great, let's put those on the list for this week and circle back about what worked and what didn't next week. Bottom line: You have to get more sleep. Good idea?"

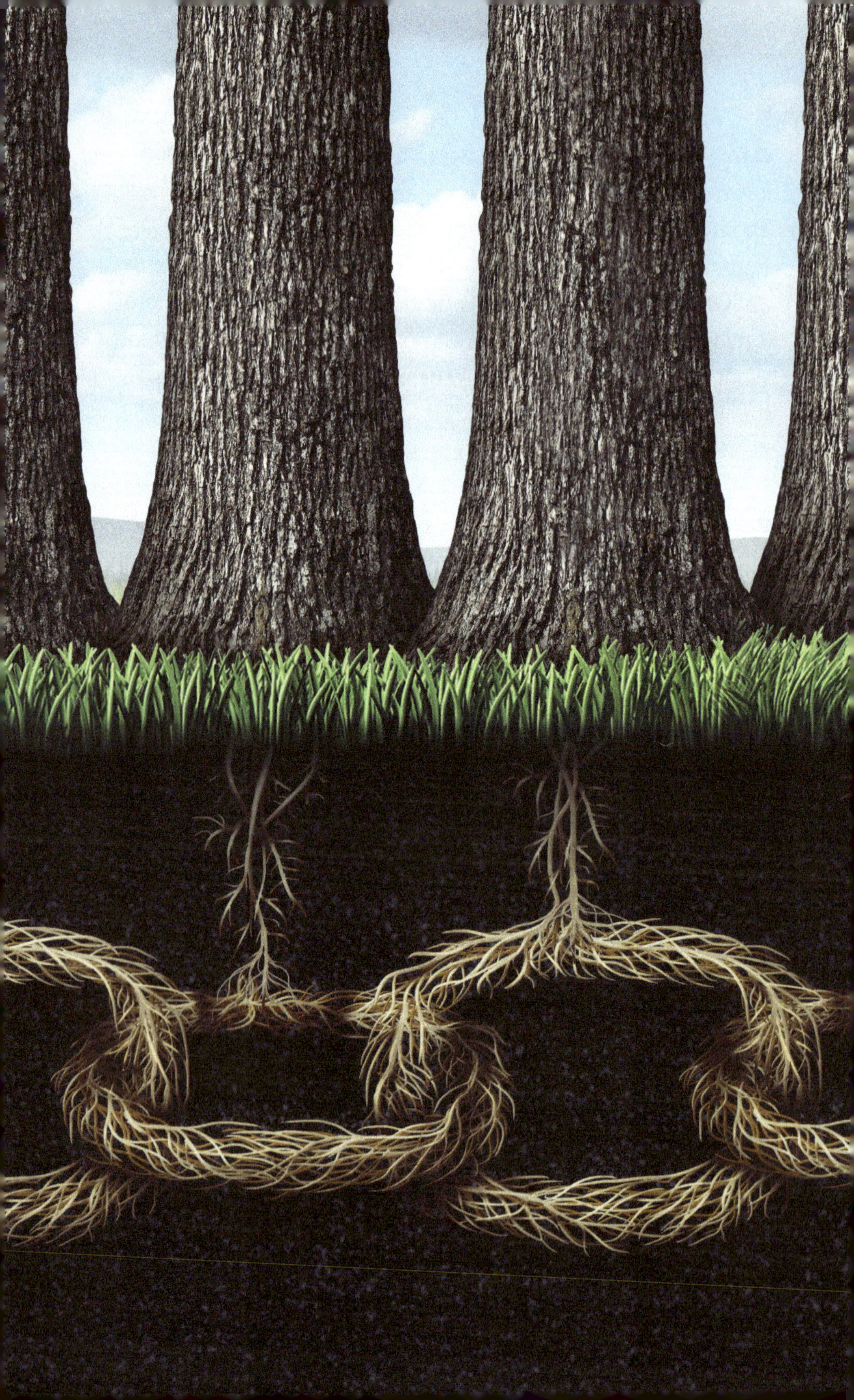

Structuring a Series of Questions

> Think of this like the links in a strong discussion. Great conversations form links of questions, statements and responses. Much like the strong roots of mighty trees, these chain links form the underpinnings of trust and rapport that cannot be seen.

Now that you know a few questioning techniques, let's continue by learning how to string different kinds of questions together. Great conversations form links of questions, statements and responses. Much like the strong roots of mighty trees, these chain links form the underpinnings of trust and rapport that cannot be seen.

By definition, leaders take charge and set the path forward. This includes guiding people through a series of questions. Blurting out questions without adequate thought either to consider your purpose or to take into account what the responder might be thinking isn't what great leaders do. Getting to the heart of the matter, uncovering information, and holding people accountable all require that the leader structure their questions properly.

In coaching sessions, it's often the case that you have to ask a series of questions to get to the bottom of the matter, to the root cause.

Often, one question lead to a follow up question, which in turn leads to another. Ideally you would pose a series of questions that start at a logical point and progress through the various nuances and levels until your curiosity has been satisfied.

Remember: Questions have two primary purposes:

1. To uncover new information
2. To confirm or disprove your assumptions or suspicions.

Series of Questioning – Models that Work

5 WHYS

There is a technique called the 5 Whys that is designed to get as close to root cause as possible. The 5 Whys is a process of asking "Why?" numerous times in a row to detect the root cause or meaning of a particular problem or situation. Asking "Why?" is necessary when people do not truly understand the situation or when a deeper understanding is necessary. Stopping to ask "Why?" causes people to use higher order thinking skills, cut through layers of rules and regulations to find the true reasons they might be doing something. Asking a series of Why's also might have them begin to challenge their ways of thinking or behaving, current situation, or problem.

Transitional Timeline Model

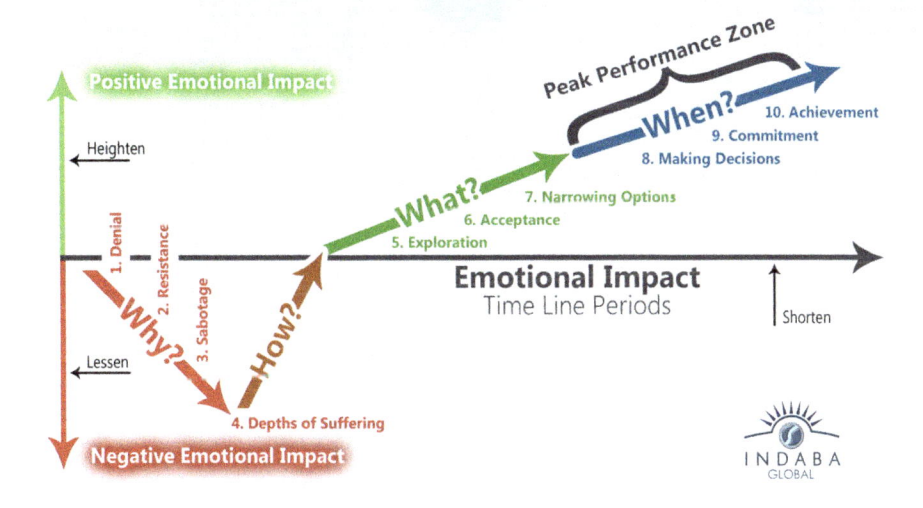

In the Transitional Timeline Model (discussed in the Change Course), a series of questions asked in the correct order can:

- Lessen the negatives associated with any change.
- Heighten the positive motivation during change.
- Shorten the time it takes to implement changes.

In the Transitional Timeline Model, questions are posed in this order:

- Why?
- How?
- What?
- When?

Big Broad Narrow Detail Model

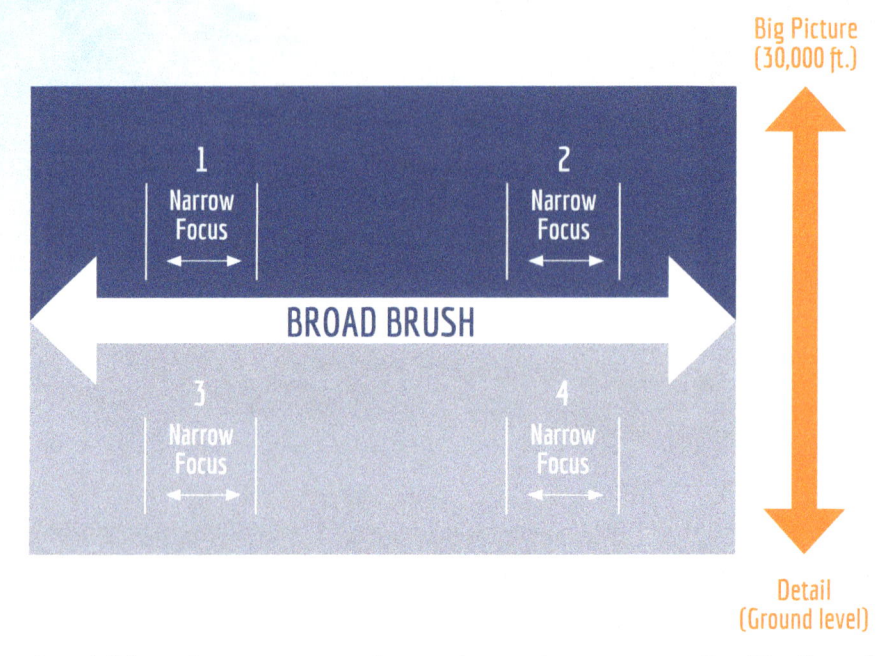

[Diagram: A rectangle divided into four quadrants labeled 1, 2, 3, 4, each marked "Narrow Focus" with horizontal double-arrows. A horizontal double-arrow across the middle is labeled "BROAD BRUSH". A vertical double-arrow on the right is labeled "Big Picture (30,000 ft.)" at the top and "Detail (Ground level)" at the bottom.]

In addition, the sequence of questions when you use the Big Broad Narrow Detail Model can either:

> **a. Reduce confusion: Make addressing and answering questions easier and less unclear.**

Imagine streamlining your questions. You start at the 30,000-foot level, explaining that you want the person to focus at the top level, without going into details or Action Steps yet. After you've satisfied your questions at that level, you pick a Broad-Brush timeframe (like next quarter or next year) and focus your questions and follow ups in this area only. Next, you pick one month or a single week (Narrow Focus) and concentrate on addressing this in your Q&A. Finally, you tackle the relevant

Detail and/or Actions needed in your Detail Questions. As you can imagine, segmenting and posing questions purposefully and logically can build trust and get to the heart of what you need to know far quicker and with less stress for all. By guiding the person logically through a series of well-thought questions, you will control the direction of the conversation and keep the other person focused on the appropriate areas and topics.

b. Frustrate and confuse people.
If you ask someone a Big Picture question, then immediately jump to a Detailed or Action or How To question, and follow that quickly with a Narrow Focus question, then drill back over to more details and fly up to the 30,000 foot more strategic level, this jumping around will bewilder even the brightest on your team. Hopping all over the place before you set context for your questions will put people on the defensive. They'll wonder what you're looking for and will try to uncover why you are bouncing around. When you question people in this manner, it puts them on edge. It can erode Leadership Currency and trust.

GET UNCOMFORTABLE ISSUES ON THE TABLE: USE FAIR WARNING

In Leadership Coaching, coachees are sometimes adept at 'dodging'. A series of well-thought-out questions can stop them from avoiding the issue and will get them to start discussing what's at the heart of the matter. Make no mistake, it may take asking a few well-thought-out questions to get the coachee to open up about things they'd prefer 'dodging' and not discussing. These behaviors are not healthy.

In these situations, especially if you suspect you'll have to deliver pointed feedback or hold someone accountable, you might want to set the tone. If you know you're going to talk about uncomfortable subjects, it's usually a good idea to tell your coachee that you're going to start a series of questions that are designed to drill down until all the issues are on the table. This gives the coachee Fair Warning of what's to come.

The definition of giving 'Fair Warning' is to let someone know you are going to do something before you do it. In order to be classified as

Fair Warning, you need to give the person adequate forewarning or notice of what you are going to do. The key word is 'adequate'. As an example, if a surgeon is going to perform an elective procedure, the patient should be given Fair Warning about what will happen, including how they might best prepare for a successful outcome. The timeframe for Fair Warning of the potential impacts should be 24 hours to a few weeks. If a football player is going to set up a play, Fair Warning for their teammates might be between 1 and 5 seconds before the action takes place. In coaching sessions, the Leadership Coach determines adequate Fair Warning based on the situation. Break the phrase down to determine what you and the coachee might think is 'Fair', then give warning about what's coming. Then, follow through in the timeframe you stated.

HERE ARE SOME SUGGESTIONS:

FAIR WARNING IN THE COMING DAYS:

"Harold, in our next session, we're going to start delving into your communication style. I am giving you Fair Warning that I'll be asking some pointed questions about your history of angry outbursts. We've only brushed on these in past sessions, but I think you're ready for a deeper dive. If you can prepare for this by thinking through some past examples that you might feel ok talking through, no matter how explosive they were, that would be great. I just wanted to tell you this is coming up and that you'll get through it just fine. We'll use the examples to go through some of the models I mentioned. They'll form the basis for learning Anger Management techniques and exploring your Self-Talk."

FAIR WARNING IN THE COMING MOMENTS:

"Judy, I just heard you say something contrary to what you told me just 20 minutes ago. I am giving you Fair Warning that we are going to circle back and fact-check in a moment. I suggest you think through what I'm saying for the next few moments. (Silence) Ok, now let me ask you a couple of tough questions. I expect you won't like this conversation, but we have to delve into what's going on here. The goal is for you to provide direct and fully honest responses to the questions I am asking. I also would like you to consider the intention of the questions before you respond. This way, you'll probably provide clarification and information that we both know will be helpful in having me better understand this situation and working out where you're coming from with all this."

This technique of giving the coachee Fair Warning' is powerful for two reasons:
It provides permission for you to begin.

It gives the coachee time to prepare and permission to feel the discomfort you and they know is inevitable.

Informing of intent to drill down usually makes the process of asking tough questions a lot smoother. Provide any background information or model that you would like to discuss at the beginning of the drill down for even better results.

Prior to starting the series of questions, make sure you go into the reasons why the drill down is important for their leadership efforts.

By doing this, the coachee usually is more open to a long series of questions. Also, remember that many of the questions you are supposed to ask probably would seem overly intrusive in any other situation. Coaching sessions are supposed to be where the coachee gets asked tough questions. Remind them this is part of the process and let them have a little time out for a few minutes if stress levels get too high. And remind yourself: It is acceptable for you to be asking them and why this is critical to their success.

HEADS UP TO TOUGH QUESTIONS

Another way you can lower the coachee's stress is to give them a heads up about the type of questions that are likely to come up. Example, "Susan, in order to help you with building trust with your team, it will be vital for me to ask you about that straw that broke the camel's back – as you said it was the event that brought everything crashing down. Can you tell me about your emotions, health, state of mind, and the circumstances that led up to the incident? After we talk about those, I am going to ask you a series of questions about what has changed in the last six months since the incident. Ok? Some of these are going to be hard for you but we need to get through them all. Are you ready to start?"

USING SILENCE DURING QUESTIONING

Being silent after delivering questions has a powerful impact. Pausing and waiting for the coachee's response can help to emphasize important points. Being quiet can give the coachee a few moments to gather their thoughts before responding. When you start your coaching sessions, let the coachee know that it's ok to think before they respond. In fact, this is desirable! One of the things you hope will come from coaching sessions is that the coachee will learn to think before speaking. It's a skill that many need to learn.

- Training yourself, as a Leadership Coach, to be quiet after asking a question has a few benefits. It can prevent you from asking another question, potentially destroying the impact of the first question. If you keep talking after asking a question, it can confuse the coachee. You must avoid doing this unless you are doing so for a specific reason.
- Silence is also good if the response the coachee gives isn't detailed enough. If you don't speak, they most likely will.
- Pausing again after an initial response can encourage the respondent to continue with their answer in more detail. Pauses of less than three seconds have been proven to be less effective.

BROAD-BRUSH OR LASER-LIKE QUESTIONS

Many people never consider that different types of questions can lead to different outcomes. You can steer a conversation one way or another by asking the right kinds of questions, or the wrong questions. You can broaden the aperture of the topic, expanding the view of the issue, topic or problem you are focusing on by asking *Broad-Brush Questions that stimulate general answers*. Or you can narrow the focus and ask *Laser-Like Questions* that require *detail-focused answers*.

TANDEM FOLLOW-UP QUESTIONS

Tandem Follow-Up Questions are posed to bridge onto related areas that the coachee might not want to discuss, but should. These can be either Broad-Brush or Laser-like. Examples: "How would this concept of listening before judging apply in a different context, perhaps something like building up your relationship with your Sarah again?" or "What are two other ways, beside directly helping yourself inside your head, that you can use the Self-Talk Chart this week to communicate better?" Another example, asking "How would these insights apply in your leadership meetings?" during one-on-one coaching sessions can open the coachee's mind to using the techniques they are learning in other environments outside of the 'safe zone' of your coaching sessions. Often, a person's natural narrow focus on only what's in front of them or an immediate task will hinder them from probing about related topics that should be explored. By asking more Tandem Follow-Up Questions, the coaching sessions become richer and broader. This means you can reach into other areas of the coachee's profession experience more easily. Behavior touches nearly every aspect of a coachee's work life, so this is an important consideration.

HERE ARE SOME SUGGESTIONS:

1. What would it look like if you were entirely successful in your leadership efforts?
    a. **Tandem Follow up:** What would you see if you popped into a time machine and thero it was, you maintained your goal of reading at least one business book a month for 30 years?

- Why do you want that goal to drive your long-term future?
    b. **Detail Follow up:** Why do you want that knowledge in the short-term for your career?
        - Why do you want that to help grow your organization?
2. In six months, if things were going exactly the way you want, what would you see?
    a. **Tandem Follow up:** What would be your next communication-based goal after you achieve good habits in your current one of learning how to listen better?
        - Why?
    a. **Broad-brush Follow Up:** What would you do if you had unlimited resources in the next six months?
    b. **Detail Follow Up:** What about it is so important to you that you would defend it at all costs in the next six months?
3. **Detail Follow Up:** What would be the precise impacts on you (and others) if things don't change right now?
    c. **Broad-brush Follow up:** What are some things that you can accomplish that don't depend on others?
    d. **Detail Follow Up:** What currently is your biggest problem or challenge?
        - **Narrow then Broad Approach Follow Up:** If this weren't a problem, what would be your biggest problem?
        - What is working well?
        - What has contributed to your success so far?
4. **Detail Follow Up:** How exactly might your unwillingness to set and live by the boundaries with others on the Executive Team get in your way?
    a. What about professional boundaries might keep you

from getting where you want to go?
- b. What obstacles have you faced when you tried to set and enforce boundaries on yourself, what did you do, and what did you learn?
- c. What particular obstacles do you expect to face when you are setting accountability parameters for you and others for your leadership efforts in the next two weeks?
  - How specifically do you plan to approach them?
  - What particular communication do you think needs to happen?
  - Who will be your biggest supporters?
  - Who will be the people who will not get on board as easily?
- d. What resources do you have access to help with the accountability parameters you have to set?
- e. What are your biggest mistakes and challenges in trying to hold yourself to deadlines and budget constraints, and what did you learn from them?

5. If a trusted colleague were in your shoes, what particular individual advice would you give them about what they should be concentrating on?
  - a. **Follow Up:** How can you use your answer to help yourself?
6. What is one step you could take right now that would indicate you were moving forward with your influencing goals?
  - a. **Follow Up:** How would you suggest I help you hold yourself accountable?
    - What are the things you least like about accountability?
7. Are there any important questions that have not been asked?
  - a. **Follow Up:** Have you ever found yourself avoiding answering questions or dealing with issues?

Planning a Broad then Narrow Questioning Approach

You will find that most coachees don't like to discuss touchy or negative topics until they get comfortable. If you start with Broad-Brush Questions then drill down further into the issue by asking a series of Laser-Like Questions, you might find your coachee opening up more to you, and with less stress.

HERE ARE SOME SUGGESTIONS:

Broad-Brush Question: "You said you spoke at three leadership meetings this week, at two different locations? How did that go?"
Response: "Great, I was happy that I made it to them all and got the chance to meet a couple of great people on my team."

Broad-Brush Question: "In our last conversation, you were worried about the message you had to deliver."
Response: "Yes, that's true. I was anxious."

Laser-Like Questions: "What specifically happened that made you feel better about it?
Response: I walked in the door and Sandy, my right-hand in Phoenix, came up and greeted me. She said she was so happy to see me, and after I spoke she said she loved the presentation. I needed to see a friendly face."

Laser-Like Questions: "That's great but why did you think you needed that?"

Response: "The last time I went there - three months ago - I was stressed. The result: I was a tad sarcastic. I actually gave one or two of the guys a really hard time during the Q&A session. I got called out the next day by our HR Lead for being rude. I was seriously worried that I'd have a repeat performance. My default is sarcasm. It's not pretty. It isn't what I imagine a leader to be. I don't want to be that type of person."

Laser-Like Questions: "That's interesting, John. Why didn't you bring up the real reason at our last session?"

Response: "I didn't want to say anything because we started right in with Anger Management techniques and the disadvantages of using sarcasm with people in our coaching session. I didn't want to talk about it since I screwed it all up in front of so many people at the site not so long ago. I was still raw from it. I was going back there, addressing the same employees and I was really afraid that I'd fail in my leadership responsibility to keep calm and monitor my emotional temperature. I also wanted to choose leader-like words and responses. But I was so embarrassed to tell you."

Laser-Like Questions: *"John, this process of building leadership skills takes time. No one, especially me, expects you to be perfect. What I do expect is that you try and learn from things as you go along. I expect you to be able to communicate what you're going through – especially things you're afraid of. This vulnerability will make you a better leader. Listen, as long as the impact of what you did caused you to get better for next time, to be a better leader, I'm good with that. And you should be too. But learning some additional skills to help with specific events and specific behavior is exactly why we get together. There is no reason to stall developing your leadership* *skills or create unnecessary stress by keeping things hidden. I am not judging you. This is a safe place. You have to believe that at your core. I simply want to help you become the very best leader you can become. That in mind: Was there anything else about this that you might want to tell me or learn about, knowing this is a safe place and I'm not judging you at all? The goal is to help you grow your skills and provide tips and tactics so that you don't repeat prior mistakes. Don't forget: It's also important to rehearse when you're facing a tough situation. Perhaps that would have helped if we practiced what responses leaders should give during a Q&A session – especially when they think they might get push-back. Don't you think this would have helped you prepare and also might have lowered our stress?"*

<u>Response</u>: "Actually, that would have been very helpful. I'm really sorry I didn't mention all of this in our last coaching session. But to be completely honest, I didn't have the guts to bring it up. I was really worried about it when I promised the site director I would go there. It gave me sleepless nights and a lot of stress. The closer I got to the date, the more it impacted me. I kept imagining bad things! And it was so silly because none of them happened. That's a real lesson. We talked about expectations and worry conceptually in several of our coaching sessions, but I hadn't lived through an event that I blew completely out of proportion yet. I realized that I am my own worst enemy when my Self-Talk spins out of control. I actually practiced pithy and snippy responses to a hundred possible questions. Then I batted them down because they were inappropriate, un-leader-like or petty then crafted some more. Round and round and round for hours when I should have been resting! You taught me the Self-Talk process, but I didn't work through the steps. I completely ignored what my logical self was telling me I needed to do. Even though I recognized it, and I knew the model I needed to work through, I

resisted big time - and it hurt me. But, there's a great ending here. I did a stand-up thing that I wouldn't have done before our coaching sessions. What I finally did was directly based on one of our session conversations. I went up to that guy and said 'sorry'. I was open and honest. I told him I was in a bad place – going through the tough decisions about a big downsizing - and that I shouldn't have taken it out on him - especially in a public setting! Now that you know all this, I can tell you that I am a little proud of myself! What the heck was I thinking?!? I was so lucky that he is a great human being and he absolutely respected the effort it took to do it. He thanked me and shook my hand. I let myself be open and honest about my failings. I could see the trust building and even better, I saw the respect he had for me as a leader take a giant leap right in front of my eyes. The guy sent me a thank you the next day. I did exactly the same with two other people and even though I didn't get a thank you email, I could see they respected me apologizing. I told each one of them what I had learned, and I promised to be a better leader and make them proud. It was amazing. What most people would have considered weak build the most trust and respect. It was so powerful! I took responsibility and tried to make amends. It felt good!"

Laser-Like Questions: *"All-in-all, you did great. I'm really proud of you for stepping up and taking on what you did and making it a lot better for you and that guy, too. Is there anything at all that you'll do differently next time? Be specific about your behavior please, then we'll talk about your thinking."*

<u>Response</u>: "Well, for a start, I was kicking myself that we didn't talk about it prior. I knew I was going into a stressed situation. I think if I had rehearsed what I was going to say, I would have done an even better job of keeping my stress low, and looking like the leader I

want to be. I would have appreciated your listening ear and maybe some suggestions on how to make it sound better too. I felt I hashed it up a bit. I actually stuttered and repeated the apology a bit much. Granted, I shouldn't have been sarcastic last time and I was. I shouldn't have called the guys out last time, and I did. I shouldn't have ever embarrassed them, but my ego took over and because of that, I was a bad leader. You would have laughed or been horrified at how badly I communicated my apology! But I did try to make amends and that's the most important thing. I saw the guys I didn't do well with last time when I was presenting my slides. Not surprisingly, they were guarded and quiet during my presentation and in the following Q&A. What did I learn? That apology should have been BEFORE the meeting, not after. Here's how my apology went down: After my presentation, I went up to the first guy and tapped him on the shoulder. I started with "Do you remember me?" I thought the guy was going to faint! I think he thought I was going to get into it with him again instead of apologizing. I'll tell you, he looked worried! Good thing Sandy was standing right next to me and smoothed the beginning part over quickly! We practiced an opening line and she delivered it beautifully! She said: "John owes you an apology and he wanted me to tell you he apologized to me too." I meant ever word of that apology. I grew through this whole thing. I learned what I don't ever want to do again. The biggest lesson is that if you don't behave like an un-leader you won't lose leadership currency and have to unwind everything. Commonsense I know, but I lived it and felt pain that I don't want to repeat."

Tandem Follow Up Question: *"John, well done on that one! It was smart to include Sandy. Along that note, do you think it might be good to solicit some feedback from Sandy about how others thought you did and include a follow up and a thank you?"*

DEVELOPING FOLLOW UP QUESTIONS & LISTENING

It's important to remember that people rarely say everything in the exact order, use the perfect words, or address the topic with appropriate depth, thoughtfulness, and detail. That's why the primary tool of a good leader is to become a great listener after posing a series of good questions. Well-crafted questions with great follow up questions can stimulate, draw out, and guide wonderful discussions. But this only happens if the leader LISTENS carefully.

IDENTIFY YOUR PURPOSE.

The series of questions should help you gather either facts or confirm or refute assumptions. Decide which type of information you need and frame your questions accordingly. Questions are a leader's most valuable verbal tool. Questions will keep you and your organization safe because they uncover vital information and shed light on assumptions. Great leaders ask purposeful questions in a timely fashion. There are a few important points to consider when you pose questions:

> If you don't really care about the information that's likely to come from your question, don't ask the question.

- **Asking questions erodes Leadership Currency.** Think of everything you do in terms of making deposits or withdrawals from your Trust Bank. Praising someone for going the extra mile and accomplishing a task deposits Leadership Currency in your

Trust Bank. When people feel good and respect each other, it builds trust. Doing the right thing doesn't always deposit currency in your bank. Creating stress by holding people accountable or providing feedback can build trust if done well, or erode trust if done poorly. It's often about the skill and the intent. Asking questions can often erode the Leadership Currency in your Trust Bank because it creates stress. Please consider that even if you are doing what is vital, your Trust Bank takes a hit. The good news is that if you become skilled at asking questions, this erosion won't be as significant. And hopefully, if you are fair and consistent in the questions you ask, people will learn to trust that your questions are vital to the organization's health. **Tips:** Guard your Trust Bank well. Spend your Leadership Currency well. You will find that you can ask tough questions if your Trust Bank is full. You will also find that people will be more forthcoming and honest in their responses if they know that you are willing to make a withdrawal from your Trust Bank for them.

- **Ask only necessary and important questions.** If you don't really care about the information that's likely to come from your question, don't ask the question. Remember that the purpose of asking questions is to:
  - Uncover new information
  - Confirm or refute assumptions.

USE WORDS THE OTHER PERSON UNDERSTANDS.

Asking questions that are not clearly understood is a waste of time. Plus, they make the conversation somewhat awkward. Who's going to admit they don't understand? If you confuse the responder, you risk they'll respond in a way you didn't anticipate. Then you have to go back and unwind the conversation. In this you'll probably destroy some of the trust you have. Acronyms, obscure words, or phrases that are specific to a limited understanding are dangerous unless you know for certain the other person is completely on the same page as you are. If you suspect, by observing body language or by listening to the other person's response that they don't seem to understand what you're asking, you should restate, rephrase, or reshape your question, and/or provide better framework, perspective, context, or background. Know your audience. If you've spent a fair amount of time with the other person, they probably know your questioning style and you most likely have a good idea of their answering style. The less you know this, the more you'll have to focus your questions to one thing at a time. To get more information or to flesh out answers, craft short questions. Design each to address limited scope or to cover a single point. In this way, you'll channel the person's focus to precisely the information you require.

USE UNBIASED PHRASING.

If you pose biased or leading questions, *"Sarah's team is great to work with, aren't they?"*, you're going to get a biased response. The responder is predisposed to agree. The alternative is that they go into conflict with your lead. Most people won't do this. Just because the person responds, doesn't mean they're necessarily being completely forthcoming. An objective, unbiased question will get closer to the other person's true opinions: *"How's it going with your new work assignment. What do you think about working with Sarah's team?"*

PLAN YOUR QUESTIONS AND TARGET NATURAL BEHAVIORAL TENDENCIES.

Outline your information goals and a sequence of related questions to help you steer the conversation to uncover what you need to address. A series of well-crafted questions will certainly help you uncover information or refute or confirm your thinking. The choice is yours whether to follow general questions with specific ones or vice versa. Please remember that when you build a hierarchy of questions that begins with the big picture and gradually drills down into specifics with follow-up questions, you'll be moving from strategic questions to action questions. On the other side of the coin, if you want the person to step back from discussing the day-to-day more tactical 'to do's' and begin thinking at the 30,000-foot strategic level, you'll start with a narrower timeframe with a more detailed focus before expanding that to a broader more philosophical set of questions. Know your audience and start where their natural behavioral tendencies gravitate. For people who have a naturally higher Dominance Factor, get into their world and start with the tactical. Do the opposite for elevated Steadiness/Strategy Factor folks. For these types of higher S people, beginning with a broader more philosophical starting pint and them drilling down to the associated actions and time constraints often helps them work through the steps you need them to get done.

UNLOCK DEEPER CONVERSATIONS.

Determine which types of questions will suit your purpose and remember that open-ended questions invite the respondent to talk more than closed questions do. Additionally, you'll get more information and build a deeper level of understanding and trust, too. "What do you like best about working with Sarah and her team?" will probably open the person up more than "Do you like Sarah's team?" Another line of questioning rephrases an open-ended question in the declarative or directive format: "Give me some information on what you think about working with Sarah and her team." "Tell me about that project." Often, coachees who dodge or give partial answers will reply in more detail to a directive.

CRAFT SEGUES, SHIFTS, AND TRANSITIONS.

Conversations should flow naturally and logically from one question and response to the next. By thinking about how you'll transition or shift towards where you intend to go with your line of questioning, you can make this more natural. People open up more when conversations seem to flow naturally from one question and response to the next. As a leader, you can certainly facilitate this 'flow'. Anticipate the person's response to a well-framed question and use something in that answer to transition to your next question. Even if this takes you off on a slight tangent for a little while, it shows that you're listening and willing to go with the other person's thoughts. But you have to get back to your purpose, so you'll have to shift the flow to where you need it to end up. To do so gracefully, make sure you have a couple of segue or transition questions at the ready to get back on track. Make sure you never appear to be just hammering through your agenda. Crafting segues, and transitions ensures that the conversation flows naturally. You can artfully shift by asking questions like these:

"Oh, by the way, I forgot to ask about...(topic) when you mentioned it a little while ago. Can you expand on that for me?"

"Before we end this, I wanted to get your take on....(topic). Can you spend a few minutes explaining what happened?"

"I wanted to get your opinion on ....(topic). What do you think the team should focus on next week to avoid a repeat of last month-end?"

Never interrupt. Ask your question and remain respectfully quiet. Listen to the full response. Think about this: If you've asking a purposeful well-crafted question, why would you interrupt the responder? It makes no sense to interrupt someone when they are trying to provide exactly what you asked them for!

Aggressive Assumptive Questions

Questions that are really statements of assumptions or suspicions posed as a question can be viewed as antagonistic. They typically are equally destructive to trust, which often leads to argumentativeness. Look at this question: *"Can you name one employee on the finance team that never overran a deadline?"* or *"Why does your team insist on fighting every suggestion from the sales team who are out in the field every day interacting with the customer?"* It's clear from looking at these that the underlying intention isn't to get new information. It's to state something the asker believes.

Why choose a question format? The asker might be using sarcasm. They may want to hide behind the question, sensing that a statement might be viewed as even more hostile. It would be far better for the relationship to ask a series of questions. Then the responder has an opportunity to provide information that can increase rapport and understanding. Taking the two examples, they might be better posed like this:

AGGRESSIVE ASSUMPTIVE QUESTION:

"Can you name one employee on the finance team that never overran a deadline?"

Alternative: "Several members of my team voiced concerns about timelines being slipped when it comes to deliverables from the Finance Team. I asked them for facts and data to discuss with you. I didn't want this to be a finger pointing exercise. Here is a log on deliverables promised between both of our departments: Finance to Operations and vice versa. It looks like the slippage is coming from three specific individuals, and not the whole Finance Department. From our side, it looks like it is isolated to one team. I instructed the Team Leader to address this and let them know I am tracking it and expect immediate improvements. I'll let you know what happens and I would like your perspective on this. (waits for response) Back to the Finance team: Have you noticed anything like this when you ask for deliverables, or has any other department head or employee mentioned it? Why do you think the discrepancy in timelines and deliverables for these employees exists?

AGGRESSIVE ASSUMPTIVE QUESTION:

"Why does your team insist on fighting every suggestion from the sales team who are out in the field every day interacting with the customer?"

Alternative: "Several members of my team voiced concerns about how conflict seems to arise with the Marketing Team whenever they make suggestions about customer care-abouts and changes they'd like to see in their marketing materials. I asked them to put together a list of their suggestions, rather than bring them up verbally. I wanted you to look at them and let me know if these are completely off the mark. I want to help my Sales Team understand how to best get dialog running smoothly and openly again with their counterparts in Marketing. I realize that their temperature is up right now, and they feel they aren't being heard. As leaders, we need to address this and figure out how to address concerns without Marketing Team feeling they are being singled out in an open-sided finger pointing exercise either. Have you had any feedback from Marketing on how they feel about Sales Team members? Do we maybe have an internal spat going here? Is it a tempest in a teacup or a bit bigger and more serious than that? What do you think we can do to address it before it hurts Sales and Marketing efforts?

a sympathetic sibling in your feelings about Thanksgiving, or perhaps go with one to Thanksgiving with your family? I know that you've really been worrying about that for a while now. We haven't been able to lessen your anxiety over this even after a good few chats. Maybe a similar approach that you used for the Main Street meeting would help? What do you think of that?"

Response: "I think that if you would have said that last coaching session, I would have said 'no way'. But now, I think it might be something to talk over. I shouldn't exclude it like I have before."

Ask a Question to Discover Intention

The reasons why a question is asked is called 'the intention'. Intention is the DNA of communication. Seeking clarification and understanding of the coachee's intentions might help you gain insight into why the coachee is behaving in a certain manner. If you step back and challenge your basic assumptions and/or affirm your understanding, you'll be a better Leadership Coach. You must do this if only to feel more confident in your conclusions. In many instances, Leadership Coaches request clarification about what a coachee just said about a topic.

> *The intention is to gather information to better understand the context and content of the coachee's communication and/or responses.*

A Leadership Coach may prompt coachees to share more information about thoughts, behaviors, actions, and or feelings they are experiencing. Setting the appropriate timeframe and context makes these conversations more efficiently.

Present: *The intention is to openly discuss what the coachee is going through in their mind right now and to prompt about past and/or future thoughts.*

Past: *If the coachee talks about the past, ask them to be specific in their memories and check to see if these have been based on reality or have been distorted by their perceptual prism.*

Future: *The basis of behavioral coaching is to have the coachee make the right choices inside their mind (Self-Talk) that results in appropriate behavior for the situations they'll face. Rehearsing the decision making, Self-Talk and thinking patterns for the future actions they might take is what great coaching forward-driving conversations are all about.*

Accountability and Tag Up's from Prior Coaching Sessions

Leadership Coaches should always start a coaching session by asking for or confirming some basic information about what happened with their coachees since the last time they spoke. *The intention for the questions is to tie up loose ends, bring the coachee back to where*

the last session left off, and to start the ball rolling on this session without losing continuity.

Coaches ask follow-up questions after assignments, milestones, or tasks were due. *The intention is to assess what the coachee thought of the assignments. Another intention might be to ascertain the motivational components associated with these. Did the coachee like them? Or did they find them boring, ineffectual, or uninspiring? Were they too simple or complex?*

> Successful people ask better questions, and as a result, they get better answers. -Tony Robbins

Four Questioning Techniques

You can be intentional by using one of four different questioning techniques:

1. Closed
    a. yes/no
    b. information specifics
2. Opened-ended
3. Leading
4. Options and the 'Illusion of Choice'

1.A CLOSED QUESTIONS: YES/NO

The simplest form of questioning is the Yes/No question. As its name suggests, the answer expected is either yes or no.

Yes/No Questions can be a great way to:

- **Check accountability:** *"Did you complete all the tasks and go through all your responsibilities this week?"*
- **Boundaries:** Figure out the boundaries a coachee wants/needs for their leadership efforts: *"Right now, you have an open-door policy. I get why that's important to you. Do you think that setting some quiet time every day – with your door closed - to work through your individual responsibilities and tasks will help you have better work/life balance?"*
- **Next Steps:** Ascertain what appropriate next steps might be: *"Do you want to start learning how to change your _____ habits this week?"*

Sometimes this question is answered with a modifier or 'hedge'. If this is the case, the answer might be perhaps, maybe, or sometimes (or the like). In coaching sessions, when the coachee doesn't answer either yes or no, you must delve deeper.

1.B CLOSED QUESTIONS: DATA/SPECIFICS

Closed Data/specifics Questions look for a specific and quantifiable response other than a Yes or No. They are most often posed to gather information and to negotiate limitations or boundaries.

Closed Data/specifics Questions can be a great way to:

- **Look down information:** What time will you be available on Tuesday? Was there anything on your responsibility list that slipped?
- **Quantify particulars:** You said that you wanted to complete

the hiring process for your successor by what specific date?
- **Negotiate limits and boundaries:** What would an acceptable method for communicating with you be? Do you prefer text, email, or phone call to set appointments? What times are best for contacting you? Are there any limits on when I can text or call?
- **Gather details:** In the last session, we talked about how meetings were killing your personal efficiency and ruining your scheduling options. You said you were going to log the meetings you attend by importance, gathering information and adding value that no one else could. Let's discuss the results. How many times did you attend a meeting last week that you could have sent a proxy or not attended because you didn't learn anything new or add value?

> The art and science of asking questions is the source of all knowledge. - Thomas Berger

2. OPEN-ENDED QUESTIONS

As a Leadership Behavior Coach, it's very important to have an inventory of powerful open-ended questions. Opened-ended questions are answered by more than a simple yes or no. Make no mistake: Open-ended can be one of your most powerful coaching tools.

> Asking the proper questions is the central action of transformation. Questions are the key that causes the secret doors of the psyche to swing open. -Clarissa Pinkola Estes

By using open-ended questions on a consistent basis, you can help your coachee 'program the way they respond to themselves internally', visualize a result, envision how they'll respond/perform, and/or put positive motivation and emotional involvement into play. As a Leadership Behavior Coach, your focus and your questions determine to a large extent the direction the coaching session will go. Most leaders understand how important the subconscious mind is in leadership efforts. One of the best ways to tap into the coachee's subconscious mind and its power is to employ open-ended questions. **Remember this: Where the subconscious** (deep thinking) **leads the conscious mind** (decision making) **follows. The conscious mind is the place where 'actions are decided and acted on'.**

So how exactly does this process of tapping into the subconscious mind work? When our subconscious mulls over questions, it kicks into gear in trying to answer or respond. If the question requires a 'yes' or 'no' answer, the subconscious mind shuts itself off thinking "I'm done." When it hears opened-ended questions, it can't get to 'done' easily. Answering open-ended questions requires a more thoughtful response and deeper way of thinking. By posing the appropriate open-ended questions during your coaching sessions, you can make sure that your coachee is more thoughtful. You can stage your questions to illicit various responses. These can help the coachee become motivated, energetic, remorseful, talkative, angry, open to debate, etc.

The key to a great coaching session is posing the appropriate questions to invoke appropriate response.

WHAT DO OPENED-ENDED QUESTIONS DO?

- *They can help you establish rapport, trust, and credibility. How did today's session help you?*
- *They make it easier to gather information. You said you were unhappy with your team's results last Monday, what happened to cause that?*
- *They help your coachee open-up. Can you tell me more about that? How did that make you respond?*
- *They help you in digging deeper, perhaps to qualify what you've heard. You said you conducted three extremely tough performance reviews last week. Can you tell me about each and what you learned?*
- *Opened-ended questions help the coachee become directly involved in the coaching session's discussion. You seem a bit distracted/stressed. What do you think is creating my observation today?*

HOW DO YOU LAUNCH OPENED-ENDED QUESTIONS?

Ask the question and let your coachee respond.

- DO NOT interrupt.
- DO NOT prompt.
- DO NOT lead. (Note: A leading question pressures, prods for, or encourages a preconceived or desired answer. Example: Why don't you get more excited when you see how much revenue has increased in your department? Can you see how beneficial it is for you? Assumes coachee isn't excited. This question calls the coachee out about their level of emotions

and is judgmental regarding this.)
- **DO** be quiet.
- **DO** be respectful.
- **DO** be patient.

Warning: Please note that opened-ended questions are a tool, but they are not the only questioning tool. There are times when leading questions, yes/no questions, etc. are more appropriate for your purpose.

OPENED-ENDED QUESTIONS (SAMPLES)

- What other concerns, opportunities, and/or topics should we discuss today?
- Can you help me understand that a little better?
- What exactly does that mean?
- Can you give me a bit more insight into your thinking on this?
- How did that work out and what would you change for now?
- What challenges does that boundary or accountability measure create?
- What challenges has that kind of boundary or accountability measure created in the past?
- Let's get specific for you/those impacted?
- What are the best things about _____?
- With whom have you had success with boundaries or accountability in the past?
- With whom have you had difficulties with boundaries or accountability in the past?
- What prompted you to act like that given the situation?
- What made you want to investigate this more?

STRUCTURING A SERIES OF QUESTIONS   167

- What are your expectations/requirements for this solution to be right for you? What is it that you'd like to see yourself accomplish in the next day/three days/week/month/year/3 years?
- What process did you go through to determine your current work/life balance needs so far/right now?
- How do you see this unfolding if you do have that conversation?

OPEN-ENDED QUESTIONS CAN HELP CLARIFY

When you ask clarifying questions to better understand what has been said, your coachee will appreciate it. Please remember that often people speak past one another. Asking illuminating questions can help uncover the real intent behind what is said. Have you ever had someone ask a question that, if you probed a little, you might uncover the actual intention, emotions, motivation, or purpose? Digging deeper can provide better understanding and help you understand the coachee better. It can also lead us toward even better and more relevant follow-up questions. *"That's interesting! Can you tell me more about that?"* and/or *"Why did you think that when you...."* or *"That response makes me ask why...?"* In general conversations between people, the participants rarely dig deeper to ask 'uncovering questions' for fear of being rude, of prying, or appearing overly curious, or just plain nosey. The result is they tend to make assumptions and complete any missing parts themselves without first unearthing appropriate facts, necessary context, or background information. By clarifying with open-ended follow-up questions, you will dig deeper and get to a better place of understanding. It often takes a bit of uncomfortable questioning to get to the heart of the matter. But that's your responsibility as a Leadership Coach.

3. LEADING QUESTIONS OR 'SUGGESTIVE INTERROGATION'

> None of us is immune to suggestion. We are social beings and live in a social world. -Siri Hustvedt

Leading question or suggestive interrogation is a question that hints at the answer. The Leadership Coach is looking for a certain type of response or for a way of answering from the coachee. Leading can be most beneficial to confirm decision making, future actions, new ways of behaving or the like.

EXAMPLES:

"After you've practiced mirroring and matching to build rapport in this session, do you think you'll use it the interviews you have coming up this week?"

"Since reading Noble Intent, and looking at how the principles can positively impact workplace relationships and communication, do you agree that it might change how you think about your interactions with Tom and his team?"

CONSEQUENCES OF LEADING QUESTIONS

The problem with leading or suggestive questions is that coachees will often 'tell you what you want to hear'. If you use this form of questioning, you must bear this in mind. The question itself contains the information the Leadership Coach wants the coachee to confirm.

> *A fact is a simple statement that everyone believes. It is innocent, unless found guilty. A hypothesis is a novel suggestion that no one wants to believe. It is guilty, until found effective.* -Edward Teller

DELIVERING LEADING QUESTIONS EFFECTIVELY

Whenever you deliver leading questions, as much as possible, keep neutral tonality and make sure your body language doesn't further cement the 'leading'. If you don't do this, there's a risk that the coachee might think you are trying to overly influence them or skew their responses to ones you'll deem 'acceptable'.

If you ask a leading question about emotions, you also want to find out the degree of emotional involvement the other person may have experienced. For example: If your question references excitement, don't be a bounding puppy! Tone it down! Otherwise the person might automatically mirror your excitement. If you want to know if they were stressed or anxious, make sure you keep those particular 'emotional tells' in check. When this happens, it is called transference. Transference often occurs unconsciously when one person 'picks up' emotions, feelings, fears, or reactions from another. This is a normal part of conversations, but can be detrimental in a situation where transference of emotions has the potential to skew responses.

Warning: You should never transfer your emotional involvement to your coachee when you pose a leading question. Transference can occur when a coach transfers emotions to a person in coaching sessions. This transference can occur because the coach's body language, tonality, words or gestures stimulate emotions.

BENEFITS OF LEADING QUESTIONS

Leading questions do have a benefit in that you can use them to watch a coachee's reaction. *"In our last coaching session, you said that you would call two people from the New York City office. You wanted to work on your influencing and relationship building skills. The context was accountability. You said you wanted to let them know how important accountability is. You mentioned that you wanted to reiterate that you treat all remote locations fairly across the board when it comes to hitting their numbers. You said you were going to mention to the front-line sales managers that you wanted some thoughtful ideas on how to hold remote office reps a tad more accountable without locking them down with unnecessary and/or unproductive paperwork. Did you find out anything about the folks over there that you found concerning?"*

The risk is that if the coachee didn't find anything at all to be concerned about, the coachee will be less forthcoming than had the Leadership Coach asked an opened-ended question: *"How did your call with your NYC office go?"*

However, if you do want to get a positive response or reduce fear, a leading question may be the best tactic. *"Last session I asked: What's the worst that can happen if that conversation with the NYC office does bring up some concerns for you? You don't think letting your front-line sales managers know that you want more accountability with the numbers is fair? Don't you also think that soliciting their input on how to do this might really be helpful? What's the worst thing that could happen? You don't think they're going to bite your head off do you? Don't you think that regardless of the response, you've broken the ice on a subject your predecessor let get out of control? Isn't that worse thing actually a good thing?"*

Depending on the circumstances, leading questions can be objectionable or appropriate. Additionally, leading questions may often be answerable with a yes or no: *"You had a conversation with your sales managers in the NYC office this week that made you concerned?"* OR leading questions can be opened-ended questions: *"How many concerns did you unearth on your NYC office conversation this week?"*

HOW TO MAKE LEADING QUESTIONS MORE EFFECTIVE

> I try to create an environment where it's okay to make a mistake, though it's not okay to be unfocused or come in unprepared. I'm challenging and demanding, but very patient. I don't tell you how to get there and I don't show you what to do, though I'll ask leading questions. - Ruben Santiago-Hudson

Here are some samples of leading questions and how to change them to be appropriate and effective:

The goals is to determine how much 'leading' is required to get the information you need or to confirm or refute any assumptions. Then the Leadership Coach should pose an appropriate leading question.

Do you have any problems with your peers/employees/team member/boss?

This question assumes the coachee is experiencing problems and prompts a response detailing those problems.

A neutral question would be: *Do you have anything you'd like to discuss regarding maintaining the best relationships possible with your peers/employees/team member/boss?*

"Did you enjoy your strategy session? Wasn't it fantastic?"

Including the word fantastic can lead respondents.

A neutral question would be: *What did you think of the strategy session? What did you learn about yourself? Did you make the adequate progress?*

"If you were to think about the next market to address perhaps London, NYC, or San Diego, where would you like to focus resources first?"

By giving examples within the question, you're providing answers, swaying the thoughts of the coachee. If you'd like more thoughtful answers don't give any leading examples. If you'd like coachees to narrow down a list of options, ask them to choose their top 1 or 3 new or emerging markets.

A neutral question would be: Can you speak to emerging markets? What are your top choices for regions or cities where you might allocate resources.

"Do you agree that hiring a new COO should be your next step in putting your team together room?"

Stating a question with "Do you agree..." makes this a leading question, meaning a 'Yes' from the coachee would be more likely. Additionally, by prompting the exact person or position that would fill a future role, the 'lead' developed into a more strongly biased question. To adjust for this, change the question to one that is more impartial.

A neutral question would be: *"Have you considered what the next hire for your leadership team would ideally be?"*

AVOIDING LEADING QUESTIONS

Below, we'll examine how to avoid leading questions during your coaching sessions. Please note that the third question will get you the most reliable response, because each of the first two questions are leading questions. Leading means that the phrasing of the question itself **includes or implies the desired answer**.

Question 1: *"I suspected you were having difficulty with Joseph when we discussed your day yesterday. What happened?"*

Problem: The coach's question may not be an accurate representation of the coachee's experience with that employee. The coach may anticipate the coachee had difficulty but that's not what happened at all! The coachee may have already resolved the issue, could found it was an isolated event, been misinformed or simply have been venting, or a host of other experiences. Posing the question like this puts a point of view into the conversation that might potentially skew the response. Additionally, by asking a leading question, the coach may inadvertently break rapport because the coach and coachee are no longer on the same page.

Question 2: *"Why do you think you had difficulty talking with Joseph?"*

Problem: Again, this question implies the answer and assumes that coachee had difficulty. It is a blunt leading question which the coachee may find objectionable.

A neutral question would be: *"What was easy, challenging, exciting, or that gave you something to think about regarding your interaction with Joseph?"*

This opened-ended question steers the coachee to the topic of interest (the activity) without suggesting what the experience may have been like for them. It also puts forth a variety of possible responses with none being in command. The coachee can say pick one or add to the list, without disagreeing with the coachee. Here the Leadership Coach offers a 'general frame' for the topic of the question, rather than suggesting a response (leading).

USING LEADING QUESTIONS FOR COMPLIANCE

> We see and hear and otherwise experience very largely as we do because the language habits of our community predispose certain choices of interpretation. - Edward Sapir

As with any influencing technique, there are good ways to use leading questions. One way is to promote compliance. The key is to structure the leading questions around a goal. Tagging the You will notice in the examples below that you can increase the motivational impact by using leading questions.

HERE ARE EXAMPLES OF HOW TO ACCOMPLISH THIS:

Goal: Getting the Board presentation completed in a timely and less stressed manner.

Leading Question: We discussed ways to cause less stress prior to a Board Meeting. Since they always happen on a Thursday, do you all think that getting the final draft out to everyone by the Thursday prior for any last-minute edits and then a two-hour tag up Friday at noon is one way we can avoid ruining everyone's weekend four times a year? *Don't you think that Thursday or Friday we should have a rehearsal of the most important slides with a mock Q&A?*

Goal: Making sure the team understands how important cooperation is.

Leading Question: Do you think Nasa could have landed a man on the moon in the 1960s without a thousandth of the computing power we have today if they didn't cooperate with each other? *What can we do to make sure we have that type of cooperative thinking in our organization?*

Goal: Motivating a sales team to bring in at least 15% more revenue than last quarter.

Leading Question: Looking at the talent in our organization and the foundation we've laid, it struck me that we can genuinely achieve what we set out to do. We are on track for at least a 15% increase this quarter, but like we said in our strategy session last month, the key is religiously tracking the front end of funnel. We all agreed this has to be our primary focus. What are some suggestions to do this at our level? *And what can we do to make sure this tracking happens at every single level of our sales team?*

Goal: Making certain the metrics and dashboards enhance accountability.

Leading Question: There's no doubt in anyone's mind that accountability has been spotty. We've had four mergers in two years. It's been great for the business as a whole; but it's been chaotic. We have to make some tough decisions about staff in the next six months. Consolidating the data and getting to the heart of what people are doing versus what they should be doing is something we've talked about at length. Now is the time for the rubber to hit the road. Bottom line: At all levels of our organization, timely feedback is an issue. Holding people accountable is still an issue. Making decisions on who to reward, what to recognize and who to promote is too subjective. Knowing that we have to concentrate on this and solve this, what can we do to demonstrate our skills in proving feedback so that all of our employees can model our behavior? *Since we've all agreed we need to do better in this, what can we do this quarter to bring up our skills?*

LEADING USING RHETORICAL QUESTIONS

The purpose of rhetoric, or the art of influencing, persuading and convincing, is to speak or write in a way where a. your point is clear; and b. without having to say something directly. Rhetorical questions are the inquiring way of making a point using something that is obvious. Rhetorical questions are often humorous and don't require an answer. But we suggest that you avoid them during coaching sessions unless you want to lighten the mood and you have built up a lot of trust. Please remember: A rhetorical question is a question that is used to make a point, rather than to actually get an answer. You should want to open dialogue, not shut it down.

> Rhetorical questions tap into the experience base of the listener. You can pose one based in intellectual, emotional and/or motivational

> power. They are best when anti-literal, relying on metaphor, allusion, and other linguistic devices. Most important, the questioner assumes there exists knowledge within a community of listeners.

RHETORICAL QUESTIONS ARE:

1. Obvious or verifiably true (and most of the general populous would agree to the point) or
2. Impossible in reality or meant as a metaphor.

Often rhetorical question can be used to challenge or provoke a response by pointing out something that is quite obvious to drive home your point. Professors, teachers, politicians, lecturers, religious leaders, and others use rhetorical questions to help keep attention of their audiences. *"Who wouldn't like to win the lottery?"*, is not a question that requires a direct response. Nor are these examples looking for a response:

- *"Who in a leadership position doesn't want to be respected?"*
- *"Do you really think people are all bad or all good?"*
- *"Nobody thinks accountability isn't important, do they?"*

Why do rhetorical questions influence us? The human brain is programmed to answer any question it is asked. This is true even if the speaker doesn't wait for a response. It the answer is obvious; the responder and speaker are generally in agreement.

Example:

- These resources are your wish list. I get that... You didn't possibly think I would say yes or agree to all of this, did you?
- The decision is already made. We all agreed. There is no point in beating this to death again, is there?
- You guys delivered on time and profits are up over 8% again? Are you kidding me?
- You did a fabulous job with this proposal! Is there anyone smarter than you?
- I know that you stressed your team to the max reworking the numbers. Can we do better next time not killing our employees please?
- Ideally, if you want to be a success in this world, you have to figure out what you love and work at that, right?
- How do you think we're going to hire people if we aren't competitive?
- These numbers aren't going to fly with the customer's budget. Is this proposal supposed to be some kind of a joke or am I in a bad dream?
- You haven't had time to read at least one business book in the last year? Do you truly want to stop learning and growing your leadership skills for the rest of your life – one year on knowledge slipping away at a time?

Rhetorical questions are often used by speakers in presentations to get the audience to think and are, by design, should be used to promote thought. Rhetorical questions can make people think along the same lines. They can effectively unite the asker and responder. But the listener and the speaker should be on the same sheet of music for them to hit home. Example: *"No one wakes up and says: 'I want to be a crappy bossy leader, do they?' And no one says they want to be the worst at delivering feedback, do they?"*

The biggest possible benefit for using a rhetorical question is that they make people smile and possibly agree with each other about things that might not be spoken aloud – but are elephants in the room. *"We all have to pull our weight on this team or people will get resentful. It would be a sorry world indeed if this weren't the case, wouldn't it?"* If you are going to use this tactic; do so judiciously. Why? Because the pitfalls can far outweigh any benefits. Another word of caution: Rhetorical questions can seem sarcastic. There is no place for sarcasm in Leadership Coaching.

WHY SHOULD YOU AVOID RHETORICAL QUESTIONS DURING COACHING SESSIONS?

Asking rhetorical questions might make the coachee feel like foolish. These types of questions can also come across as very rude. Therefore it's not advisable for a leader to use them unless people clearly know you are making a point or that they are used to drive home a point and not directed at anyone maliciously. If you ask a rhetorical question regarding a person's behavior, the coachee would know right away that you are very unhappy about what they are doing. But since the question doesn't promote a response, it isn't a terribly healthy way to bring up a point about the coachee's negative, disappointing, or underperforming behaviors. Best advice: Avoid asking negative rhetorical questions.

Here are some negative examples:

- *Don't you think that you should have known what would happen?*
- *Can't you do anything that you promised during our coaching sessions?*
- *Would you like to say that a little bit louder so that I know you're serious this time?*

These are extreme to make a point. But, as you can imagine, even if all of these are true, the coachee could feel that they are being attacked. From a historical standpoint, most people will only use rhetorical questions when they are terribly frustrated and will probably want/need to apologize about it later.

4. OPTIONS AND THE 'ILLUSION OF CHOICE'

As a coach, you'll soon realize that coachees often need help coming up with options to move forward in their leadership efforts. They just don't know what might work for them. As a Leadership Behavior Coach, you IDEALLY NEVER want to direct. You should ALWAYS provide options. The key is to provide options that work with the coachee's individual goals, value system, and resources, where either choice is basically the same (and leads to your outcome) but is worded differently. One way to do this effectively is to use the fourth questioning methods: Options and the Illusion of Choice.

OPTIONS QUESTIONS

Movement forward by providing options is a highly effective method for getting coachees who are 'stalled' to take action. Because this questioning method is designed to propel the coachee forward toward any choice and get them thinking proactively and doing something to advance the ball. The specific goal when using an Illusion of Choice Question is to get the coachee to think about making a forward-progress decision based on picking between options that move them toward any decision or action. To produce an effective Options Question, you use two options stated as 'commands' or 'action statements' that would propel forward momentum and pose them as a question. **Please note: With Options Questions, the choices could be vastly different.**

By using at least two alternatives or options within an Options Question during your coaching sessions you can:

- Create the illusion of choice (The coachee will pick one and move forward.)
- Utilize that illusion to install suggestion (The coachee doesn't know which way to go and you provide suggestions/options.)
- Hide your suggestion so that it is unrecognizable (By using a question, you are not directing. Therefore, the coachee might 'own it' or think it was their own idea. They can get moving ahead without as much energy, time and emotional expenditure.)

THE ILLUSION OF CHOICE OPTIONS QUESTION

An Illusion of Choice Options Question is a structure that subtly influences the coachee by giving them the illusion of choice within a narrow set of options that lead to a particular objective. The specific goal when using an Illusion of Choice Question is to get the coachee to think about making a decision based on picking between two similar options that align with a predetermined outcome. The options/suggestions you provide inside the question allow the coachee to make a decision on which option might be best given the situation and the desired outcome or objective. The question's suggestions ideally will propel leadership efforts forward.

The differences in the options might simply be:

- the time frame in which the coachee's goal will be met,
- the specifics of how the process of meeting the goal will come about,
- how the details of deal will be structured,
- which day you will meet,
- the time/s of day that is best, etc.

EXAMPLES OF OPTIONS QUESTIONS:

Betty, you've been talking about the personnel changes you need to increase sales and you've said you want to stabilize the organization. These two can work against each other from a morale standpoint. You told me that you have to do something because your boss is getting frustrated because the Sales Management position is still open. Bottom line: You have to do something really soon – like yesterday!

The way most people would look at this is fairly simple: You can tell people you are looking for a qualified candidate either outside the organization or from within while explaining that you are looking for a candidate who will keep the same goals and culture – someone that won't rock a smoothly sailing sales organization. Or you can tell your boss that you can't make management changes in the timeframe she wants. If you go this route, I suggest that you show her the results of the survey detailing that the sales people need reassurance and stabilization. It shows quite clearly the last Sales Manager before you took over was an unmitigated disaster for morale. You might be right that your organization needs Behavior Coaching time. If you bring a new person in right now you might destabilize the sales organization risking that your top producers might leave. But that means you have to communicate forthrightly to one party or the other – sales guys or your boss. Which option do you think is better right now?

John, you said that you want to get better at speaking in front of the Board. There are several ways to do this but from what I know of you, two choices come to mind. You can either retain a speaking coach which is expensive but will ramp up your skills quickly or you can use systematic desensitization whereby you slowly put yourself out there more and more – sink or swim - building up your tolerance through grit or you can go to Toastmasters and do it in a structured but less expensive way.

> The bottom line: You get someone to do what you want them to do by giving them two options – and you don't really care which one they choose! You get closer to your goal – they feel that they are in control.

Note: During the coaching session, you are not necessarily looking for an immediate answer to the question. You can assume that the person will consent to any of the options and move forward. Sometimes it's best not to wait for a response, and simply assume they'll make the correct choice. You can circle back to it later to make sure they thought about it and decided what they'll do. Often, it's a much better coaching tactic to use your senses (observing, listening, and feeling) to gauge whether a person is moving forward or not.

GUIDELINES FOR THE EFFECTIVE USE OF OPTIONS QUESTIONS

- Make sure the coachee trusts you.
- Progress from mental to physical. Always try to bind a person's thoughts first, then work progressively towards binding physical movement. If you want them to do something, give some alternatives about the thinking behind that before they actually go do it! Plan, then do!
- You must deliver the double bind effectively and meaningfully, with the best of intentions without leading the coachee towards one or the other. Remember, all the options are just fine if the coachee picks one and moves forward!
- From the chart below, you'll see that it really doesn't matter which option your coachee picks from the pairings. Either choice will move them forward.

EXAMPLES OF ILLUSION OF CHOICE OPTIONS QUESTIONS:

Betty, you've been talking about the personnel changes you need to increase sales. You told me that you haven't been successful promoting from within because every viable candidate doesn't want the Sales

Management position. Bottom line: They like selling not management. You've had this information for three months. The way most people would look at this is fairly simple: You can either get a headhunter to start looking for a qualified candidate in a retained search or use several recruiters, you can ask for referrals (which is slow going) or you can get your internal recruiter to start looking and posting on job search boards. Let's narrow it down to one or two that you can commit to doing starting this week. What are the best ones for you right now: Recruiter, headhunter, referrals, or internal recruiter?

John, you said that you want to get better at speaking in front of the Board. There are several ways to do this but from what I know of you, two choices come to mind. You can either retain a speaking coach which is expensive but will ramp up your skills quickly or you can use systematic desensitization whereby you slowly put yourself out there more and more – sink or swim - building up your tolerance through grit or you can go to Toastmasters and do it in a structured but less expensive way.

PAIRING COMBINATIONS FOR DOUBLE BINDS	
Learn to let go and support this process	Continue with your leadership efforts by learning more about how to trust the process
Be open	Be receptive
Be interested	Get excited
Use a headhunter	Get the internal recruiter to help
Make it a habit	Use it daily
Work it into this month's budget	Set it up to start paying that debt next month

STRUCTURING A SERIES OF QUESTIONS

Get enthusiastic in a few minutes	Build up your excitement as you succeed one step at a time
Invest meaningful time with your coworkers building high morale	Get on board with reconnecting with your team and just having some downtime
Consider the cost savings	Let it positively impact your bottom line
Agree to new ways of acting	Think about how to create new habits
Recognize accomplishments	Look at personal wins
Apply it	Use it
Consider alternatives	Choose an option
Make an appointment	Sit down over lunch/coffee
Accept it as fact	Take it as truth
Use this knowledge daily	Integrate it into your daily life
Invest in your future right away	Understand how you can use this to help your leadership efforts after you figure out a few more details of your plan
Get excited immediately	Think about how motivated this will make you

EXAMPLES

The illusion of choice happens during communication a lot more than you think! Look at these historical sentences. We've underlined all the options in each statement.

When will a man discover that he is the master-gardener of his soul, sooner or later? (Does it really matter when this enlightenment occurs?)

Ask ourselves this: We must all hang together or assuredly we shall all hang separately?

- BENJAMIN FRANKLIN, to the other signers of the Declaration of Independence

Will I accept if nominated or serve if selected? No!

- WILLIAM TECUMSEH SHERMAN, message to the Republican National Convention

TRAINING AND DEVELOPMENT

I know you've been thinking about training your operations team and starting an accountability program now that you're through the restructuring. You've talked about it for months. This might make you feel even better in general. It's clearly been bothering you that your people haven't had the opportunity to learn more about providing feedback too. So today we'll set some time aside to discuss this. Bottom line: If you've already decided this is something you want to do, you must decide how and when to start. The choices of 'how' aren't completely clear yet. And we don't know which options will work for you. There are lots of ways to go about this. Have you started the research yet? Ask HR for some viable consultants or internal coaches or just recommend some required reading each week to all operations staff to start? Can you think of some more that might work for you as a starting point? How about coming up with some benefits to your overall leadership efforts and tap into this as motivation, too?

COMMUNICATION

So far, you have been learning different ways to speak to people to make it easier for them to understand what you and your team are going through right now. As you continue to learn to use the natural strengths in your behavior pattern to lead your people, do you think that you will find thinking about them and using your strengths as an approach will help you? Finding a way to have critical conversations is important to your leadership efforts. How do you think you'll do this in your work life in general or to enable you to be a more thoughtful leader and peer?

192 LEADERSHIP BEHAVIOR COACHING: THE ART OF ASKING PURPOSEFUL QUESTIONS

DISC-based Coaching Session Questions

The Leadership Behavior Coaching Program is very different from other coaching programs because we focus on DISCflex and behavior patterns as a foundational approach. We believe that if you ask questions designed to resonate at the coachee's behavioral level, they will have more impact on the outcomes your coachee will see.

Back to the Beginning

Now that you've learned what types of questions to ask, we are going back to the beginning, in a sense. This section contains suggestions of questions that are DISC Factor specific. You will notice these suggested questions can tie into the coachee's DISCflex Leadership or Business Behaviors Report. We have provided targeted questions to match each of the DISC Factors. Ideally, you'll know your coachee's scores in each factor and tailor your coaching sessions and line of questioning to the coachee's unique behavioral pattern.

> My mother's openness has remained inspiring to me. I strive to be a skeptic, in the best sense of that word: I question everything, and yet I'm open to everything. And I don't have immovable beliefs. My values shift and grow with my experiences - and as my context changes, so does what I believe. - Amy Tan

UNDERSTANDING BEHAVIORAL GOVERNANCE

There is a fundamental in understanding behavioral governance: Anytime you make the choice to behave, you make the choice to use a behavior governed by a DISC Factor (or two). Most people's choices are automatic which means they are ruled by their natural DISC Pattern. This isn't always the best in terms of outcomes or efficiencies. Enlightened people learn that making conscious choices and training themselves to make the appropriate behavioral choice is preferable.

HOW DO DISC FACTORS TYPICALLY RESULT IN BEHAVIORS AND ACTIONS?

If you want results, you use your Dominance Factor. Speaking to people in friendly terms means your Influence Factor is in play. Loyal or kind? You picked your Steadiness/Strategy Factor to govern the situation. Deciding to stick to the rules means your C is dominating.

Behaviors and actions are determined by which behavioral factor is the most 'overriding' or 'governing'. How does this play out? If you want to be friendly but have to get something done in a particular way, your Compliance Factor has to have preferential treatment. It has to trump your Influence Factor to be most effective. If you understand that you have to make the correct behavioral choices for the situation, you're well ahead of the game. The benefits to this knowledge are profound in terms of reducing stress and underscoring appropriate behavior for leadership situations.

WHY IS IT IMPORTANT TO ASK QUESTIONS IN DISC-SPECIFIC WAYS?

From a Leadership Behavior Coaching viewpoint, you can tap into this insight and have substantial impact on the client's thinking if you ask DISC-based questions. Your coachee's DISCflex Report will indicate which behavioral tendencies they are naturally inclined towards. These DISC Factors and Sub-Factors rule your coachee's behavior, while the opposing subfactors are the behaviors they'll typically use the least. We think that being able to use all the factors and subfactors consciously for the correct situation builds behavioral strength. At the very least, your coachee should know where their natural tendencies lie. The coachee's behavioral tendency will fall somewhere on the spectrum detailed in their report. The goal is to utilize this knowledge to drive the coaching sessions toward success. Ultimately, with this knowledge, the coachee will be careful to choose which DISC factors to use wisely given the situations they face. Additionally, with your coaching, they'll become adept at being able to consciously choose to always 'dial up' or 'dial down' their behavior to bring them balance on their leadership behavioral spectrum.

YOU CAN ASK THE SAME QUESTION IN FOUR DIFFERENT BEHAVIORAL WAYS

In this section, you'll look at how to effectively swap out the same question for the four DISC Factors. We believe it's best if a Leadership Coach poses questions in a behavioral style that will ring true to the coachee. If a coachee is more thoughtful and more prone to introspection (Elevated Steadiness/Strategy Factor), the coach should pose their questions in a way that impacts elevated S verbiage. "George, in thinking through how you're going to communicate with Sarah about what you need to do for the next month, what are some of the things that are causing you internal stress or keeping you awake at night?" The same question to an elevated Dominance Factor individual (quick paced, results-oriented, impulsive) might be posed like this: "George, let's look at the conversation you're soon to have with Sarah about what you need to do for the next month. We discussed putting your thoughts together before you talk to her. What are some of the things that you are going to focus on when you are explaining the results you expect to see?"

AIM FOR THE COACHEE'S BEHAVIORAL CORE

As you can see, the message posed differently might impact different coachees at their behavioral core. When you go through this section, start looking at how the coachee's DISC Factors affect how you might pose the question and what response you might receive. The more questions you examine, the more this concept will infiltrate your mind. When this occurs, your Self-Talk will change. You'll find that you will start tailoring your questions and verbiage to other people's behavioral patterns automatically. The more you focus on doing this, the better you'll become at this Leadership Behavior Coaching skill.

Your job as a Leadership Behavior Coach is to ask questions that motivate the coachee to act in accordance with their leadership efforts. As you ask these types of DISC-based questions, you'll uncover some behavioral patterns that might help them get serious about how to own their boundaries and address their leadership efforts. One of the ways you can assess how motivated your coachee is in their leadership efforts is to monitor how they are doing in the activities you've assigned and with the reading you've recommended.

We suggest that you open up a 'Consequences Discussion' about your expectations for their assignments. As part of this discussion, we suggest using DISC-based Q&A to underscore the importance of the activities, the necessity of sticking to learning schedules and in keeping promises made in the coaching sessions.

CONSEQUENCES Q&A FOR COMPLETING OR NOT COMPLETING ACTIVITIES AND HOMEWORK:

1. Explain to the coachee that it is important they live up to their obligations and promises made in the coaching sessions.

2. Explain the potential consequences of non-adherence:
   a. Wasted time.
   b. Cause unnecessary stress.
   c. Feelings of disappointment, sense of failure, blows to self-esteem, feeling unaccomplished, self-loathing, apathy, guilt, or shame in not delivering what they promised.

d. Put these in terms of their DISC Pattern:
- **Dominance Factor:** *What were the results of procrastination or not completing assignments in the past? Did that behavior hurt or help?*
- **Influence Factor:** *What affect has procrastination or not completing assignments had on your relationships in the past? Did that behavior hurt or help?*
- **Steadiness/Strategy Factor:** *What embarrassing, or internally painful affect has procrastination or not completing assignments had in the past? Did that behavior hurt or help?*
- **Compliance Factor:** *Have you ever planned to do something but then you let procrastination or not completing assignments stop you from getting things done on time? Did that behavior hurt or help?*

3. Detail how each assignment and every activity will address an area for their leadership efforts. Ideally you should do this in terms that will resonate with their leadership goals in DISC language.

Start Asking DISC-based Questions

> I can't just say one time of the year I'm going to do something different. I have to commit to a lifestyle behavioral change and just try to be a little bit better today than I was yesterday. -Gabrielle Union

THERE ARE CERTAIN BEHAVIORAL TENDENCIES THAT ARE LINKED TO THE FOUR DISC FACTORS.

Here is a reminder of what the DISC Factors are. Remember these as you look at the suggested DISC-based questions you can ask the coachee as they go through their DISCflex reports. Please use these as a guideline and come up with additional questions and follow up questions that work for you and your coachees.

DISC IS AN ACRONYM FOR:

DOMINANCE — Your need for **control, how fast you like to get results,** and your source of **ambition.** Whenever you are feeling **self-motivated**, you are using your **'D' factor**.

INFLUENCE — Your need for **communication, interaction with others,** and your source of **persuasion**. Whenever you are feeling **talkative**, you are using your **'I' factor**.

STEADINESS — Your need for **preparation**, working things out, soul-searching, consideration and **thoughtfulness** as well as your need for comfort prior to taking action. When you are being **strategic** or **go out of your way to help someone**, you are using your **'S' factor.**

COMPLIANCE — Your need for **structure, adherence to rules,** and your source of **organization**. When you become **extremely focused on completing your tasks according to expectations**, you are using your 'C' factor.

Here are some examples of questions and their DISC-based counterparts to get your coaching sessions started:

WHERE DID YOUR LEADERSHIP EFFORTS BEGIN? AT WHAT AGE DID SOMEONE SAY YOU WERE A LEADER OR THAT YOU FELT YOU WERE? WHAT ARE THE LEADERSHIP ATTRIBUTES THAT YOU THINK GOT YOUR PROMOTED TO THIS ROLE?

Dominance Factor: What were the results of your leadership skills with team members?

Influence Factor: How do your leadership strengths affect your peer relationships?

Steadiness/Strategy Factor: What were the major pain points of your leadership style for your direct reports?

Compliance Factor: What rules did you think should have been reworked or totally broken in your last position? Did you take a while to try to make them work for your team or did you just retool them to work for what you had to get accomplished?

HOW DID IT PROGRESS?

Dominance Factor: What degree of momentum/speed of decision making do you think occurs in your behavior when you decide to do something that isn't good for you? Maybe being too blunt or forward charging? Do you think that sometimes stopping before acting might have changed some things for the better? For examples, what were some of the results of your quick pace on your team's morale and burnout rate?

Influence Factor: How did the friends change as your promotions progressed?

Steadiness/Strategy Factor: Even though you knew you were coming in to turn around a bad situation, as your new team's numbers continued to go down, did you find yourself getting more moody, depressed, disappointed in yourself or something equally internally worrisome or painful?

Compliance Factor: Tell me about how you adjusted your schedule, habits and how your tried to square with your need for order as your travel schedule got crazier in your new role.

WHEN DID YOU REALIZE YOUR COMMUNICATION STYLE WAS A REAL ISSUE FOR YOU?

Dominance Factor: When did you come to the realization that the results of your communication style when you were stressed weren't working for you anymore?

Influence Factor: Did you ever feel insecure about your future when you got frustrated with your peers seeming lack of drive and your inability to motivate them to get on the bus? Did the realization that your normally friendly communication style wasn't working for you anymore happen because of a conversation with someone else or did you come to that conclusion alone?

Steadiness/Strategy Factor: Did you ever feel anxious about your future because you and your new boss weren't on the same page? How did the realization that your communication style wasn't working for you anymore happen?

Compliance Factor: When you come to the realization that the results of your communication style weren't working for you anymore, did you immediately come up with some kind of plan to get you out and keep you on track with leadership efforts or are you looking for one now?

WHAT HAS WORKED FOR YOU SO FAR?

Dominance Factor: What are the results of your leadership efforts so far? Are things happening quickly or slowly in your view?

Influence Factor: What are the results of your leadership efforts so far? Do you feel better about talking them through now or are you still a bit unsettled and feel that you're not quite there yet?

Steadiness/Strategy Factor: What are the results of your leadership efforts so far? Do you think you are a bit more able to figure out what makes you less anxious versus more energized? And do you want talk about some strategies to help you get into a more active leadership role? Do you think this discussion might help come up with some ways to deal with the anxiety you've been telling me about?

Compliance Factor: What are the results of your leadership efforts so far? Do you think you are a bit more able to figure out some plans for this coming week to help you be less anxious and more energized about your new leadership role? You mentioned you want to talk about a checklist to help you get more actively involved in your department. I wrote down that you want help coming up with some ways to deal with the lack of accountability you've been telling me about. Have you started putting together a list or a plan yet to address this with your management team?

HABITS FORM BECAUSE OF EXPERIENCES AND EXPECTATIONS

Your DISC-based questions can help your coachee tap into their own behavior style. Let's do an activity so you can practice writing DISC-based questions.

ACTIVITY

Rewrite this pair of questions for each of the DISC Factors:

Example: What is the most important thing about accountability? What do you hope to accomplish?

> **Dominance Factor:** What is the most important thing about accountability? What results do you expect your people to deliver?
>
> **Influence Factor:** What is the most important thing about accountability? How do you expect your people to communicate their goals and promises?
>
> **Steadiness/Strategy Factor:** What is the most important thing about accountability? What strategy do you expect your people to deliver prior to launching into action?
>
> **Compliance Factor:** What is the most important thing about accountability? What metrics and plans do you expect your people to deliver so you can best track progress?

Rewrite these questions for each of the DISC Factors:

> **Dominance Factor:** What is the most important thing about leadership communication to you?

Influence Factor: What is the most important thing about leadership communication to you?

_____

_____

Steadiness/Strategy Factor: What is the most important thing about leadership communication to you?

_____

_____

Compliance Factor: What is the most important thing about leadership communication to you?

_____

_____

Did you know the accountability standard and timelines were slipping or was it a surprise? If so, what should you have done at those moments in time?

_____

_____

Dominance Factor: Did you know the accountability standard and timelines were slipping or was it a surprise? If so, what should you have done at those moments in time?

_____

_____

Influence Factor: Did you know the accountability standard and timelines were slipping or was it a surprise? If so, what should you have done at those moments in time?

_____

_____

Steadiness/Strategy Factor: Did you know the accountability standard and timelines were slipping or was it a surprise? If so, what should you have done at those moments in time?

_____

_____

Compliance Factor: Did you know the accountability standard and timelines were slipping or was it a surprise? If so, what should you have done at those moments in time?

_____

_____

Looking at the reporting mechanisms you have access to, ask yourself: "What can I do today (and moving forward) to make sure the team makes their numbers and hits expected timelines and I don't get surprised again?"

Dominance Factor: Looking at the reporting mechanisms you have access to, ask yourself: "What can I do today (and moving forward) to make sure the team makes their numbers and hits expected timelines and I don't get surprised again?"

_____

_____

Influence Factor: Looking at the reporting mechanisms you have access to, ask yourself: "What can I do today (and moving forward) to make sure the team makes their numbers and hits expected timelines and I don't get surprised again?"

_____

_____

Steadiness/Strategy Factor: Looking at the reporting mechanisms you have access to, ask yourself: "What can I do today (and moving forward) to make sure the team makes their numbers and hits expected timelines and I don't get surprised again?"

_____

_____

Compliance Factor: Looking at the reporting mechanisms you have access to, ask yourself: "What can I do today (and moving forward) to make sure the team makes their numbers and hits expected timelines and I don't get surprised again?"

_____

_____

Look at this question and change it to align with the DISC Factors: What do my boundaries have to include, sound like, and be connected to for me to really 'own' them?

Dominance Factor:

_____

_____

Influence Factor:

_____

_____

Steadiness/Strategy Factor:

_____

_____

Compliance Factor:

_____

_____

Complementing Your Coaching Sessions with DISC-based Questions

Why the Enterprise Development eLearning Suite Lessons are Important

Any Program is only as good as the work the coachee puts in. We designed the **activities and Enterprise Development eLearning Suite** to help drive knowledge and accountability. Does the Leadership Coach translate lessons from required reading, activities, models of excellence and coaching sessions into organizational excellence?

- What happens when the coach is not around?
- Do the lessons' impact stop?
- Is the coachee still working the Leadership Behavior Program and motivated to learn and self-examine?
- Are they ahead or lagging according to progress expectations?

A Leadership Behavior Coach should recognize when coachees put in the extra time and effort as they work on implementing ideas and knowledge from the coaching sessions. Keeping track of progress and checking off completed items/training in their eLearning will help give coachees a sense of accomplishment as well as providing a measuring stick for tangible work they have put in. Each time a coachee comes to a meeting and gets recognition/sign off for their efforts they will feel good and be more likely to want to continue delving deeper into the models, activities and leadership knowledge they need.

> Building this pattern of small achievements and recognition will build momentum towards more success.
> "Success is the sum of small efforts - repeated day in and day out." - Robert Collier

Questions that pair to the Executive Coaching topics:

VALUES

Initial question: As far as the values you hold dear: What do you feel it takes to maintain and develop a successful team?

Questions if the coachee does not know what his or her team's core values are, you can probe to personal core values with these types of questions:

WHAT ARE SOME IMPORTANT THINGS THAT WERE TAUGHT TO YOU GROWING UP?

D – How can you channel these to help your leadership efforts?

I – How can you tap into the warm feelings and important lessons you remember from childhood to help foster your leadership skills/efforts?

S – How can you tap into the respect you felt for your parents/teacher/professor/coach to capture the important lessons you remember from childhood or your college years to help your leadership efforts today?

C – How can you reach back and remember the important lessons from childhood or your college years to help you better structure and make plans to lead your team?

THINK OF SOMEONE YOU RESPECT. WHY DO YOU RESPECT THAT PERSON? WHAT IS IT YOU VALUE ABOUT THEM?

D – How can you let them know you appreciate them and what they've done for you?

I – How can you let them know you appreciate and respect them and their friendship?

S – How can you let them know you appreciate their loyalty and the deep connection you have?

C – How can you let them know you appreciate how they've helped shaped your life as a leader?

WHAT WOULD YOU LIKE PEOPLE TO REMEMBER ABOUT YOU?

D – When you think about the results you want and the things you value in your professional life, at the end of the day how would you like people to remember you for your leadership efforts and determination?

I – When you think about the friendships you want and the people you value in your professional life, at the end of the day how would you like people to remember you for your leadership efforts and personality?

S – When you think about the connections and caring you have for others and the things you value in your professional life, at the end of the day how would you like people to remember you for your leadership efforts and thoughtfulness?

C – When you think about the preparation and planning you've done, the progress you hope you'll make by working your plan, and the things you value in your professional life, at the end of the day how would you like people to remember you for your leadership efforts and follow through?

WANTS VERSUS NEEDS ACTIVITY

WHAT DOES THE WORD "NEED" MEAN TO YOU?

D – When you think about things you need, how do you think they affect your leadership efforts/results, specifically talking about motivation, follow through, and determination in two ways:

1. If you have them?
2. If you can't get them yet?

I – When you think about things you need, how do you think they affect your leadership efforts/results, specifically talking about motivation, insecurity, friendships, and determination in two ways:

1. If you have them?
2. If you can't get them yet?

S – When you think about things you need, how do you think they affect your leadership efforts/results, specifically talking about motivation, strategy and changes they require (and you might not like making) in two ways:

1. If you have them?
2. If you can't get them yet?

C – When you think about things you need, how do you think they affect your leadership efforts/results, specifically talking about motivation, organization and planning in two ways:

1. If you have them?
2. If you can't get them yet?

Use similar verbiage for each of the four DISC Factors to adjust these questions to the coachee's behavior:

What does the word 'want' mean to you? What does the word 'want' mean to you?
How can you tell the difference between the two?
How does it feel when you get what you want?
How does it feel when you have all you need?

FEELINGS AND EXTERNAL SENSORY INPUT MOTIVATIONAL INTERVIEWING QUESTIONS

D – How can you direct/command your feelings to be positive even when you know the deck is stacked against success. How do you do it when you can't let the team know how bad the situation is and how much energy it's going to take to turn something around?

I – How will your negative feelings affect others on the leadership team?

S – If you are going into a negative situation, what tools can you bring to help you stay positive and be a great leader?

C – What are some self-governing rules you can make to stay positive and be a great leader?

REPROGRAMMING MEMORIES

D – What would you like your memory of that unpleasant incident be like right now and in the future?

I – How would it sound if you told your positive/negative memory to others?

S – What kind of energy would you like others to feel about your new memory?

C – How can you structure your new memory to be more productive and positive from a lesson's learned standpoint?

ESCALATION OF EMOTIONAL INVOLVEMENT

D – How can you prevent your negative emotions from manifesting into unwanted behaviors?

I – How would it affect you if others saw you negatively?
    S – What steps can you take to prevent your team members and direct reports from getting side-railed by any person's negative emotions?
    C – How can you organize your thoughts to stay on a positive track?

WHAT DOES MY CURRENT CHARACTER REFLECT?

D – What are some unwanted characteristics that prevail even when you don't want them to?
I – What have others stated they don't like about you?
S – What positive traits do you possess that can benefit yourself and others from a leadership perspective?
C – What negative traits do you carry that disrupt the way you want to lead and be perceived?

FEAR - WHERE DOES IT COME FROM?

D – Tell me about a time you made a snap decision that you instantly regretted.
I – Tell me about a time you made a decision that made you feel rejected by others.
S – Tell me about a time you made a decision without thinking that hurt others unintentionally.
C – Tell me about a time you made a decision that made you feel uncomfortable and unorganized.

SYSTEMATIC DESENSITIZATION

D – What has been the result of a fear you have been unwilling to confront as a leader?

I – How could you use your 'good fears' to help other people on your team?

S – What does avoiding your fears say about your self-acceptance as a leader?

C – What do you think could happen if you maintained your courage in adverse situations?

OVERCOMING FEAR

D – What negative thoughts overcome your positive thoughts and how does that feed your 'bad fear'? What could you instantly tell yourself to feed your 'good fear'?

I – How could you influence your thoughts to feed your 'good fears'?

S – What is a solid strategy/plan to assist you in overcoming your 'bad fear'?

C – What rules could you set for yourself to help you accomplish overcoming your 'bad fear(s)'?

DEALING WITH FEARS

D – What is a fear-based belief that hinders your progress as a leader?

I – How does your fear inhibit your work relationships?

S – How does fear prevent you from being bold with your team's strategy and stretch goals?

C – How have any fears you might possess affected the leadership standards you have set for yourself in the past? Has it pushed them down or pulled them up?

TIPS TO KEEP A POSITIVE ATTITUDE

D – What is something you have said to yourself in the past that has had an immediate positive effect?
I – What is something positive you said to someone in the past that made a marked difference in their attitude? How can you apply that to yourself?
S – What is a thoughtful statement you told someone and how can you apply that to yourself?
C – What positive thoughts can you tell yourself that will keep your growth as a leader on track?

TIPS TO OVERCOME MY OBSESSION

D – What is a persistent thought that immediately stops your progress from being free of worry? What is something you could tell yourself or remind yourself to break that worry and turn it into resolve to get to the heart of what's going on? What can you do or say instead of just worrying, that helps solve the problem? How can you address concerns and bring issues out in the open with great questions.
I – What is an obsession or continual worry that has a negative impact on your team dynamics or leadership results?
S – How does obsessing interrupt your ability to effectively lead and work your strategy?

C – What are some rules you can create to practice when you begin to obsess?

CHANGING NEGATIVE HABITS

D – What is something you want to see happen in the near future? (30 days)
I – How can having a stretch goal help those around you excel?
S – How can having positive habits add to your team's overall strategy?
C – How can practicing positive communication habits help your desired outcome for a team capable of open and respectful communication?

WHAT MOTIVATES ME?

D – What is a results-based motivator that you can use to help your goals get accomplished right now?
I – What is a people-oriented motivator you can use to help those around you to support your team's objectives and work together more cooperatively?
S – What is a thoughtful or kindness-based motivator you can use to help people work better together?
C – What is a process-based motivator that will assist you and your team to establish operational protocols that foster innovation and cooperativeness?

Active Listening without Judgment

> Too often we underestimate the power of a touch, a smile, a kind word, a listening ear, an honest compliment, or the smallest act of caring, all of which have the potential to turn a life around. -Leo Buscaglia

If we as Leadership Coaches hope to get people to open up in coaching sessions, allowing us to see what really makes the coachee tick, we need to engage in high level active listening. When we do, Leadership Coaches create circumstances that encourage coachees to open up, engage more, and have a deeper level of communication with us during the coaching session.

Always try to remember that we were all born with two ears and one mouth. That is the same

ratio that makes you a good communicator during coaching sessions: minimum of 2 parts listening; one part talking. Active listening involves the use of your highest level of auditory skills. Active listening can be very effective if you want to understand more about a person's values and beliefs, as well as what's truly important to them. It is also important to first listen before we can logically expect others to trust us.

ACTIVE LISTENING HAS SEVERAL COMPONENTS:

1. **Context and content:** Understanding the words spoken in the context they were intended. Pay attention to make sure you

As a Leadership Behavior Coach, each day holds a surprise – some pleasant – others not so much. If we expect to be surprised can we see, hear, or feel the emotions of wonder, astonishment, disbelief, shock, admiration, bewilderment, or amazement when it comes to us. Believe me: We see and hear it all!

Let's not be afraid to receive each day's coaching surprise, whether it comes to us as sorrow or as joy, as a shock or a pleasant disclosure; a revelation or bombshell. If we listen – actively and fully – we will open a new place in our minds, a place where we can welcome surprises and process the consequences and opportunities more completely. This is how we provide great value to the coachee and their organization.

hear the actual words the coachee says. Have agreement of the framework, issue, opportunity, or the situation being discussed.
2. **Clarification:** Ensure that you clear up any potential misunderstanding of basic meanings.
3. **Evaluation:** Determine the present state versus desired state of the situation according to communication goals. What needs to be done with the information being communicated? Does something need 'fixing', or does the coachee simply need to vent? Are you expected to be a sounding board or are you expected to offer options and ask to follow up questions?
4. **Reaction/Response:** Provide verbal or body language messages that relay that you have a grasp of what the coachee is communicating. NEVER interrupt. Interrupting is disrespectful because you haven't listened until the end of the person's words. If you interrupt, you've already thought of your response before the person finished. None of these are appropriate for active listening.

SHOWING THAT YOU'RE LISTENING

Active listening involves giving the person who is speaking certain communication cues so that they get the impression that you're really listening to what they have to say. It gives the impression that you care about what is being said. Let's look at how this might work. Imagine that you were a coachee trying to get a point across and that you felt nervous opening up. How a Leadership Coach listens and responds might make a big difference in the trust the coachee has. This simple act of active listening may assure the coachee that opening up, being vulnerable and/or and communicating in a blatantly honest manner is ok. And that's precisely what great coaching sessions try to accomplish.

IMAGINE YOU ARE AN OBSERVER DURING A COACHING SESSION. HERE ARE TWO DIFFERENT SCENARIOS:

1. Suppose the Leadership Coach is looking in a notebook the whole time, making notes, and never making eye contact with the coachee. Occasionally, the Leadership Coach might mutter "*mm-hmm*", but other than that, nothing indicates they are PRESENT in the conversation.
2. Now, imagine that the Leadership Coach nods along with the coachee, interjects at the right moments, and asks the coachee relevant questions about the information he is relaying. The Leadership Coach tilts their head giving the impression that their ears are working. They also smile at the appropriate moments and never interrupt the coachee. Even better, the Leadership Coach pauses for a moment before they answer or respond to the coachee. In this way, the coachee clearly understands that their coach has taken the time to listen thoughtfully to their comments and respond to their words appropriately.

Obviously, the second situation would make a coachee feel more comfortable.

> One of the sincerest forms of respect is actually listening to what another has to say. -Bryant H. McGill

SIGNS OF ACTIVE LISTENING

Active listening essentially amounts to putting across the 'signals' of active listening. When you communicate, the more you send the signal that you're actively listening, the more likely someone will be open with you.

Active listening involves the use of your highest level of auditory and thoughtfulness skills. It also involves giving the person who is speaking certain communication cues so that they get the impression that you're really listening to what they have to say. When you communicate, the more you send the signal that you're actively listening, the more likely someone will open up. Here are some signs of active listening:

- Eye contact and taking note of eye accessing cues.
- Nodding along with what a person is saying.
- Giving emotional cues to show that you're engaged such as laughing, smiling, and frowning.
- Adjust the tempo and match the other person's cadence. Your face and posture, your eyes and breathing all show that you're really engaging with what they're saying.
- Appropriate responses are crucial. Take care to laugh when appropriate, or to smile or frown when the occasion calls for it.

> We change another person's behavior by changing our own.

Be fully present. Remind yourself 'be in the moment'. If you feel yourself drifting off somewhere inside your head or pre-thinking responses, remind yourself to come back to the moment and show that you are listening intently to precisely what the other person is saying. Whenever you listen responsively there's an excellent chance the other person will naturally do the same. This is a truism: **We change other people's behavior by changing our own.**

EMOTIONAL RESPONSIVENESS

In responding, take on the appropriate emotional tone. If they are excited, you should be somewhat excited, too. Mirroring their emotions and feelings is a powerful way to connect. Of course, always remember to 'be appropriate' in your mirroring. What else can you mirror to show you're listening intently? If they are serious about the subject matter, you should be serious. Remember that body language and facial expressions are critically important in establishing trust and rapport. Creating and maintaining trust and rapport is critical during coaching sessions.

VERBAL RESPONSIVENESS

You can respond verbally to show you are listening. When appropriate, you can interject with a statement that shows that you've been through what the person is talking about and that you understand it. Often, a simple statement of *"I've been there before,"* or *"I understand what you're saying"* are enough to really get a person to open.

VERBAL BACKTRACKING, PARAPHRASING, AND SUMMARIZING

Other effective techniques for reading and understanding another person is to use verbal backtracking, paraphrasing, or summarizing:

VERBAL BACKTRACKING:

1. Verbal backtracking is used to clear up any possible confusion or misunderstandings before they arise. You circle back to an earlier place in the conversation, asking for clarification, or asking questions during a conversation. It is basically just asking questions during a conversation to:
    a. Give the impression that you're listening intently, and
    b. Make sure that you truly understand and appreciate what the other person is saying.

2. To use verbal backtracking effectively:
    a. Every so often repeat back what the coachee just said in the form of a question.
    b. Get your delivery spot-on: Try not to seem confused, but rather open-minded and curious, as if you're really trying your best to understand them.
    c. You can say something like: *"So if I understand you correctly, you're trying to put the point across that your peers need to be more effective in working together on group activities? I am hearing frustration. Is that accurate?"*

3. In addition to aiding your understanding, verbal backtracking also

has the benefits that it forces the person in question to actively question and/or clarify what they've said to you. **Here's what happens:**

a. As you ask a person about what they've said, they must consciously call it to mind and ask themselves if they really meant it.

b. They also are forced to explain their standpoint more clearly or to clarify their expectations a bit better. As you do this, you're naturally setting them up to engage in intellectual banter with you.

PARAPHRASING:

Paraphrasing is a little different from backtracking. Paraphrasing involves taking a set of facts or opinions and rewording them. When paraphrasing, it is important to keep the original meaning and to present it in a new form. Basically, you are simply stating something in your own words that expresses the original idea.

You use paraphrasing to let the person know that you understand what they're saying from your experience and standpoint. When you use active listening and paraphrasing together, you restate a portion of the conversation with the explicit purpose of clarifying the points or letting the person know that you understand their message and expectations. When you paraphrase you should try not to use all of the exact same words that the other person used. The literal meaning of 'para' is 'near' or close to. When you paraphrase, your words should be close but not exactly the same. Additionally, you shouldn't use their tonality or inflection if these are different from your own traits. This could look like you are mocking them!

Paraphrased words and phrases do however need to convey the same meaning. Also paraphrasing doesn't need to be posed in the form of a question. It is important that paraphrased words and phrases always be your own words, not the coachee's. With paraphrasing you restate a portion of the conversation with the explicit purpose of clarifying it in terms that you would typically use.

HERE ARE SOME SENTENCES THAT HAVE BEEN PARAPHRASED:

Original: Mary's professional life spanned years of incredible change for women. She was the first in her field to be awarded a patent. The first to win a Nobel. She said she tired of firsts because if she was the first, it meant that other women weren't progressing as quickly as she would have preferred. It annoyed her until the day she passed away.

Paraphrase: Mary lived through an era of liberating reform for women. She was a pioneer in her field having been awarded prestigious awards from the world's greatest institutions. Prior to her death, she lamented that she wished other women had procured greater success faster.

Original: Sales Managers in our firm like our new logo and have ordered 998 golf shirts within three days of the unveiling.

Paraphrase: The managers in charge of revenue at your firm seem to like the new corporate image since they've ordered nearly a thousand shirts for their team members in a very short time.

Original: Any trip to your Home Office should include a visit to the factory floor to see how they 'make the sausage' so to say.

Paraphrase: I heard that you are heading to Houston. You said you wanted to make sure you arranged a factory tour with the Head of Manufacturing when you go. Great idea to see how they put things together!

SUMMARIZING:

Although paraphrasing usually makes the segment shorter than the original, another option is to use a summary of what the person said. Summaries are comparatively much shorter than the original message. They are most importantly an overview or synopsis of the main points the person was trying to convey. Summarizing is another tactic to show people that you were listening properly to them. When you summarize, you usually take large sections of the conversation and reduce them to their essentials. In summarizing you provide the gist of what your understanding is of what the person said. You should only summarize the key areas or the main points -- those that are worth noting or going over or those that need clarifying. When you summarize, you put the main ideas or points of the conversation into your own words. Remember, this summary is the general idea in a brief form where you focus on the heart of the matter.

> Basically, it's hard for me to assess myself, a hardship not only prompted by the immodesty of the enterprise, but because one is not capable of assessing himself, let alone his work. However, if I were to summarize, my main interest is the nature of time. That's what interests me most of all. What time can do to a man. -Joseph Brodsky

HERE ARE SOME SENTENCES THAT PROMPT A PERSON TO SUMMARIZE:

- *I think can put together an outline that summarizes all the previous topics and the results from our coaching sessions thus far, don't you think?*
- *"You said that your marketing materials are overwhelming prospective clients. Is it possible to summarize the relevant features and main points of the product you offer on one concise page? If you can't do it, can you ask your marketing department folks to get it done and explain why this is urgent?"*
- The coachee kept circling back to the same issue without coming up with an action plan for resolving their team member's problematic behavior. Because the coaching session was going off track again, the Leadership Coach asked: *"I understand the choices as well as the pros and cons of what you are facing. Can you please encapsulate the ten-minute description you gave into three salient points? Then we can deal with each and come up with some focused actions."*
- Can you summarize what it is that makes you think you would be suitable for this position?
- I think that it would help if you summarized the main points from the Board meeting last week including your high level outlook on what the Board Members had agreed. If you consistently do so after every Board Meeting, you'll find that you'll have far less rollback of decision making after the fact. AS an added benefit, you won't be as frustrated with a couple of your Board Members!

MAKE SURE YOU AGREE ON EVERYONE'S UNDERSTANDING AND THE YOU CAPTURE THE ESSENCE OF THE MESSAGE

> Try this experiment: Pick a famous movie - 'Casablanca,' say - and summarize the plot in one sentence. Is that plot you just described the thing you remember most about it? Doubtful. Narrative is a necessary cement, but it disappears from memory. -Peter Greenaway

dialog

When you paraphrase or summarize another person's words, phrases or entire conversation, make sure that you are looking for body language and vocal quality clues as to whether they agree with your summarization or paraphrasing. This is critically important. Active listening depends on feedback. Showing you have a deep understanding of what the person is trying to say and an agreement from the originating messenger is vital. Your responsiveness will fill in a lot of what is lost by the process of paraphrasing or summarizing. Just like you cannot condense a book's entire substance into an outline, nor can you capture the entire essence of another person's words by summarizing or paraphrasing. But, by showing that you 'get it', the other person can rest assured they are being respectfully understood.

FIVE INEFFECTIVE LISTENING BEHAVIORS

Let's step back for a moment. If you know that people want to be understood and accepted: How do you let them know that they are? People feel valued and acknowledged when you show that you are willing to understand them, which means you must listen. However, effective listening is harder than it might seem. In fact, many people who engage in ineffective listening don't even realize how often they do so. Let's look at what these ineffective listening traits might be.

Simply put, there are five major types of 'less than optimal' or ineffective listening behaviors that people tend to engage in. To help you identify if you might have fallen prey to these, let's take a critical look at each one. Just as important, as you are going through this section, think of what you might do if you see your coachees are ineffectively listening.

HERE ARE SOME INTERESTING QUESTIONS TO ASK OF YOUR COACHEE:

How might you bring this to the coachee's attention?
How do you think this information might help the coachee in their relationships?
How do you think it might help/hurt the coachee's leadership efforts?

1. PRETEND LISTENING

The first type of ineffective listening is pretend listening. When you engage in pretend listening you give someone else the impression that you're listening to what they're saying when you're tuning them out. Oftentimes this isn't malicious. You simply might have too much on your own mind to listen to what is being said. You might be composing a response because you 'got it' so quickly. The coachee might have told you all this before and you have already figured out where this is going and what their next words will be.

In pretend listening, you don't pay enough attention to the subject matter at hand or listen to the precise words being spoken. How can the speaker pick up on pretend listening? When asked for a response, the listener typically looks like they are brushing off the speaker by giving a response too quickly, perhaps without providing information or much thought about the issue.

Listening is hard work! Often underneath it all, the goal of pretend listening is to look like you're listening, but to get out of conversation without much listening investment. We've seen jokes about spouses who do this all the time. It's a habit that happens when people know each other well. But it will, over time, make people feel that they are not being respected, heard at the level they need, or that their words are being discounted.

Other times, pretend listening, or brushing people off, occurs deliberately. When you participate in this type of listening, you might look as if you are actively listening, but you really are not. Even though you might be making eye contact and giving off receptive body language, you are completely missing or ignoring what the person in saying.

Here's an example of pretend listening:
Person A says: "I then told him that I was really going to have to put some thought into this
issue before I gave him a firm answer. I just don't know what to do. Got any thoughts?"
Person B responds: "Yes, I think that you always come up with the best solution. I don't think my input would be any better than yours."

CONSEQUENCES AND SOLUTION TO PRETEND LISTENING

As you can see person "B" is not really listening to person A. Because of this, they do not fully

understand each other. Person A really is looking for understanding and input from person B. By pretend listening, Person B is being disrespectful. Of course, this should be avoided!

The first step to doing this is to be consciously aware of whether you're really paying attention to what the person is saying. To do this, turn off your self-talk and internal dialog so that the conversation between you and the other person is the only conversation filling your thoughts. The best way to accomplish this is to be *fully present and attentive*. Put all other thoughts out of your head except for what the person is saying at that moment. Imagine yourself in their shoes, and how important this might be to them. This will go a long way in getting rid of the negative ramifications of pretend listening.

2. SELECTIVE LISTENING

The next type of listening is selective listening. When you are participating in selective listening

you are taking a positive step from pretend listening. With selective listening, you are listening to what the person is saying, but only hearing parts of what is being said - the parts that interest you. Once again, this might not be intentional. Sometimes it's an unconscious process or worse, a habit. It could also be that your subconscious mind is filtering out only the parts of speech that you find most important for very good reasons. You might be trying to remember only the pertinent points to summarize what the speaker is saying.

THE FOLLOWING IS AN EXAMPLE OF SELECTIVE LISTENING:

Person A says: "I told her I would go to a client meeting to shadow and support her three months ago, and she picks this day to ask me! But this is a once in a life time opportunity to present to the Board that you're talking about here. I wonder what I should do."

Person B responds: "Speaking of Board Meetings, did you see that horrible expose on the news yesterday about how many Board

Members don't prep for Board Meetings? It reminded me of one of our Board Members on the Finance Committee from a few years ago."

CONSEQUENCES AND SOLUTION TO SELECTIVE LISTENING

Whatever the case, selective listening will not lead to a complete understanding of others, and as you can imagine from the last example, it can really tick someone off! Paying conscious attention to how you listen to people will be the best way to put a stop to this. Selective listening can lead you to misidentify the real topic of someone's communication. With selective listening you hear only what you want to hear. In this example, person B was probably thinking about last night's TV show in their subconscious. The word 'Board' triggered their subconscious thoughts and it became all they could focus on. As said, it takes real conscious effort to take listening a step farther and pay attention to the whole conversation - the content and context of what the person is trying to say. To truly understand someone, you must listen to all that they are saying. As you can imagine, this is imperative during coaching sessions.

3. ADVISING TOO SOON

The next form of ineffective listening is called 'advising too soon'. 'Advising too soon' occurs

when you give someone advice without them first seeking it. It also happens when someone tries to 'fix things' rather than allowing the coachee to explain ALL of the situation they are grappling with. Much like rapport, advising someone or even providing options to consider is something that you must earn. When you give someone advice too early, they might naturally be resistant to it. This will happen regardless of whether the advice or suggestions are valuable or not.

> Therefore, for the sake of communication, building relationships, and showing that you understand the other person and respect them, you should avoid giving advice or offering suggestions and options until the time is right. You must listen for the appropriate moment to provide suggestions and/or give advice. You also must decide if your advice is wanted or appropriate.

NOTE #1: Please remember, that as a Leadership Behavior Coach, we cannot stress enough that you should not direct the coachee. You should always provide multiple options and talk through the pros and cons. The same is true when asked for what to do or suggestions.

NOTE #2: Sometimes, advice is exactly what isn't needed. Sometimes simply letting the person talk things through will help THEM come up with their own answer, so that you never have to provide any options, much less advice!

Back to 'advising too soon'. Minimally, you must listen for when they solicit advice or information from you before you leap in to 'advising too soon'. Advice in the form of options and suggestions should only be given when you truly understand the other person and when a degree of rapport has been established.

Look at this example:

Kim meets up with her coworker, Sarah, and is introduced to Sarah's new coworker, Matthew. Kim and Sarah are having a conversation when Kim says "I never feel like going out any more, especially to networking functions. All I normally do is go home straight after a rough day at the office. If I drag myself to a networking event, I don't go early or stick around afterwards." Before Sarah has a chance to respond, Matthew gives Kim some advice, "You've got to get out and interact. Networking is so critical for your career. If you don't interact and build your network, you won't have the contacts you need to get ahead or when you change jobs you'll be at a disadvantage, and that's not cool!"

CONSEQUENCES AND SOLUTION TO ADVISING TOO SOON

This is an example of when someone offers advice when the timing is not appropriate, and the trust isn't high enough. Matthew does not yet understand Kim or her situation. How could he? He's only just been introduced to her. He has not yet gained trust and rapport with her. At the very least, it's presumptuous of him to offer advice without understanding. It's easy to see that Kim isn't going to be very receptive to the advice, however on point or valuable. Kim would be more likely to take the advice if it came from someone who fully understood her and at least picked up on the context and intentions of what she was saying at that moment.

4. JUDGING

Another type of ineffective listening is judging. Judging occurs when you immediately make

a decision without first actually listening to what they have to say. Judgment is most often based on a bias. Perhaps you are swayed in a direction by your personal values and beliefs, and when a subject comes up, these are what guides your judgment. Maybe you have commitment bias because you've been working on a project for six months and are nearing the end of a tedious last stretch. A change in plans or new information isn't something you'd necessarily be open to receiving. When this happens, you immediately shut down open-minded communication and along with it any possibility of understanding precisely how the other person thinks.

For instance, take this example:

Person A says: "I'm starting to think that I just don't fit in with past coworkers I used to hang out with anymore. I find myself avoiding them more and more. I'm not returning their texts or calls as quickly. When we were all working on the same project I thought we had so much in common but honestly, we just don't have the same outside interests, likes, or experiences."

Person B responds: "You just need to lighten up and no feel so badly about this. It happens to almost everyone on intense teams. You don't have to avoid them completely. You can control how much or how little you see them. Who knows, another project might come along, and you'll work with them again. You just don't like the fact that you might feel or look disloyal or unfeeling about them. Things have changed. You have a new team to connect with right now and not a lot of time for family much less friends. Time is precious. They'll understand that. You need to try to help them feel it's ok to interact less but still value them as coworkers, too."

Not only does this count as advising, but person B also made a negative judgment about the

first person saying they might look disloyal or unfeeling. This destroys rapport instantly. To avoid this type of listening, don't just jump to conclusions. Take time to find out why the person you're communicating with feels the way they do or why they made the comment they did. Take the time to discover what will help build trust and rapport. The person you are communicating with will be more accepting of your 'judgments' and/or preconceptions when you give them at the appropriate time.

5. PROBING

Probing is a method of questioning designed to make the person provide information they might not want to give out. Probing often makes people uncomfortable and wary. When a person probes, they ask a targeted question, and then listen for the response. If the response isn't 'enough', the person probes again, until they are satisfied they have the information they need. In coaching sessions, you sometimes must probe. Coachees rarely answer all the questions that need to be addressed without probing, prompting, or the like. That's the nature of the beast.

So how do you probe and keep the relationship strong? The first thing to do is tell the person what you are doing. This is called 'fair warning'. Whenever you are going to do something you know might break rapport, tell the person. Here's an example: "John, I know that we've been dancing around your leadership efforts and activities last week. I'm going to ask you some pointed questions to figure out what's happening, and I'm going to keep probing for the facts until we get to something close to reality."

The secret of effective probing is a 'Catch 22'. Probing will not work unless rapport is established first and the person is open and willing to provide answers to your questions. The only reason they'll do this is when they feel that you are not going to use the information against them. So, knowing this, you should tell them why this information must come to the surface. "John, if we know what happened last week, we can get through it. If I don't know what's happening, how can we discuss some solutions?" or "John, you know that full transparency, being vulnerable and brutally honest, no secrets, discussing things that are uncomfortable, is all part of knowing yourself best. This is a coaching session. That's what we do here. So, let's just get it out on the table. The information will stay right here in this room. I promise. I can't help you help yourself if it doesn't come out."

If the person doesn't trust you or isn't responsive, they won't answer your questions no matter how deep or 'hard' you probe. It will be an awkward process that will get you nowhere. And if they do provide the information, they'll resent it. That's not great for coaching sessions at all! But on

the flip side, if you have established a high level of trust and rapport with the coachee, probing isn't really needed. They should trust you enough to answer your questions without you 'digging' for the answer; the simple act of asking the right type of questions - not 'probing' - starts a conversation. How do you know the difference (if you feel like you are)? Additionally, if you only ask closed-ended questions when probing, your results will be less than desirable. If the questions are like 'pulling teeth' during a coaching session, you're probably probing.

Here is an example of probing that doesn't go well for the person trying to probe:

> A: "How did your conversation with your operations manager go last week, Mary?"
> B: "Okay, I guess."
> A: "Learn anything about why he's been avoiding you?"
> B: "Not really."
> A: "Are you planning to call him out on the costs and schedule slippages again this week?"

B: "I don't want it to look like I'm picking on him alone. Sales and Marketing are just as guilty of skirting around me as their new leader. Haven't particularly thought about how I'm going to address this with him again yet."

A: "Why not?"

B: "I just haven't."

As you can see, probing did not get person A detailed answers to any of the questions that they asked person B. Person B clearly didn't want to be engaged. If probing continues, both participants are likely to become frustrated with each other. If you are the person probing, and you are not getting the appropriate responses from the person you're talking to, you should stop probing. It's as simple as that. If you don't stop, probing can make the situation worse. That doesn't mean that you're not going to circle back to address this. Timing is important. The tactic you use is just as important.

When probing puts someone's back against a wall, recognize it and let them know that you are giving them space. You have to let them know that your questions need to be addressed for their own growth. A suggestion might look like this: *"I realize you are getting aggravated with these questions. How about figuring this out another way. Maybe we can negotiate between us when you'd prefer to have me poke at this touchy subject."* If you say this with a smile, it will diffuse tension. Additionally, they'll know you are sensitive to the topic but will insist that it be discussed.

There are times however, when probing is appropriate and highly beneficial. When rapport is high, probing is an excellent way to procure information and keep the conversation ball rolling. Let's look at an example of what this would be like:

> A: "How did your conversation with your operations manager go last week, Mary?"
> B: "It was really great. My anxiousness was all for nothing! We talked for 45 minutes. Mostly about life. You know, like how we got to this point in our careers, how we hold people accountable, and how we both want the department to thrive."
> A: "Learn anything that you particularly liked?"
> B: "Well, I knew that Keith was a really good team leader. And I knew that his family had a lot of military folks in their background. So does mine. His grandfather took part in the invasion in Normandy. It suddenly dawned on me that he was probably in the D-Day invasion. I asked how old his Grandfather was, and we figured out he would have been about 24 years old. My Grandfather was 24! We both wondered if that's one of the reasons we were both so driven, trying to live up to our past heritage. We figured out that's where our values came from, too. He didn't recognize where I was coming from until we talked. And that's my fault. He thought I was being hard on him and his team. He admitted that he didn't appreciate that I was brought in to change the entire organization to one where accountability and performance matter again. He told me that with the last VP, he was continually undermined when he tried to hold certain people on the prior management team accountable. So he just gave up being the lone voice crying into the wind. I explained that I truly value people

and know that his team will need to make sacrifices to get our numbers back up. We connected at a profound level. I can work with him and get this ship back in the water! I'm excited!"

As you can see, there's a vast difference between employing probing when the other person is receptive and when they are not. When using this tactic, make the choice when to use it based on the response that you get in the person's willingness to be open. Active listening can be highly effective if you want to understand more about a person's values and beliefs. It is important to first listen before you can effectively ask someone to trust you.

Do's and Don'ts for Active Listening

DO:

DO ASK: If you are unsure, ask questions: Never guess when you can simply ask the person directly. Hoping you guessed right does work for effective coaching sessions. Clarify. Clear up misunderstandings. Avoid confusion.

If you're not sure what the person means, ask them questions like:
"Do you mean this?"
"Am I correct in my thinking that you meant…?"

DO Overlook speech problems or when they don't choose the exact word you think they should: Please ignore anything that isn't perfect in a coachee's speaking or communication. Such things as twitches, tapping, an unusual voice, a high-pitched or squeaky voice, or a heavy accent are inappropriate to comment on. This is the same advice for any ill-chosen words the coachee might pick. There is one exception to this: When you are given permission to address such speech matters as part of the coaching assignment. A good example of this is if your assignment includes executive presence. Speaking is a critical leadership skill.

Please remember that communication isn't perfect, especially in a safe environment where stressors are sometimes brought to the fore. Err on the side of caution and cut people a lot of slack in this area. As a rule of thumb, when people are in a coaching session, they aren't necessarily concentrating on their words especially when emotions run high or when they are thinking about their past and how to best move forward. Confusion inside the coachee's head sometimes exhibits itself in strange and wonderful ways.

Listen, listen, LISTEN! Don't nitpick petty inconsequential things while you are listening. Never let those things distract you from what's truly important during the coaching sessions. Just focus, focus, focus on listening! When you notice something different it may make it difficult to concentrate, but you must focus and do exactly that. You should concentrate on what is being said - always.

DO Be open minded: Always be willing to consider new ideas and suggestions, especially when they come from the coachee. Just because you're a coach doesn't mean you know best or have all the answers! If you don't listen, you never learn anything new. Never assume you know exactly what the coachee should do. There are many paths to Leadership Behavior. There are many options in how to communicate and connect. An open-minded approach insists on an impartial and unprejudiced style. Showing that you are **receptive to new ideas or arguments** or that you're neutral, nonjudgmental, and nondiscriminatory is powerful.

DO Give a reaction: Make eye contact, nod if you agree, and interject phrase like *"I'm happy to hear that"*, *"How interesting!"*, *"I can see that"*, or *"I understand what you mean"*, assuming they don't interrupt the person's words. Provide confirmation: *"Yes, I agree"* or *"No, you were right not doing that."*

DON'T:

Don't assume or jump to conclusions: Human nature has people thinking a step or two ahead. But forming conclusions too soon, without adequate time to listen and evaluate is a sure-fire way of being wrong in many instances. Even worse, pre-thinking what you think the coachee is about to say next shuts down discussions and can really make a coachee frustrated or angry. Many misunderstandings and trust breakdowns occur because of this. Doing this is dismissive and rude!

Don't interrupt or self-talk/listen: Be present. Pay attention and take note of what is being said Confuse and HOW it is communicated. This takes concentration. If you are thinking ahead, talking to yourself inside your head, or thinking about your response, you aren't in active listening mode!

Don't judge: Judgment and bias are coaching session killers! Examine your personal biases (you all have them) and figure out a way to curtail them during coaching sessions.

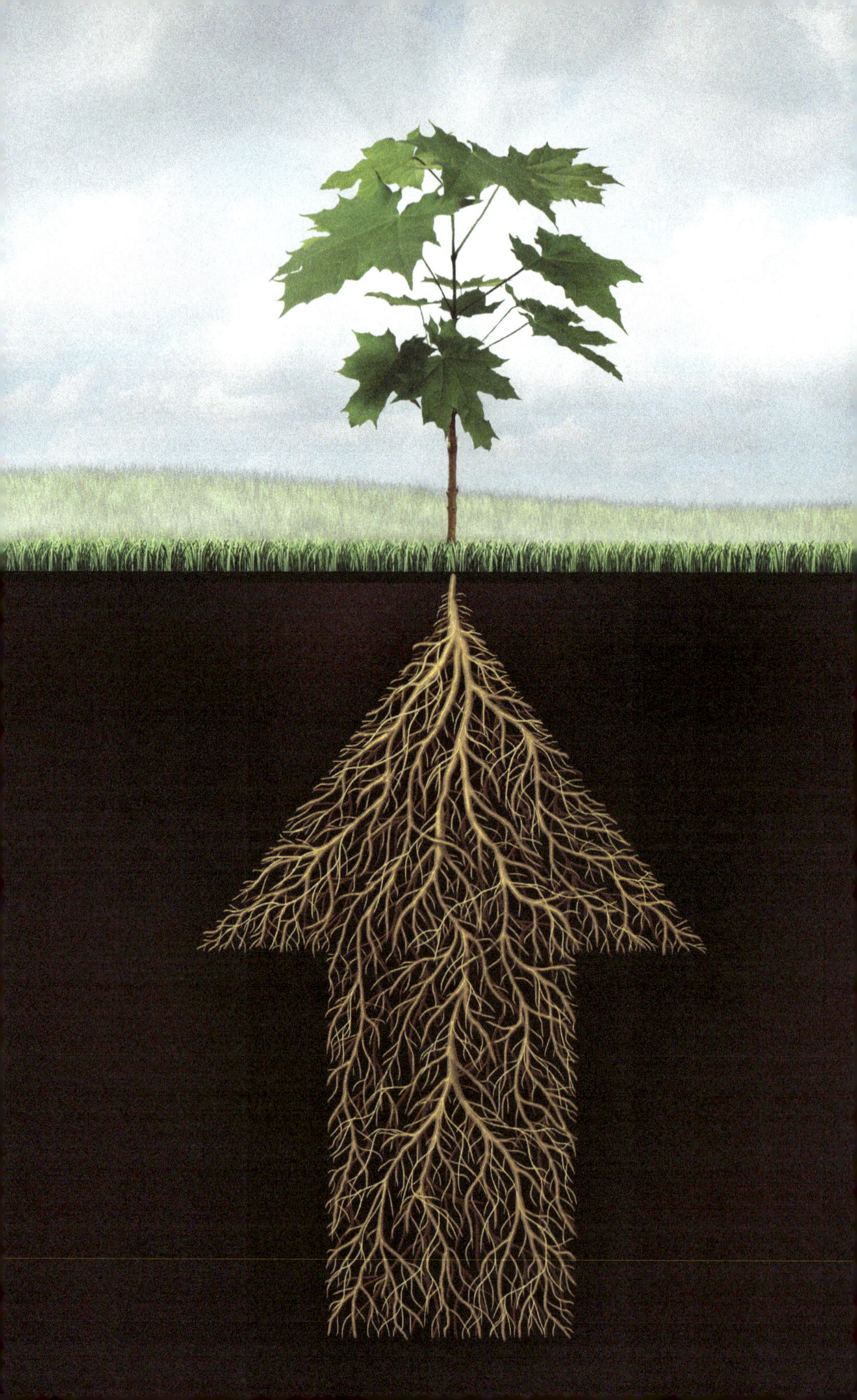

Provide Feedback to Provoke Thoughtful Responses

> Feedback, like nourishing rain, should be gentle enough to nurture a person's growth without destroying the roots.

PREPARING TO PROVIDE FEEDBACK DURING A COACHING SESSION

> We all need people who will give us feedback. That's how we improve.- Bill Gates

WHY GIVE FEEDBACK?

Ongoing feedback is of critical importance. So is ongoing praise! But, often more important than the giving of feedback are the conversations and responses that happen because you've delivered it, and then praised your coachee for what they did to take that feedback onboard.

Feedback coaching sessions are not an isolated, nor a one-sided event. When your coachees respond to you about the feedback you've given them, you must take in what they say, process in effectively and reply, addressing all their concerns, perhaps dealing with negative emotions. You must anticipate some of the things they'll say or do and sort through their responses to get to a place where they understand why you gave the feedback.

Next, the coachee should realize that feedback is given with a view to them taking corrective actions. The dialog should occur with a view to making plans to come up with suitable ways to resolve the feedback issue. Likewise, make certain they understand you'll keep your finger on the pulse of this issue, making certain you circle back to it until new behavior and/or habits are in place. Reiterate the reason for feedback: To make sure leadership efforts stay on track. This view should fuel momentum and make feedback a bit easier 'to swallow'.

LESS EXPERIENCE, MORE FEEDBACK

The primary goal of Leadership Coaching is to engage coachees towards Leadership Behavior. Coachees ideally will take on accountability for their responsibilities and make improvements in their habits. But that's in an ideal world. This is Behavior Coaching and that sometimes puts a different spin on things. This means that you'll probably be spending more time initially on coachees with less experience in behavioral change. In your initial coaching sessions, you'll need to ramp up their skills and knowledge around Behavior Coaching accountability. While at first it might seem counter-intuitive that you have less to talk about Behavior Coaching accountability with your 'star coachees' or those whom you've been coaching a while, think about this: By the time you've been coaching them for a while, they should have the 'Behavior Coaching accountability thing' down pat. If they don't, you're doing something wrong.

> Feedback is a gift. Ideas are the currency of our next success. Let people see you value both feedback and ideas. – Jim Trinka and Les Wallace

Feedback and corrections take less time with coachees who know how to make changes because you've already established what the process is. Teach the process early and you'll have better results. Hold coachees accountable and they'll learn even faster.

Coachees who already fully understand that by giving feedback you're doing your best to shine light to help their leadership efforts won't be as reluctant to listen or change. Therefore, as a Leadership Coach, you don't have to spend as much time 'explaining the process again' or 'dealing with feedback feelings'.

As coachees initially engage with you and start to receive feedback from a Leadership Coach, it's sometimes tough for them to sort everything through emotionally. Many times, this is the first really tough feedback high performing high potential employees and leaders have been given. Executive Coaches are typically engaged for key employees. Key employees rise to the executive ranks because they are very bright and really good at what they've done. Bright gifted people know it. They have confidence and most haven't had tough feedback.

How can you get through to them quickly and still maintain trust? Explain this exact concept to them. Add this: What got them to where they are right now probably isn't enough to pop them up to the next level. It might not even be enough to keep them in the job they're in right now. I've seen many an executive flounder. The book, The Peter Principle, explains how this might happen. Its basic premise is that people get promoted to a level of incompetence. And they stay there or figure out a way to overcome their incompetence. If you suspect this is an area where feedback needs to be given to one of your coachees, have a look at the Unconscious Competence Model. It will help you explain what the coachee is going through and will give your coaching sessions a pathway to success.

> Leaders cannot work in a vacuum. They may take on larger, seemingly more important roles in an organization, but this does not exclude them from asking for and using feedback. In fact, a leader arguably needs feedback more so than anyone else. It's what helps a leader respond appropriately to events in pursuit of successful outcomes. -Jack Canfield

Nowhere is this tougher than receiving critical feedback. This is especially true if they're already feeling 'down on themselves' or a bit hopeless. Add this to the fact that most people aren't trained in how to RECEIVE FEEDBACK and you'll begin to get a sense of why spending lots of time upfront is important.

Logically then, inexperienced coachees require more time to deliver and talk through your feedback. However, this doesn't mean that you stop providing consistent and timely feedback to ALL coachees. You must do this on an ongoing basis, whenever warranted, if your coachees are to have any hopes of improving their behavior and staying on track with leadership efforts.

At the same time, you must be certain not to alienate those star players we mentioned. Always recognize their efforts and let them know why it is that you spend less time on their feedback as your coaching sessions progress. Explain that you realize they are on board and on track – because you know that they can take care of themselves better and better as your coaching sessions and their learning improves. This is a natural byproduct as your Leadership Coaching and time together continues.

PLAN AHEAD

You should always prepare for Providing Feedback or Delivering Evaluation Documentation During a Coaching Session ahead of time. There are many tactics that we'll discuss that you can use to give yourself the edge when facing a potentially tense coaching session. Each one of these should be exploited to make the best of the situation. Going into an evaluation blind, without facts and data to back you up, is never a good idea. You'll just be setting yourself up to get blindsided. The coachee could have an emotional outburst or become defensive. Therefore, with due preparation, most of this can be avoided.

SET THE TONE FOR THE SESSION

An evaluation should set the tone for the coming 'accountability period', establishing what goals and deliverables are important to leadership efforts now, having discussions and perhaps offering suggestions for how to best work towards those goals. What is an 'accountability period'? It's the agreed timeframe for deliverables and measurements. Ultimately, upcoming 'accountability periods' should provide coachees with a frame of reference by which they can work more productively and effectively, improving themselves and advancing their goals (short and long term).

DO NOT DISCUSS...

There are certain critical matters that you must never discuss or criticize during a feedback coaching session (or at any other time for that matter). This might include subjects such as race, age, religion, politics, and sexual orientation. In general, avoid the kind of topics that might lead to allegations of discrimination or might get you and/ or your sponsor into hot water.

NO IMPROVISATION!

Never, under any circumstances, improvise during a performance evaluation. Never 'wing it'. In a very literal way, lives might hang in the balance because of the feedback you provide. Feedback can help turn someone around, especially if it is delivered well. So, you should always approach the matter with that sense of importance and gravity.

By preparing thoroughly ahead of time, you can make certain that no matter what happens, you get your points across and the coachee leaves the coaching session knowing what it is that is expected of them performance-wise in the future. By winging it, you risk failing to properly communicate your ideas, or worse, running into conflicts that you're unprepared to dissolve or avoid. Possibly much more important, you will botch your dialogue and suggestions for improvement. Additionally, you might forget to set appropriate goals and metrics for the upcoming accountability period.

HAVE A CLEAR AGENDA

Just like conducting regular coaching sessions, when you perform a coachee feedback session, you should have a clear agenda. Prepare a list of points that you want to go over during the session, and define an order to hit them in. Having an agenda laid out beforehand will help you to remember critical points if you get sidetracked by other discussions that come up. In general, the more organization and preplanning you can bring to the feedback process, the better it's likely to go.

> Mistakes should be examined, learned from, and discarded; not dwelled upon and stored. - Tim Fargo

USE MEASURABLE CRITERIA

The criteria that you use to constructively criticize or praise a coachee's leadership efforts and results should always be objective, which means that these should always be measurable. Don't just say that a coachee did "pretty good" or "rather badly". Instead, provide facts and figures that show what was expected of the coachee, compared to how the coachee behaved and performed.

With hard numbers on the record, it's hard for a coachee to disagree with a Leadership Coach's feedback. For example, a coachee might have had the goal of becoming more mentally alert and less stressed at work. Angry outbursts were something he never wanted to do again. In the coaching sessions, Heinrich mentioned that his best stress reliever is physical activity. He said that he also thinks best on long solitary walks. Heinrich vows to do some adjustments to his behaviors. You discuss some quick fixes to pop some activity into the day. He promised to take the stairs between meetings instead of the elevator. He said he was going to use his earpiece and pace instead of sit during long conference calls. When he is on the road, he told you he'd eat less high calorie foods and drink less alcohol. He wanted to start exercising more in the evenings and on weekends.

As a coach, you know that new behaviors stand a much better chance of sticking if the person has clear accountability and metrics to live by. It doesn't matter what the goal is – by measuring progress or lack thereof you can start to adjust behavior in a methodical and fact-based manner. Monitoring this goal is easy if Heinrich wears a tracking sensor.

Heinrich asked you to bring this up at every coaching session. By looking at his sensor tracking stats, when his numbers were examined, the first two weeks went better than anticipated. You congratulate him on great progress. The third week you notice a marked downturn in his steps. His sleep data is problematic, too. The change of habits is not happening. Based on this, you give him a call. "Heinrich, was just taking a pulse on your stress levels the past two days. What's happening?"

"Funny you should call this morning! I was just about to tear someone's head off their shoulders. Our quarterlies came in 2% below what we promised the Board. I am shocked my guys didn't tell me sooner. This is unacceptable!" After discussing the numbers and having Heinrich reiterate his plan, you circle back to the new habit he was working on. As you can imagine, the coachee argued that he was focused on business as a top priority, not himself. Heinrich was getting annoyed!

> The measure of a Leadership Behavior Coach is the behavior of the Coachee. The measure of a leader is the behavior of his followers. Therefore, the impact the Leadership Coach has on the organization can be profound. Leadership Behavior Coaching is a great responsibility. -Hellen Davis

However, you must address this as part of their promises they didn't deliver on. This is a Leadership Behavior Coaching moment. You say: *"Think of this: What if everyone could argue which metrics should count and which shouldn't, after their agreements were made? I do understand that you are busy with different priorities but not living up to this goal is actually a detriment to all your leadership efforts. If you don't get the stress out of your system, your temperature when you communicate won't be appropriate. Plus, what message would this send to your subconscious? How can I as your Leadership Coach, to allow this to go unchecked? How would leadership efforts progress if coachees weren't held accountable for all the goals they agreed to were part of their coaching responsibilities? If this were allowed, why bother with goals, measures, objectives or Behavior Coaching accountability at all? Remember these words because one day you'll have to have exactly the same type of accountability discussions with your folks, too."*

BE OBJECTIVE

As we've mentioned before, being objective is one of the most critical aspects of conducting a feedback coaching session. During a feedback meeting, you must stick to the facts and rely on evidence when proving instances to back up your observations. Discuss specific incidents rather than relying on fallible sources like memory and hearsay. For example, you should say to the coachee: *"You were determined to get your strategy docs completed by the morning of October 10th so that we could review them and work on your delivery on the 11th. The reason is simple: You are presenting for the first time in front of the Leadership Team on the 12th. You need to prepare and have time to make adjustments. Let me get the facts before I speak: Today is the afternoon of the 9th and one of your team members, the person in charge of putting the slide deck together, just told you they haven't started and asked for another day? Did you get your deliverables to him on time? Did the other inputs from finance and HR come in on time? Is this the same team member who slipped several deadlines in the past?"*

"Yes, this is the same type of procrastination issue with the same person. They had everything they needed when promised by all other team members."

"Bottom line: Then I assume there is no justifiable reason other than poor planning and/or procrastination on this issue. One team member's procrastination shouldn't put your reputation as a leader at risk. I also assume that you were very clear on the reasons why you needed this and when. Are you asking me what you should say? Here are some words: "Gordon, the original deadline cannot change. This looks like the result of poor planning, lack of communication, and/or procrastination because you didn't come to me earlier asking for a delay or for help. Please note that the team and I expect the same quality product that would have been delivered had there been better planning. This can be a defining moment for your career. We all make choices. I hope you choose well, step up to the plate, make arrangements to get this done, and learn from this event. After the LT presentation, I want to circle back and find out what adjustments need to happen so this type of thing doesn't occur again. Please write down what you think the root causes are so that we can go over them. We have all had to overcome things like procrastination, putting too much on our plates, and/or being overly optimistic about how long things take to do. I think that spending some time thinking about this and other prior events might be time well spent. I would like to hear your thinking on this and if you like, I can provide some coaching or suggestions.""

The first way of dealing with this is clearly more objective than this statement. *"You need to tell him that you will not tolerate deadlines slipping."* The first method asks relevant questions and seeks understanding before communicating. It leaves little room for pushback because it uses hard facts and data. The more objective you are, the more specific you are with the facts, the less opportunities there are for the people to argue, debate the information, or get into unproductive conflict.

In general, the question of who is meeting expectations, who is exceeding them, and who is lagging is often steeped in subjectivity. Your responsibility as a Leadership Coach is to be objective and have the facts for any feedback your deliver. What makes feedback sessions go 'wrong'? These four things can lead to quite a few emotional encounters with coachees and compound how badly feedback coaching sessions might go:

- Less than adequate communication of expectations
- Not enough feedback by the measurements
- Not being objective
- Being ill-prepared or improvising
- Having inadequate communication skills in the realm of providing feedback.

NO SURPRISES, PLEASE!

In addition, coachees who feel they were doing well do not take kindly to getting surprise feedback or when a Leadership Coach says something vague like: *"I feel you could do better."* Be specific. Remove opinion and subjectivity from feedback coaching sessions as much as possible.

By using measurable data, observation, and information gleaned from other sources, you can deliver feedback, results, and behavior in an objective and predictable matter. If they listen to the feedback you consistently provide them, coachees will have a good sense of their own leadership efforts versus expectations. They can do a 'gap analysis' at any given time to move forward with the Behavior Coaching goals, locking in good decision making and acquiring better habits. Feedback can give a coachee very specific information about what is expected of them, and who (the coachee) is accountable for failure or not reaching desired Behavior Coaching results.

Empower
Enable
LEADER
Encourage
Motivate
Reward
Initiate
Coach

Preparation for Your Feedback Coaching Sessions

> What is the shortest word in the English language that contains the letters: abcdef? Answer: feedback. Just like your ABCs, feedback sessions are the foundational building blocks of a great organizations.

MAP A COMMUNICATION PLAN AND REHEARSE YOUR DELIVERY

It pays to mentally rehearse for any feedback sessions. Mapping out a feedback communication plan means that you go over the topics that you plan to cover with the coachee. The flow of feedback sessions is important to Behavior Coaching success.

Based on your knowledge of the coachee, you can anticipate the things that they're likely to say in return. You can anticipate your own reactions to their reactions. By doing this, you help yourself not to be taken off guard by unexpected turns in the flow of conversation. Be careful, however, not to get locked into so rigid a conversation structure that you end up totally unprepared to follow along with how the conversation goes! As a Leadership Coach, you must listen and allow the coachee to discuss their agenda points too. Remember, we advise the coachees to do the same as their Leadership Coach. Come prepared and have agenda points to discuss.

REHEARSE 'INSIDE YOUR HEAD FIRST'.

Make any adjustments to the feedback you're going to provide. Next, say what you plan to say out loud. This works even if you are the only person who will hear it. A lot of feedback comes across by way of your gestures and tonality. You can get a sense of how it's going to sound and look to the coachee if you practice in front of a mirror. Sometimes by doing this, you can not only develop a more confident delivery, but also catch things that may be ambiguous, confusing or will take the discussion down a 'rat hole'.

Using vocalization, you also might pick up words or sentences that may sound subjective rather than fact and/or data based. Additionally, view your words through the coachee's lens. Have you listened to hear what the coachee might think of as frustrating or insulting? Have you tested your phrases to listen to what might make the coachee unnecessarily angry, combative, or defensive? Your delivery is important because it often forewarns how well (or badly) the coachee might take in your feedback. Your rehearsal allows you to change things so that the coaching session goes as well as it possibly can.

Focus on the coachee's behavior, never their character.

Discuss the Actions and BEHAVIOR; Never Criticize the Person's Character. When providing your findings and feedback, be certain to always phrase statements to the coachee in a fashion that makes it clear that it's the deliverables, actions, and behaviors you are specifically discussing, not the person's character or personal core values. Coachees might still react negatively, but it's much more likely they'll take kindlier to "For the past two coaching sessions, you haven't completed the activities we agreed were important for you." This behavior makes it difficult to keep sessions productive. Plus, you must focus on doing things on time. Working on procrastination is one of this month's goals." rather than "Why can't you ever do what I ask on time?!"

MAINTAIN NEUTRALITY

It's important to maintain a sense of neutrality while providing feedback. The bottom line is that your life as a Leadership Coach won't change if your coachee doesn't live up to their responsibilities. This is their leadership efforts, not yours. If you must go over someone else's observations or negative comments from another supporter, and give your coachee some tough feedback, you might be tempted to say something like, *"They sure can be hard sometimes, can't they?"* to make the news go over easier. Resist this temptation. You cannot take sides on this. 'Putting down' the observer lessens the impact of their observation. It is what it is. It's their reality and it needs to be brought out. Relationships are at stake. As a Leadership Coach, you must remain as neutral as possible in all matters such as this, so that if emotions rise or conflict begins, you're in the best position to defuse it.

BE CLEAR

When preparing your feedback, be sure that you plan your statements concisely.

- It's best to avoid artistry or wordiness altogether.
- Explain that you are going to be forthright. Then speak as bluntly and plainly as you possibly can. Communicate with Nobel Intent and a good heart.
- Use common words.
- Be direct and forthright. Being vague for the sake of sparing feelings will just lead to your ideas being misrepresented and misunderstood.
- Using clear, easy to understand words and keeping your sentences short and to the point will help the coachee to digest and remember them more easily.

THE MEETING PLACE MUST BE PRIVATE

All feedback and coaching discussions should be private. There is only one exception - when giving feedback during a dangerous situation where you need to bring in other parties such as a supporter/representative to ensure order and safety. For this session, we will assume this is not the case. Never conduct a feedback coaching session in a public place. The potential for it going awry is simply too great. On one hand, the coachee might feel uncomfortable responding to what you say openly if there are other people around. On the other hand, if you provide feedback, they'll likely resent you for it if others are around to overhear. Before you conduct a feedback coaching session, make sure that you have a totally private and secure meeting place, where both parties feel comfortable. As a bonus, conducting a feedback discussion in private will make it seem more formal and thus more meaningful and memorable to the coachee.

AVOID CONFLICTS

Avoid conflicts when conducting a feedback coaching session by sticking to the facts and remaining neutral and objective. If you sense that the coachee is trying to take the discussion in an argumentative or unproductive direction, do what you must to reign them in. Once conflict begins, it's harder to defuse than if you cut it off before it ever has a chance to escalate. Study anger management and 'becoming defensive' to pinpoint the root causes of coachee frustration, anger, and/or 'desire to battle'.

BE COMPOSED AND CALM. NEVER LOSE YOUR COOL

The worst thing that a Leadership Coach can do during a feedback coaching session is to lose his/her cool and get into a heated discussion or an argument with the coachee. If this happens, the coachee will know this is an acceptable behavior during a coaching session. Plus, they'll potentially lose respect for you, try to goad you into doing it again in a future session, or not take your words as seriously as your actions. Instead they will be more likely to rebel against the process just for emotional gratification.

As such, if you're not confident that you can keep your cool during a feedback coaching session, use one of these tactics to keep a cool head. Reschedule the coaching session. Have someone else be present with you when you deliver this feedback. Rehearse with someone and get your delivery perfect. Stick rigidly to your agenda and insist that all counters or objectives be addressed at a later coaching session and or in writing. Pick a time when the coachee will be most receptive, and you will be most calm. Ideally, of course, you should be able to remain calm no matter who you're providing feedback to, but in extenuating circumstances where you have repeatedly delivered feedback to problematic coachees with less than stellar responses, keep these options (and others like them) in mind.

POINTS FOR DELIVERING FEEDBACK DURING A COACHING SESSION
ESTABLISH THE GROUND RULES

Before you carry out a feedback discussion, always set forth ground rules for how the conversation will proceed. These can be simple things like 'no personal attacks' or rules for moving through the 'housekeeping' issues, responses, follow up, paperwork or the agenda. It can include communication guidelines such as who should speak and when (no interrupting). No matter what the guidelines are, make sure that they help rather than hinder communication. Also, check that everyone involved is aware of them up front.

HERE ARE SOME SUGGESTIONS FOR GROUND RULES DURING THE FEEDBACK COACHING SESSION:

1. Confidentiality first. What is said in the coaching session, stays in the session unless parties agree to discuss with others. If anyone thinks harm to self or others will occur, they have a responsibility to share with predesignated appropriate parties.
2. Be fully present. Silence all cell phones, pagers, and sideline other distractions. If they have to be on, set the rules for looking at tests or answering calls. Remember, they are running a business and coaching sessions do need to empathize with that. Be somewhat understanding and flexible.
3. This is a 'haven' where it is expected that people will always be honest.
4. Be respectful and sensitive to others
5. Refrain from using offensive language.
6. Listen to each other. Give everyone an opportunity to speak

without interrupting.
7. Share feelings and experiences openly. Discuss options but never give advice.
8. Have a positive attitude. Accept the feedback without making judgments. Be thoughtful in any responses.

STATE THE PURPOSE OF YOUR FEEDBACK AND HOW IT MIGHT BE USEFUL TO THE COACHEE.

THE PURPOSE OF A FEEDBACK DISCUSSION IS TO GO OVER ANY DELIVERABLES OR PROMISES MADE SINCE THE LAST ACCOUNTABILITY PERIOD.

The goal is to discuss 'results versus expectations' with a view to moving forward with any changes or corrective actions. Tell the coachee what you'd like to cover is important. This opening statement gives the other person a heads-up about how the conversation will go. If the other person has requested feedback, a focusing statement will make sure that you direct your feedback toward what the person needs. Remember: Be clear and straight-to-the-point. Start with a strong statement:

"In reviewing what you said, I noticed that..."
"I went through my notes about what activities were due, and have a concern about...."
"Leadership efforts require discipline. I want to give you some of my observations…"
"I have put together some talking points from our last conversation..."

REITERATE THAT FEEDBACK IS SIMPLY PART OF THE PROCESS AND THAT IT CAN BE USEFUL.

A great Leadership Coach helps a coachee overcome any shortcomings and realize their true potential. **But does the coachee know that?** Some coachees may view every feedback discussion as something like a 'disciplinary action' and be defensive from the start. In such cases, you can help them to relax and ensure a better feedback session if you're clear about what the point of the feedback is from the very beginning. Plus, it always helps to go over this just to make sure that everyone is on the same page.

Start off the meeting by saying, *"Thank you for meeting with me today. The purpose of this segment of our coaching session is to ensure your leadership efforts continue toward success outcomes, and help you reach your Behavior Coaching goals. One of my responsibilities is to continuously provide you with feedback to make you aware of how your actions and behaviors might impact your leadership efforts. My goal in giving you feedback is specifically to help you see things you might not otherwise see. Hearing feedback is tough, but I hope you know that feedback, however painful, can be a great gift if taken well and with a view for improvement."*

DESCRIBE SPECIFICALLY WHAT YOU HAVE OBSERVED ONLY DISCUSS FACTS, DATA AND VERIFIABLE INFORMATION.

1. **Make a list of the specifics of a bounded event or situation.** You never want feedback to be broad in nature. The more specific you are, the better. Plus, you don't want the coachee to go off on tangents because you've opened the door and/or

'muddied the waters'. The thing you want to avoid is that the coachee will be able to diffuse the feedback by talking about something unrelated or insignificant. Compile your thoughts in a logical format. Include details that will substantiate the feedback you are giving. Example: Dates, times, people involved, promises made, and results can be important details. In addition, make sure that the specific situation you are there to discuss has enough detail to make it valuable feedback. In addition, whenever possible, remain objective and stick to what you have observed.

> Every improvement, no matter how small, is valuable.

2. **Be impartial.** When conducting a feedback coaching session, always be as impartial as possible. There may well be times when you must provide feedback to coachees you really like, know that they've tried their best and you feel bad that you must tell them something that might make them unhappy, demotivated, or angry, or with whom you have had feedback problems in the past. It's ok that you might not 'like' your coachees actions or current behavior. But you must be impartial and objective. You can never let your personal feelings, preferences, biases, or the like, enter the feedback coaching session. If you have trouble with this with some coachees, take a cold hard look at why this might be happening. Try a different tactic. Have others look at your evaluation if possible to make certain that you're being objective. You cannot let your personal feelings influence your Leadership Coaching Sessions or decisions.

3. **If you are providing third-party information, state that and allow that this information may be biased or blatantly**

untrue. **Keep confidences that you've promised and be as transparent as possible.** These may sometimes seem at odds. If there is a pecking order in which is more important, I suggest that you foster an environment where full transparency is the preference. You must tell the coachee that you are open and listening to their view of the incident. You also must make them aware that you are not passing judgment of any kind, and that you are specifically providing feedback to discuss behavior and/or corrective actions for the future. Please note that you should only discuss the specific feedback that you have said you were going to in your opening statement. If you need to provide feedback on more than one thing, state this at the beginning of the meeting and discuss the order and process for segmenting these different feedback points. As much as possible, speak in absolutes and not generalities. An absolute uses words, like 'always' and 'never' versus 'sometimes' and 'not often'. If you use specific words, feedback coaching sessions tend to go better. "On Wednesday, when we chatted, I heard you raise your voice twice to people in the background when we were interrupted." For example: "Yesterday afternoon, when you were speaking with customers, I noticed that you kept raising your voice. I don't know if this was because you were upset, frustrated or excited but in general, raising one's voice with anyone in the workplace isn't desirable."

> The ways you get results are as important as the results themselves.

4. **Be Consistent and stick to your agenda.** Go over all the points that you intend to make and be certain that none

of them contradict with one another. Also, if you make one statement, continue without detracting from it. If you make one proclamation about what is expected of the coachee but then retract it without evidence to the contrary, they'll never know which feedback to take seriously and which is "okay" to ignore. Consistency is also important when conducting feedback coaching sessions in general. You must treat all coachees fairly and equitably.

ASK THE COACHEE TO THINK ABOUT THE SITUATION AND LET THEM KNOW YOU WANT TO GET THEIR VIEW OF THE SITUATION.

1. Give the other person an **opportunity to respond** without judging.
2. Make sure your words are **heard and understood**. Consider this rule literally. Make sure that your 'words' are heard. Oftentimes, the content, context or intent of your actual words will get obscured by other matters like an unintentional tone of voice, or the mood or state of mind that the coachee happens to be in. If they seem to be reacting inappropriately to something that you said during your feedback coaching session or during a formal evaluation, stop and confirm that they understood the content or context of your message. You must check that they're not reading into things that you didn't intend.
3. **Listen!** A feedback coaching session is best with a robust dialog. This means that you must remember to listen openly to what the coachee has to say. If the coachee is unwilling to respond or is tentative be ready with an opened-ended question. Keep quiet and look at the coachee which is a signal that you are waiting for a response. Ask:

"Tell me, Jane, what are your thoughts on this?"
"What's your view/position of this event/situation?"
"What's going inside your head right now, thinking about this?"
"What is your reaction to this?"

DESCRIBE THE POSSIBLE CONSEQUENCES AND OTHER PEOPLE'S REACTIONS.

1. Ask about what the coachee might think would happen if the behavior were to continue. Explain the consequences of the behavior from a Leadership Coach's perspective, specifically as it relates to leadership efforts. If you can, depersonalize the event by providing examples of others that might have exhibited similar behavior and describe what happened to them and those they care about. By looking at what happened to others, the coachee can look more objectively at the behavior that is not desirable. Hopefully they can then figure out a way 'the other person' could have dealt with it better and relate that to themselves.

2. After this discussion, steer back to the coachee's specific event and behaviors. Discuss the desirable behavior and ways to avoid repeating the decision making or mistakes of the past. Ask them who in their circle might be affected by continued behavior and ask them to figure out the specific impact to that person. Having the coachee work through the potential reactions or consequences allows them to understand the impact their actions have on others. Example: *"You told me that your boss appeared angry, frustrated and embarrassed when she found out that you had not attended any operations meetings in the past week. You just told me that she was furious that your team was not represented and because of that decisions*

made in those meetings have to be undone. She was extremely harsh in your view, telling you she felt she couldn't trust your judgment. She also told you had basically lied to her, saying that you were going when you didn't, nor did you think to send a proxy. I know that you didn't think those meetings were a big deal. But, they were to her and that's important. You made a judgment call that didn't square with her expectations. What are the consequences for these actions on the lack of trust now in your relationship? What do you think you can do in the future to not disappoint her and to deliver on your promises to her, the broader organization, your team, and yourself? Do you have a plan to get back on track and repair this?"

ASK THE COACHEE TO THINK THROUGH SOME OPTIONS.

1. **Link Feedback and Suggestions to a Solution.** It does very little good just to provide feedback and then not have an improvement and follow up plan. While matters of not meeting Behavior Coaching expectations on following through with Behavior Coaching accountability deliverables need to be directly addressed, it's always critical to link any feedback you provide to the coachee to future outcomes and expectations. This means the coaching sessions must provide suggestions for improvement and a plan to move forward without the same behaviors repeating themselves. This 'feedback then plan to move forward' thinking will help the coachee to feel as if they're truly being assessed with their best Behavior Coaching interests in mind.

2. **Consequences and Benefits:** As the coachee goes through their options, have them talk through the consequences and benefits of each. You are looking for specific suggestions from

the coachee to move forward with this event/situation from this feedback coaching session.
3. **Options:** Whenever possible only offer other options as a last resort if the coachee has exhausted all their thoughts and they still haven't come up with feasible solutions.
4. **Understand limitations in coming up with solutions.** One exception to this is if the coachee isn't thinking through the options that might make sense to others who might be in a similar situation. Not all coachees have the answers for every situation they find themselves facing. Some do need help coming up with suggestions and options. If this is the case, please make your suggestions helpful by including practical and realistic examples.

RECAP

1. **Restate and go over the decisions the coachee made.** At the end of the coaching session, as well as any next steps and actions. Take note of the action items, not the negative points of the other person's behavior. Recap the main discussion points and add anything you've discussed that the person could do differently regarding their decision making, behavior or that might develop their life and Behavior Coaching skills, avoid misunderstandings, and check to make sure that your communication is clear.
2. **Communicate the goals for the next feedback coaching session.** Be sure that you devote some portion of your agenda to going over the coachee's Behavior Coaching goals for the upcoming accountability period. As we've mentioned a few times, one of the core strengths of effective feedback coaching sessions is the ability to integrate the goals and actions of your

individual coachees with the overall large-scale leadership efforts, including plans and short-term, mid-range and long-term goals. To do this, you need to make sure that your coachees know what those other Behavior Coaching goals are. You want them to keep these in mind while carrying out their assignments and Behavior Coaching responsibilities. Touching on them during feedback coaching sessions is a good way to keep coachees on track with these all-important points.

> Catch people doing something right!

3. **End on a positive note.** It's important to always wind-up by expressing confidence in the person's ability to improve their current situation. Example: "You've really thought this through properly today. The way you jumped in and came up with the path forward for this is great! I have no doubt that if you do what you say you'll do, that this will be a lot less stressful this time next week. If you remember from last month, when you followed through on that tough problem with Sarah, you did awesome! Please keep taking the initiate on problems like this as soon as you can, so they don't fester like they used to. If they fester, they cause undue stressors and that's a risk for relapse. You definitely don't want that!"
4. **Reiterate your ongoing support.** Coaching sessions can be an opportunity to reiterate your support for the coachee and their leadership efforts. This is the perfect way to round off a feedback coaching session.

After the Feedback Coaching Session

TAKE NOTES

1. **Agreement:** Take notes during feedback coaching sessions and encourage your coachees to do the same thing. Look at what they've written and make sure you are both 'on the same page'. There's something about putting pen to paper that just solidifies next steps! Plus, some coachees are 'wiggly'. They will ignore the spoken word session after session. Additionally, if your deliverables and promises and next steps are in writing, that is a 'lock it down' mechanism. Having this will shorten negative discussions. The points are the agreed points. It's not easy to 'wiggle away from' written documentation. This will help you to have a written documentation of what has transpired.

> Always state the facts; they are hard to argue with.

2. **Writing is better than memory.** Taking notes and documenting also helps to secure the points in your and your coachee's memory, so that they're more easily recalled at a future date. It's all too easy to forget minor points. Taking notes will help to prevent this. It also helps with Behavior Coaching accountability. How can you remember what people promised to do for themselves if you don't keep notes?
3. **Writing things down makes them 'stick'.** For many Leadership Behavior Coaches, an important aspect of their service is a session recap that is delivered to the coachee regarding the talking points and actions steps including any promises made. That which you track, write down and deliver to the coachee has a much better chance of 'sticking'. Written words have much more 'weight' than spoken words. If you want the better outcomes for your coachees, you'll consistently provide documentation to them after your coaching sessions.

LAY THE GROUNDWORK FOR PRAISE

A successful feedback coaching session should begin with a result in mind. It should inform the coachee exactly what he/she needs to do to become better equipped to achieving the Behavior Coaching goals and objectives that a coachee is seeking. This gets the coachee to "listen up" because it directly affects their personal interest and goals for their leadership efforts.

Discuss Strengths and Weaknesses. When discussing strengths and weaknesses during a feedback coaching session, and setting up 'praise', it's often helpful to look to the DISCflex Leadership Behavior Report and recommended eLearning section on strengths and weaknesses, as well as the SWOT. Make sure that you draw your conclusions from the available facts and not form any 'baseless presumptions'. For example, look at the available data, verifiable actions and behaviors, metrics, and documented instances of the coachee's behavior to determine what they might need to work/focus on, instead of basing it on something that you 'heard through the grapevine'. Likewise, be sure that a coachee is doing well in a certain area before you praise or reward them for it, or else you'll inadvertently reinforce unwanted or negative behavior.

ADDITIONAL TYPES OF EVALUATIONS

Not only is there the traditional 'sit down with Leadership Coach and receive feedback meeting', but evaluations can take on many different forms. Different forms of evaluation are particularly useful in gathering information that a Leadership Coach may have overlooked, can be used as additional resources for a formal evaluation, and provide the perspective of an outsider.

COACHEE SELF-APPRAISAL/SELF-EVALUATION

Have the coachee conduct a Self-Appraisal/Self-Evaluation on his or herself a few days before you're scheduled to provide feedback. You should already have the coachee's DISCflex Leadership Behavior Report and recommended eLearning but this Self-Appraisal/Self-Evaluation should be focused on "How I Think I Am Doing" They should turn this self-evaluation into you, giving you time to go over it before you meet. Be warned that you should always let the coachee talk through their Self-Appraisal/Self-Evaluation prior to providing your feedback. Sometimes this insight can wreak havoc on a coaching session or significantly help with a Leadership Coach's feedback. But you can't anticipate which it will be until the coachee provide their personal view of themselves and their leadership efforts thus far.

Self-Appraisal/Self-Evaluation can really be quite a valuable tool, as it can give you unique insight into how the coachee is expecting your feedback to go. If they're very far off-base, it can help you to better prepare for that. You can prevent emotionally based arguments, and to come up with a strategy to help the coachee get their perspective back on track with reality.

The Coachee's Self-Appraisal/Self-Evaluation can be an excellent tool for the Leadership Coach to self-evaluate their own effectiveness as a Leadership Coach. How? Think about it. If you consistently see that the coachees under you are of the same opinion as you about their performance, you are doing a good job setting expectations, delivering feedback, and communicating about performance. But if they are consistently off base, you might want to look at how you are 'keeping it real'.

PEER REVIEW, STAFF OPINIONS, AND THE LIKE

Peer reviews, staff opinions, and the like are all ways to get different opinions about an individual's behavior in various situations and settings. Because they are simply a 'snapshot' of how the coachee acts in different situations with different people, the information provided should be looked at in this light. As an example, people tend to be on their best behavior in Leadership Team meeting that are open to the Board. They don't appear frustrated or get angry in front of this level of persons. Ten minutes after the meeting is over, they might bounce back to their 'normal' behavior. Their Board Members might never see this.

As such, situational 'snapshots' of behavior should be taken as an important but fallible source, especially if viewed solely on their evidences alone. However, if these 'snapshots' show a lot of people drawing the same conclusions about an individual, they can be thought to be fairly accurate. It is the Leadership Coach's responsibility to provide feedback to the coachee on any areas of concern that may surface. Don't forget to speak candidly with the coachee about these concerns but refrain from 'naming names'.

If nothing else, having an approved list from whom you can gather behavior 'snapshots' should give you a great start in gathering information about how a coachee is doing (how they are behaving) outside your coaching sessions. If you can put the pieces of the coachee's behavioral puzzle together, you'll provide better feedback. More information provides better balance in the feedback process in general. It helps a Leadership Coach have further insight about a coachee's behavior and habits as they work their leadership efforts.

GROUP COACHING SESSION REVIEWS

When a coachee participates in a Group Coaching, strategy workshop, or leadership training session, a different behavior dynamic might be observed. If you are facilitating group coaching or training sessions, participants can provide insight about other participants with a view to 'lifting' and helping. In a strategy workshop, a skilled facilitator can see the innovation and decision-making skills the coachee possesses.

A survey whereby peer group are encouraged to comment on what behavior they perceive as helpful to leadership efforts pertaining to an individual is powerful information for the coachee. Peers often have a perspective that others don't. Of course, peer feedback and 360-degree feedback mechanisms aren't always perfect, but these can shed light on important areas of improvement, highlight strengths that coachees may have 'blind spots' about, and/or can provide views about the coachee's behavior based another person's interactions. Additionally, these should obviously be carefully combed through for biases, but they can nevertheless offer a unique perspective that should not be totally discounted. Remember however, that if the comments are not backed up by solid facts or evidence, you should not use them in coaching sessions as an absolute. They are for discussion and reference.

SOLICITED AND UNSOLICITED FEEDBACK FROM OTHERS

Feedback from others is always valuable. Why? Because patterns emerge. The more 3rd party feedback you can get, the better the data points. An integral part of leadership efforts is how the coachee's behavior appears from another person's point of view. The DISCflex Reports have a 3rd party insight mechanism that is quick and confidential.

A reminder: Be sure to keep within all confidentiality laws and guidelines when gathering and discussing any coachee information.

This is very important from a legal and ethical standpoint. A good rule of thumb when soliciting 3rd party feedback is to take information in but never give information out without express permission from the coachee to do so. Whenever you have permission to reach out to others for solicited feedback, it is often best to have a standard form or survey – either printed or electronic – which details what the feedback will be used for and who will be provided with an information. This ensures that the person understands what types of information you are looking for and gives them a sense that providing this information is part of the process. In other words, it puts them at ease and builds trust.

While any 3rd party information should be scanned for biases and other indications of less than ideal information (perhaps gossip or incorrect information), they are often very reliable glimpses into a coachee's behavior and 'temperature'. Unsolicited feedback can be even more interesting as it implies strong feelings on behalf of the person providing it. After all, they went out of their way to contact you with their information, without your even having to ask. Again, you must check and verify against other information and observations and discuss these with the coachee without breaching confidentiality on either side. Remember to ask what information you are at liberty to disclose and discuss and any considerations or boundaries in that disclosure. This is important because it sets up an environment where information will continue to flow.

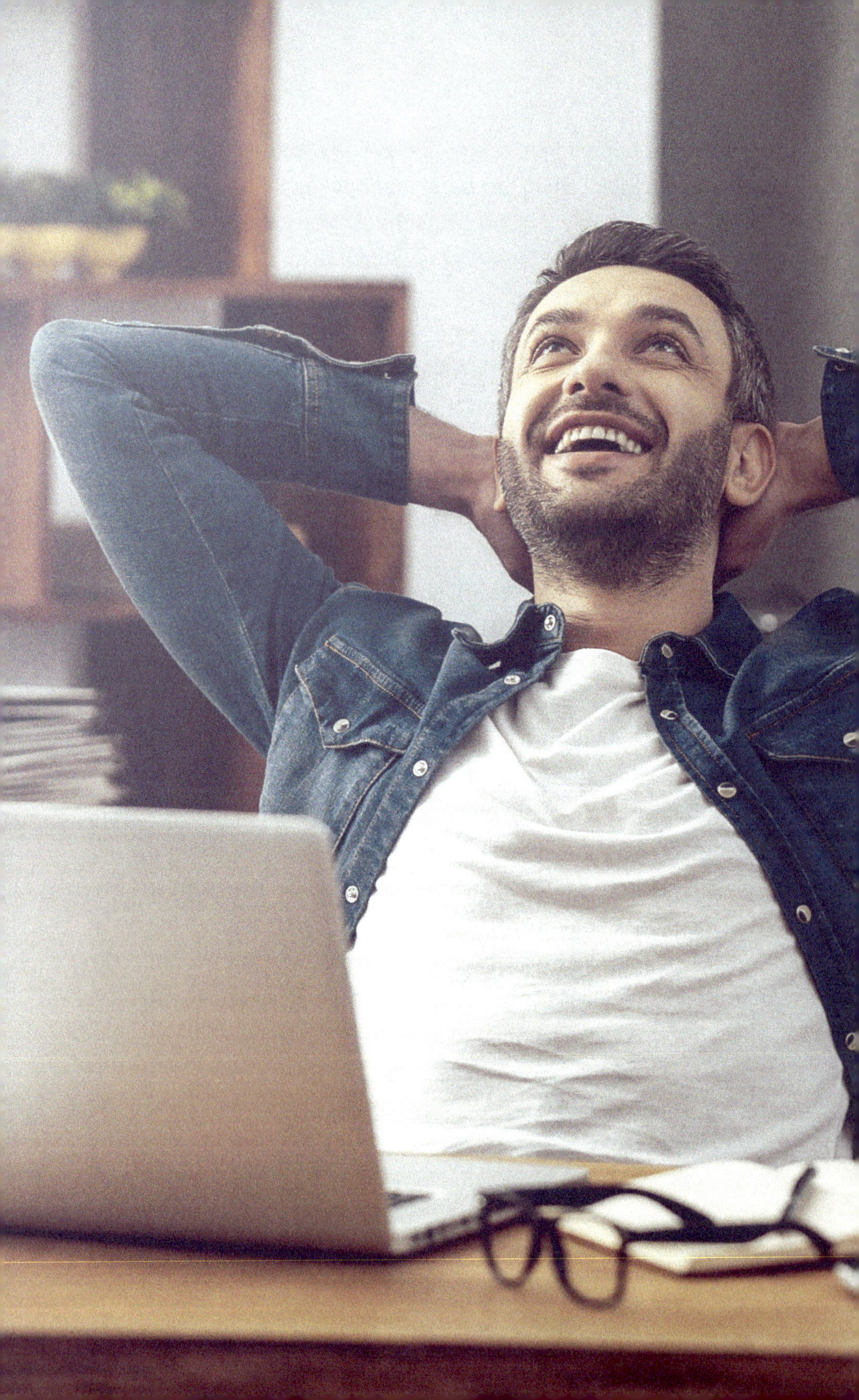

Goal Setting and Behavior Coaching Accountability

> In striving for goals, discipline, focus and a positive mindset are critical. Maintain a positive focus in life no matter what. Stay

The Definition of a Behavior Coaching Goal

A Behavior Coaching goal is defined as "an agreed upon statement of what should be achieved within a defined period of time". The goal should be broken down into SMART components detailing what the responsibility is, what the Behavior Coaching accountability expectations are concerning results, and authority or decision-making guidelines. When these are fleshed out, they'll paint a great picture of what the coachee's overall leadership efforts should be focused on, so that they have individual goals that all add up to overall strategic goals.

Part by part, let's look at what this definition means:

"An agreed upon statement" means that both the coachee and the Leadership Behavior Coach must agree upon the goal for it to be effective. A goal that is imposed upon an unwilling coachee is the kind of goal that isn't going to generate the necessary excitement for accomplishment. Nevertheless, sometimes you all must accomplish goals or tasks that you don't agree with. The key here is to have both parties agree that the responsibility will be carried out to the best of their abilities.

"What the coachee will achieve" implies that the goal must contain some sort of concrete, achievable objective leading to an outcome. A goal without specifics is unthinkable. You recommend making certain that all goals have metrics attached and that the parties discuss these prior to deployment, and that these be detailed in a SMART format.

"Within a defined period of time" indicates that a goal must have a specific deadline. Goals without deadlines tend to fizzle and die out whereas deadlines produce a great deal of enthusiasm and excitement, as well as results. Plus, often coachees who want to please you (and others) and who want to 'win' will do things ahead of time. But if they don't know what timeframe they're driving toward, you can't congratulate them on this.

SMART GOALS

SMART is a good acronym to remember while setting goals for the next Behavior Coaching accountability period. Ask whether the goal is...

- **S**pecific. The more specific a goal is, the more objective and concrete the measurement of its success will be. It does no good at all to have a goal where you can't even tell if it's been achieved or not. Establishing very specific conditions for success will give the coachee a strong sense of something to work towards. It will make it much easier to break the goal down into smaller, progressive units and/or sub-goals.

- **M**easurable. A good goal must have some ability to measure whether it has been reached. A good example would be something like 'Read 15 pages of the _____ book and complete all the activities in the Change Section of the eLearning by May 7th', because this offers some clear-cut criteria of completion. 14 pages would mean failure, whereas anything at or above 15 pages would mean success. It's very simple and clear-cut, and easy to measure using simple numbers. This is the best kind of goal to make; one where there can be no arguing or equivocating about whether it was achieved. That should be self-evident. People may argue that some goals are difficult to measure. This is indeed true. But, trust me, if you don't spend some time defining adequate metrics and measures of successful behavior and/or performance, you'll spend much more time later bickering with coachees come feedback time. Be warned: This is time well spent!

- **A**chievable. A good goal must be achievable. It must have a result that is possible given the time and resources that the coachee must work with. Asking someone with a limited time to read and work through 125 pages in a week is senseless. They just can't be expected to deliver. It's unreasonable and sets the coachee up for stress and/or failure. You'll only frustrate everyone involved. The point is that if a goal cannot reasonably be achieved, it is not a good goal.

- **R**ealistic. Much like the previous requirement, realism is a critical aspect of a good goal. There may be certain goals like "make peace with every member of your family in the next two months" that are theoretically achievable, thus satisfying the third condition, but just aren't very realistic. It normally takes a long amount of time for anyone to repair relationships. Eight weeks is a short period of time. Unless there are some serious extenuating circumstances, it's not reasonable to think that this is a realistic goal. All goals should be analyzed to make sure that they're realistic in the context of the leadership efforts and support network/environment that they must be attempted in.

- **T**imely. Lastly, a goal must be timely, which is to say that it must have a somewhat pressing deadline that establishes a sense of the appropriate urgency to get it done. Goals that are set for several years in the future tend to never get accomplished, because it's simply not possible for humans to hold focus on something for so long. set Try to set goals that can be accomplished within the next performance period. If they are longer range in, make sure that you and the coachee always set benchmarks against the longer-range goals so that you can track progress. For a goal to be a driving force, it must have an appropriate sense of urgency. Good goals must have a somewhat strict time limit. Check to see if your coachee's goals do. If they don't, consider walking the coachee through how to break the bigger ones down into smaller segments with a series of deadlines that feed into the larger goal. When you do this, make sure you keep all timelines and metrics focused on the overall anticipated result. Tie them together to achieve success in the next Behavior Coaching accountability period.

GAIN COMMITMENT TO SELF-IMPROVEMENT

> Success is no accident. It is hard work, perseverance, learning, studying, sacrifice and most of all, love of what you are doing or learning to do. -Pele

It does no good for your coachee to set Behavior Coaching goals if your coachee is not committed and/or passionate about meeting them. They need to know that meeting their Behavior Coaching goals is not just a matter of helping themselves in the short-term.

Making a commitment and achieving goals consistently leads to better habits, and a better life overall.

The degree of commitment a person has impacts health, relationships, and so much more. As such, it helps to end each coaching session by getting the coachee's firm commitment to the principle of self-improvement and growth. If you're able to motivate them to improve themselves through their education and leadership efforts, then it'll be much easier for them to meet the Behavior Coaching goals that they want. If you concentrate on the principle of driving motivation and commitment, you will see results in this area.

IDENTIFYING AND REMOVING ROADBLOCKS

> Every now and then we ask the universe for success, and we get the gifts of physical and mental strength and stamina. We beg for patience and instead faith, deeper conviction and confidence are our rewards. Some people implore the heavens for wealth and prosperity, but receive the gifts of heightened perception and increased patience. We ask for personal growth and achievement and the universe grants us the gifts of deep understanding and we are blessed with the gift of grace. What we ask for is not always what we need. Trust the universe! -Hellen Davis

A key part of Leadership Coaching is setting the stage for your coachees to succeed. In many instances, this is largely dependent upon the efforts of the Leadership Coach to identify any roadblock that could happen in the next performance period.

After you set goals for the next performance period, look at those projected goals and help walk through and identify possible upcoming roadblocks. This is a key component to goal setting because the goal should be attainable. A good Leadership Coach will be able to question the coachee about any potential roadblocks that stand in the way of accomplishing goals. Once uncovered, seek a plan to overcome and /or remove them, or at the very least they can discuss ways to deal with them.

A Leadership Coach must facilitate the coachee toward success. Ideally you assess the person's strengths and look at the opportunities that might become available. Driving toward success also means being realistic about the challenges, potentially weaker behavioral traits, and/or obstacles facing the leader. These all must be first identified. Only after assessment of both should you discuss a plan to remove negatives or deal with them accordingly.

In this way, Leadership Coaching discussions empower that coachee to think through and meet goals head on. For example, if a coachee is given a specific task to complete but finds that the resources he needs to complete that task are not available to him, and this possibility didn't come in the coaching session prior to launching into action, then the fault lies squarely with the Leadership Coach.

If you expect goals to be accomplished, then the coachee must have talked through roadblocks and whether they have the necessary resources is a potential roadblock! A Leadership Coach who is practicing good Leadership Behavior Coaching techniques checks whether all the resources are in place. By failing to identify the roadblock or discussing limited resources and then asking the coachee about their plan to remove these, the Leadership Coach has failed in their coaching session.

AFTER ACTION REVIEWS

> Leaders must exemplify integrity and earn the trust of their teams through their everyday actions. When you do this, you set high standards for everyone at your company. And when you do so with positive energy and enthusiasm for shared goals and purpose, you can deeply connect with your team and customers. -Marillyn Hewson

An after-action review is an assessment that is carried out after a major goal has been met. It is basically an attempt to look at how the result or outcome of a goal came about, what factors contributed to it, and how it might have gone differently. The goal is to assess anticipated results versus actual results. Obviously, this can be a very useful tool when it comes time for feedback and/or formal coachee evaluations.

After a goal is completed, have coachees fill out after action reviews regarding the effectiveness of the goals and how smooth the process went while working toward that goal. Set clear parameters that all statements must be based on facts, data, or other evidence - never on opinions. These fresh perspectives can be used to get a sense of what can be done better for the next time. Use information gathered from after action reviews to set goals for the Behavior Coaching accountability period. Since Leadership Coaching is a continuous process, after action reviews should be conducted after every goals period to continuously improve goals in the future.

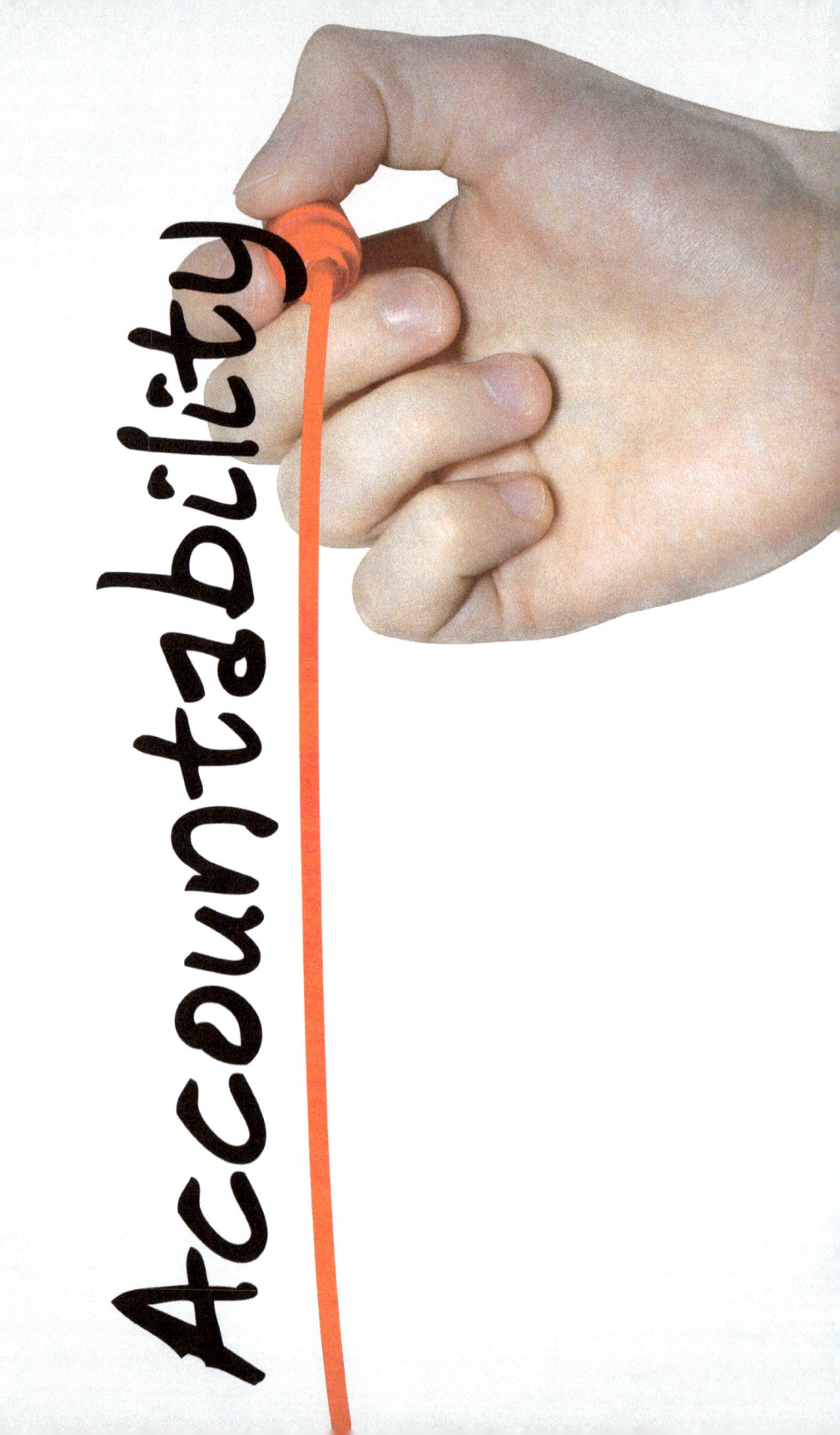

Accountability

Coaching Skills for Behavior Coaching Accountability

Now that you have the Leadership Behavior Coaching skills under your belt, one of the fundamental pillars of Leadership Behavior Coaching is holding the coachee accountable. Evaluation of how the coachee is going against expectations and feedback is a critical tool for helping to ensure that your coaching sessions are on the right track.

We'll also cover the importance of documentation, and of committing accountability reviews to writing. One objective of Behavior Coaching accountability is to help coachees grow through feedback and coaching.

Then, we'll discuss the importance of setting goals for the next steps to ensure future success. These aren't just any goals, but reasonable, attainable goals that strengthen the coachee's motivation, build self-confidence, foster great decision making, and enhance life skills.

The Definition and Goals of Behavior Coaching Accountability

BEHAVIOR COACHING ACCOUNTABILITY

To be successful at holding oneself accountable, you must first know exactly what Behavior Coaching accountability is. To put it simply, Behavior Coaching accountability is an 'ongoing process' by which you set goals, cultivate skills and appropriate behavior, put these into practice while driving toward a specific measurement. Behavior Coaching accountability also encompasses providing information and feedback to coachees based on the three fundamental areas:

- Functioning in the situations the leader finds themselves in (based on predetermined expectations)
- Conduct and behavior (how the leader acts in the situation)
- Willingness to participate and engage.

The definition of Behavior Coaching accountability is rather lengthy, but it's not complicated if you take a moment to break it up.

BEHAVIOR COACHING ACCOUNTABILITY IS AN 'ONGOING PROCESS'.

This means that it's something that should occur minute-by-minute, hour-by-hour, day-by-day, not just during the coaching sessions. Behavior Coaching accountability should be one of the foremost considerations of the relationship between the Leadership Behavior Coach and their coachee. Behavior Coaching accountability is not something that is pushed aside to be dispensed with as a chore only when things don't progress as planned. It's an ongoing process that provides continuous timely feedback to the coachee; both positive and when things aren't on track. Most important, they shouldn't only look to the Leadership Coach to hold themselves accountable. The coachee should hold themselves accountable – this is the ultimate Leadership Behavior Coaching goal.

Providing Behavior Coaching accountability feedback helps coachees stay on track because of a universal principle: *That which gets measured, gets done.*

BEHAVIOR COACHING ACCOUNTABILITY INVOLVES MOTIVATING AND CULTIVATING COACHEES.

To motivate a coachee, they must have sufficient reasons to meet a specific goal. But often that isn't enough, coachees need to know how they're doing before that goal is completed. Ongoing feedback is critical in improving the coachee's overall life skills and behaviors. When you say that you cultivate a coachee, what you really mean is that you're availing that coachee with the tools or resources that he or she needs to be successful. You're helping foster the conditions by which they can become as successful as their potential allows them to be. The feedback that is generated from Behavior Coaching accountability must be linked to suggestions and strategies for their ongoing leadership efforts. These must be equally motivating and empowering in the coachee's eyes.

Behavior Coaching accountability provides feedback in the three key areas whenever a coachee sets future goals:

- **Performing and Functioning:** Appropriately 'functioning' is a concept at the core of Leadership Behavior. In the situations the coachee will find themselves in, it is vital that they are able to perform well. Coachees must 'function well' when working with others, communicating, and carrying out their day-to-day work responsibilities so they can thrive. Operating their professional life well means they must 'function' as a leader, taking on the behaviors that are required for each circumstance they are addressing. Functioning in a work environment is based on predetermined expectations of things the coachee must do. It is a 'catch-all' term for their responsibilities to themselves and others. The coach and coachee must determine and agree upon what is expected of the coachee, so they can measure their leadership efforts accordingly.

- **Conduct and Behavior:** Conduct and behavior is how the coachee performs in a situation. It is 'how they function and perform their responsibilities'. Coachees are different in their approach to getting things done. Two coachees can get similar results by doing things very differently. And that's ok! Conduct and behavior encompass factors like personality, attitude, communication style, and how the coachee interacts with others. It doesn't make any sense to coachees working hard on their goals, if their efforts run contrary to tried and true leadership efforts or that don't work for their peers, boos, or coworkers. Part of goal setting and Behavior Coaching accountability is making sure that everything is in sync.

- **Willingness to participate and engage:** No one can force a coachee to participate. The degree of participation and willingness often reflects how well a coachee will do with their leadership efforts. NOTE: As the coachee gets some 'wins' under their belt, you might see their willingness to participate and engage go up.

BEHAVIOR COACHING ACCOUNTABILITY EVALUATION

When you say that a coachee evaluation must be carefully considered, you require that a good deal of preparation must go into the evaluation. A coach should not take the matter lightly. And remember, the goal with evaluation is to analyze expectations versus actual results.

Objective judgment means that the conclusions you come to must deal entirely with facts and recorded instances of how the coachee performed and behaved based on expectations, and their willingness to participate. Findings and feedback must deal specifically with leadership efforts' related issues and goals. These can never take the form of a personal attack. Likewise, a Behavior Coaching accountability evaluation should never be expressed in a subjective way, with the coach saying things like *"I think…"* or *"I feel…"* **One should be able to point to specific facts about the coachee's actions and/or behavior and their performance and skills, never their character.**

Consistently applied means that coachee evaluations must be based on a consistent standard. In this way, all feedback will be given equitably. By offering continual and timely coaching feedback, you can keep stress levels lower. Having feedback 'build up' isn't good for the coaching relationship. Stress builds as time goes on. The coachee might feel that you are 'keeping score' or are holding back only to unleash a torrent of feedback all at once. This can-do damage to the coaching relationship in a variety of ways.

RATING THE COACHEE

The result of your analysis of how the coachee is doing is a 'rating against expectations'. Most coaches don't really like to give coachees a rating, but this coaching responsibility is important. Coachees need to understand exactly how well they are doing, and rating how well you think they are doing versus expectation is a big part of that. This process is painful for some coaches. They simply do not like ranking coachees. It's understandable, but you must do it. It's part of your responsibility as a coach.

Think of rating as an objective way to provide impartial and critical feedback. If you can't measure and rate expectations versus actual results, it's just about impossible to provide great feedback. A rating system or ranking process is a useful tool because it allows for the coachees to set goals more effectively and provides the motivation for self-improvement. Also, if the coachee is just starting out in their leadership efforts, your rating should allow for 'wins'.

PROVIDING FEEDBACK WHILE SUSTAINING MOTIVATION IS OFTEN A DELICATE BALANCING ACT.

Expectations that are too high can be as harmful as those that are too low. As a Leadership Coach, you must gauge where the 'bar' is and adjust accordingly in your coaching sessions.

While it is often stressful for coachees to go through this process, there are usually multiple benefits and rewards for high achievers and coachees who perform well. Also, if coachees are not performing well against their expectations, this must be discussed, and a plan put in place to adjust and bring behavior and performance closer to expectations. For this reason alone, many Leadership Coaches and coachees come to accept the rating process as vital to the process.

TYPES OF COACHEE RATINGS

In Leadership Coaching, it's best to keep the rating process simple, so we suggest you use these four generally acceptable ratings:

1. Far Exceeds
2. Exceeds
3. Meets Expectation
4. Needs Improvement.

People can be at 'Meets Expectations' in one area, 'Exceeds' in another, and still rate a 'Needs Improvement' in yet another. Most important, even a coachee who consistently 'Needs Improvement' should occasionally meet expectations. These four simple ratings help categorize and standardize leadership efforts. From most desirable to least, they are as follows:

FAR EXCEEDS RATING

The Far Exceeds rating is given when the coachee succeeds and goes above and beyond what they promised to do. They might have even amazed you. If you've agreed to an assignment or task, and it was completed swiftly and decisively, with an unmistakable flair, they get a far exceeds ranking. This is the ideal that all shoot for, but realistically speaking, it is not an attainable goal for just anyone or all the time.

Several factors must line up for one to operate at this level, especially consistently. Nevertheless, the far exceeds ranking for assignments and promises is a dream come true for any Leadership Coach because congratulating and recognizing great leadership efforts is awesome! These make for the easiest feedback coaching sessions as you usually never run into any issues, problems, or conflicts.

When a Leadership Coach provides a far exceeds ranking in a coaching session, the coachee should be proud. Documenting these consistently allows the coach to establish a record of the coachee's high performance. It also shows them what path to take to continue advancing their leadership efforts towards higher goals. When a coachee consistently shows they can achieve at a certain level, you can systematically 'raise the bar'.

EXCEEDS RATING

A Leadership Coach should be able to spot those coachees who are consistently performing that are above expectations. In fact, the best Leadership Coaches, through holding coachees accountable over the long haul, can create this type of coachee! Great Leadership Coaches see their coachees' potential and then motivate them to become more successful. Consistently meeting and achieving Behavior Coaching goals needs motivation and that comes from hope and support.

Remember this: The 'Exceeds' coachee demonstrates the capacity of exceeding expectations most of the time but doesn't always manage to do so. So be gracious and kind in your feedback. The coachee is learning how to consistently raise their leadership game. They might also exceed expectations occasionally; and surprise you and themselves! Exceeds for them is not yet consistent. However, they usually never fall below meeting any coaching session expectations if their Leadership Coach and support network are strong. Coachees typically achieve more than they could have on their own when they feel people are in their corner.

Leadership Coaches look for success and are great at identifying and singling out this type of coachee's efforts. Success breeds success, but only if it's recognized. A word or two of heart-felt praise does wonders to motivate coachees. In doing so, you can draw out the coachee's individual talents. A good Leadership Coach can help motivate coachees to achieve the most they can, whereas otherwise they might have floundered for years without finding their footing, constantly moving between exceeding and meeting expectations and never consistent enough for great lifelong habits to 'stick'. If left alone, these high potential coachees may become frustrated so it's critical to grow and coach them through positive reinforcement and well-considered feedback. The leadership efforts and success with this type of coachee can be substantial with some well-placed words of encouragement.

Performance Leadership Coaching is useful to the high potential coachee because it lets him or her know exactly what needs to be done to reach his or her true potential.

MEETS EXPECTATIONS RATING

The most common type of long-term coachee is the kind who lives up to most expectations, getting assignments done and on time. But with little to distinguish them from the crowd one way or the other it is difficult to recognize and reward them other than with standard praise for keeping steady with their leadership efforts. This, however, is in no way to be thought of as bad. After all, the Behavior Coaching work is getting done, isn't it? The individual is living up to Behavior Coaching effort expectations admirably and should be praised for it. A Leadership Coach can certainly help the 'Meets Expectations' coachee by challenging them with new goals or assignments that test their limitations. This should be done to keep them feeling actively engaged with their leadership efforts.

Remember, when they are successful, tell them you are proud of them! 'Meets Expectations' coachees might never ascend to a higher level, and that's fine, especially so if they understand that it is within their power to work to succeed and thrive in life. Plus, as they get comfortable with their progress they might want to step it up and work at becoming consistently better. Explain what it would take and let them know that you would support them if they chose to do so. Remember, meeting expectations is good. If they continue to get their assignments done, and mend their relationship with self and others, that's the bottom line, isn't it?

The 'Meets Expectations' coachee will find feedback useful because it lets him or her know exactly what is expected of them, so that they can be certain that they're focusing on the things that are important for their leadership efforts always.

A word of caution however: Many 'meets expectations coachees' can become resentful if they feel entitled to the same treatment, recognition or rewards as high potential coachees. This is particularly important if you are running group sessions. Individually, and IN PRIVATE, you must explain what it would take for them to become a high potential coachee. You must also provide feedback that they are at 'Meets Expectations' and not at 'Exceeds' so that there are no surprises when it comes time for feedback and evaluation.

NEEDS IMPROVEMENT RATING

The 'Needs Improvement' rating, on the other hand, can happen often during the early stages of Behavior Coaching. When people 'slip' while trying to change habits, their effort 'needs improvement'. This also occurs when a coachee occasionally suffers some difficulties in getting assignments done or promises delivered, on time or at all. One of the biggest benefits of working with a Leadership Coach is their ability to turn around 'Needs Improvement' coachees by holding people accountable on an ongoing basis. Sometimes, it's as simple as weekly coaching sessions and making sure the coachee knows someone is in their court tracking their leadership efforts. Don't discount or overlook this critical function you play in the coachee's leadership efforts.

If the coachee is consistently in the 'Needs Improvement' zone, a Leadership Coach needs to assess the current goals and Behavior Coaching accountability parameters. It could be that they are just too high for where the coachee currently is in their leadership efforts. The goal is to build confidence and set the coachee up for some 'wins', thus proving that they have the capacity to get on track. It is the responsibility of the Leadership Coach to work with these coachees to identify exactly what problems are holding them back. Then they must provide feedback and suggestions to help them to overcome those 'Needs Improvement' ratings.

Typically, with the right degree of Leadership Coaching, a 'Needs Improvement' coachee will eventually become a perfectly acceptable 'Meets Expectations' coachee, someone who is an asset to their community. A word of caution; not everyone can be motivated towards acceptable performance. You must understand that your efforts must yield a return on investment. Keep this in mind when you decide how much time and effort you allocate to every coachee. Without this kind of intervention, however, they might have trouble initiating themselves and could eventually get discouraged and sink to the lower level.

The bottom line: The 'Needs Improvement' coachee can benefit from Performance Leadership Coaching because it illustrates to them precisely what they need to do to get back on track and become a productive member of their organization. Be aware that this is often the most frustrating type of coachee to manage. The best approach is to be extremely clear about expectations and specific measurements you will use to gauge their performance, behavior, and expectation of improvements. You must be sure to document all conversations, metrics, expectations, timelines for improvement, and goals. Without this you cannot provide appropriate feedback. Unfortunately, you might need this if your feedback doesn't get results or willingness to improve.

WHEN 'UNDERPERFORMING' IS SITUATIONAL, TEMPORARY, OR EVENT-BASED

It's often the case that tough feedback takes place soon after stressful events, new behavior or discussions, or when things are changing in the coachee's work or personal life. The result in this case is that sometimes the cause of the coachee's 'underperforming' is situational, temporary, or event-based. When a coachee is 'still learning the ropes' of new behaviors, even if they were doing great last week in other behaviors, you will have to provide feedback on your observations. You can remind them of what happens when changes take place: cognitive dissonance. You can use this topic as an opportunity to help develop the coachee's resilience and talk through the effects of cognitive dissonance on behavior and habits.

One of the main strengths of Leadership Behavior Coaching is that it can be a proactive process. It can prepare coachees that 'underperforming' is situational, temporary, or event-based forward with their leadership efforts and create new behavior and habits.

Imagine if you had a coachee who you know has the potential to be promoted into a position of more responsibility at work. But right now, their frustration levels and anger problems keep popping up. You both realize that this is an area where Leadership Coaching must focus on that promotion to happen. This is clearly a good Behavior Coaching goal. You can't wait for that promotion to be considered before you address this in your coaching sessions! You should work with that coachee now to make sure they have the skills that they'll need later. Much in line with removing obstacles to performance, making sure that coachees are working today to overcome the weaknesses that could cripple them tomorrow is a key part of Leadership Behavior Coaching.

THE IRREDEEMABLE COACHEE

The irredeemable coachee is just that. It is the coachee who has trouble living up to expectations, delivering on their assignments, living up to their commitments, and/or is unwilling to make adequate effort. They consistently turn in work late or never. In general, they have problems with all aspects of their leadership efforts as they relate to changing what has been agree needs addressing. It is not to say that the irredeemable coachee is a bad person; it might simply be the case that they're not 'ready'.

Whatever the case, if you've exhausted all possible means of turning them around through proper Behavior Coaching accountability right now. As a Leadership Coach, it's time to cut your losses and remove them from your roster. It might seem a harsh move, it might not be forever, but in the end, everyone involved will be a lot happier.

A Leadership Coach exit plan is useful in this instance, because it lays the groundwork and provides documentation and a standard process for the dismissal, setting a precedent of fairness and protection against any claims. Sometimes, it will be the case that you need to dismiss a chronically underachieving coachee. However, every termination is an affair that can easily go awry. Make sure you've given fair warning of your intention to terminate with the coachee and any other affected people in the coaching supporter ranks. Always refer to your advisors and/or legal counsel when faced with this. Litigation is entirely possible. As such, you should use well-documented logs including any evaluations as a tool to demonstrate that the coachee was assessed fairly and found to be subpar in fulfilling expectations of the coaching sessions.

SETTING BEHAVIOR GOALS AND BEHAVIOR COACHING ACCOUNTABILITY CONSIDERATIONS FOR THE NEXT ACCOUNTABILITY PERIOD

Setting behavior goals and Behavior Coaching accountability considerations for the next Behavior Coaching accountability period is an ongoing process. After a coaching session has taken place, the next step is to set goals and Behavior Coaching accountability considerations for the next accountability period. Behavior Coaching goals help the coachee to advance towards a higher level of commitment in a concrete way. They let a coachee know exactly what is expected of them and what they must do to meet or even exceed those goals. Leadership Behavior is the overall goal. When this overall goal is the focus, sub-goals fall into line. As a Leadership Coach, you should monitor the level of the coachee's motivation and ongoing commitment to their leadership efforts. It is not enough to keep giving goals that offer the same level of challenge to the same coachees repeatedly, coaching session after coaching session. This will never motivate people to excel.

Rather, coachees who are meeting their goals must be given new challenges, new education, and new opportunities to shine. They need to see they can 'better their last best' so that their rate of motivation and life skills constantly rises. By increasing these, the coachees will continuously feel actively engaged with their coaching sessions and leadership efforts. In coaching sessions, it's important for people to learn new things and be challenged.

Likewise, those coachees who are underperforming must see through the coaching sessions that they can 'win'. Small 'wins' while gradually increasing the level of effort required, and setting slightly higher and higher standards to meet, is an excellent way to build confidence in coachees. This method of inspiration and motivation does wonders to build hope, too. Some coachees need confidence so that they can improve. Additionally, setting the same level of goals at the same standards over a long period of time leads to boredom and a sense of disengagement. Therefore, be careful which goals you set as a part of your performance Leadership Coach strategy. With that said, let's take a moment to discuss the different types of coachees.

NO SURPRISES WITH CONTINUOUS FEEDBACK

As we have said, a major goal of continuous evaluations and constant feedback is so that there are 'no surprises' when it comes time for the coach to provide the coachee with an evaluation. Coaching feedback must be given on a constant, timely, and if necessary, daily basis. If this is done properly, then a coachee will always have a clear picture of where they stand and what they need to do to take corrective action.

Delaying feedback is a risk. It risks resentment, it risks relationships, and it risks trust. Providing continuous feedback is important because it ensures that a cee stays are on track. Not only does it help the coachee and their supporters know what goals are being met and which are in danger of failing, but it also helps everyone be motivated, knowing that corrections, if needed will be discussed and dealt with in a timely manner.

A coachee who receives consistent feedback is a coachee who will know exactly what he needs to do to further their leadership efforts, and ultimately lead a much better professional life. Please remember, the worst thing that can happen for any of your coachees or their closest supporters is to feel blindsided by the feedback or subsequent evaluation you give them. If a coachee has been under the impression that he was on track, or even exceeding expectations, only to be told at that they need to improve because they're falling below expectations, this is a bad situation. If you do this, expect conflict or an argument just about every time. Therefore, as a Leadership Coach, poor feedback communication equals poor coaching performance. Even worse, these types of surprises destroy trust and the fault lies squarely with you, the Leadership Coach. Avoid this scenario by making sure that you continuously give the coachee feedback on a regular basis.

TO FULLY UNDERSTAND THIS PRINCIPLE OF 'NO SURPRISES', LET'S LOOK AT A FEW ANALOGIES:

Think back to when you were in school. When report cards came out, there were those students who seemed confident in what their results would be, as well as those students who were shocked to see that their grades were less than the expected. The difference is that some students knew the grading process and kept track of the continuous feedback they were given in the form of grades on individual assignments. Using this knowledge, they could anticipate what their final grades would be. Likewise, if you provide your coachees with continuous feedback on their leadership efforts and behavior, then they'll have the information they need to move forward with confidence.

Another analogy is to consider what you would do if you had a medical problem. Of course, you would go to a person who was able to fix that problem: your doctor. Likewise, when there is a problem with behavior, there's only one way to solve it: Address it with the person who is having the problem. A Leadership Coach must take the problem directly to the coachee and make them aware of it as quickly as possible, hopefully resolving it just the way a doctor would a disease, before it spreads further and ultimately grows beyond control or repair. The bottom line: **How can a coachee 'fix' something they don't know about?**

GOAL SYNERGY

Leadership Coaching is an effective way to ensure synergy between individual and strategic goals. When a Leadership Coach takes on the role of a coach, they can provide direct, constant feedback. If they're trained to be aware of the goals, they can help to set individuals onto the right path for optimum performance.

Imagine a swim team that has been having a problematic season. Meet after meet, they constantly lose matches, but the coach remains silent. When the end of the season arrives, the coach expresses his terrible disappointment with the team and begins to go over what they need to do to improve their performance the next season. The team members look at one another as a realization dawns on them: If the coach had brought this up after the first failed meet, they could have implemented the changes earlier. They might have had a more successful season. Likewise, it is up to the Leadership Coach to give feedback in a timely fashion, at the earliest opportunity possible, so that problems and expectation issues can be corrected before they escalate into bigger problems.

Resources for Evaluation

When you are conducting a coachee evaluation, it is of critical importance that you draw all your information, evidence, and data entirely from objective sources. Use facts and information that cannot be disputed or argued about. Never use subjective impressions, uninformed opinions, baseless gossip, innuendo, or hearsay. What kind of sources are permissible, you might ask? There are quite a few good sources of objective information about a person's behavior.

Knowing where to look for them for that coachee (assuming you have permission and authority to do so) often spells the difference between a successful and accurate feedback coaching session or a disappointing or risky one.

The bottom line is that you can gauge definitively if the coachee consistently met, exceeded, or fell short of their agreed upon obligations and behavior according to expectations if you've kept adequate and appropriate notes and shared these with the coachee. Having adequate documentation is an excellent way to ensure that you have the facts and evidence to support your decisions regarding the coachee's promises to do certain things and to monitor their behavior. By establishing 'to dos' and behavior parameters up front, you can deliver the feedback that is so crucial to the coachee's leadership efforts more effectively.

Documentation and follow up removes misunderstandings about who was supposed to achieve what, and whether they ultimately achieved it.

Examining a coachee's efforts objectively, and the results of those efforts, will help you make the right decision in determining whether an individual should be given credit for a success, or otherwise held accountable and given corrective feedback.

DOCUMENTATION FOR FEEDBACK COACHING SESSIONS

Let's look at an example of how you would use documentation to hold a coachee accountable for delivering on their responsibilities. Imagine the coachee just finished a coaching session and promised to conduct at least three feedback meetings the following week. Because the coachee is reluctant to address accountability issues, it was agreed that the meetings must be in the first half of the coming week for credit to this promise. Because they have been less than honest in the past about their consistency in providing feedback to their employees, you insist that someone on their team confirm the number and times. Compliance on delivering on these Behavior Coaching effort responsibilities is easy to track and measure on a week-by-week basis. Plus, it's easy to track over an extended period. As the coaching sessions continue over time, you notice that the adherence to the promise seemed to be inconsistent.

As the Leadership Coach, you've provided feedback several times on this issue. Unfortunately, your ongoing verbal feedback has not been entirely effective. Some weeks are great, others not so much! It seemed that it was just a matter of time before the coachee slipped their responsibility in this area yet again. The habit isn't 'sticking'.

You begin documenting your findings to put formal written feedback together. On analysis of the info you've gathered, you looked at the coachee's pattern of behavior and discovered that every time you provided feedback, the coachee adhered to their responsibilities - but only for a few weeks.

Now at this coaching session, you gather evidence, data points, and relevant facts together to provide a formal evaluation. This type of documentation takes the subjectivity out of your feedback coaching sessions.

EVIDENCE VERSUS EXPECTED RESULTS

Behavior Coaching accountability deals with measurable results. These measurements, however, must be concerned with the individual's adherence to Behavior Coaching effort's expectations and goals always.

A coachee's values are just as important as their goals. Many times, a coachee wants to be rewarded or recognized simply because they met a goal. It's often more important to note **how** a coachee achieved that goal. If someone checked the box, but the methods they used go against agreed behavior, did 'things they know aren't right', or their conduct is out of line with expectations, then it can't really be counted as an overall success in the end. Coaching sessions should promote great decision making and great habits. The 'how' is just as important as the 'what'.

DESTRUCTIVE COACHEE BEHAVIOR

Sometimes a coachee will function adequately in their professional life but engage in behavior that is ultimately destructive in the long term to themselves or others. This might be the case in the example of a coachee who achieves a goal but does so in a manner that burns out team members and then they leave the organization. It might be ethical, legal, operational, procedural, or security behavior or conduct that arises that causes an issue. Documentation of these can be a good way to identify such behavioral tendencies and correct them before they become a problem. In addition, if at any time during a coaching session or assignment that you consider the coachee a threat to themselves or others, you must follow the

Leadership Behavior Coach guidelines fully. You must also comply with any legal requirements in your jurisdiction. Please review the confidentiality guidelines for Leadership Behavior Coaches when faced with destructive coachee behavior.

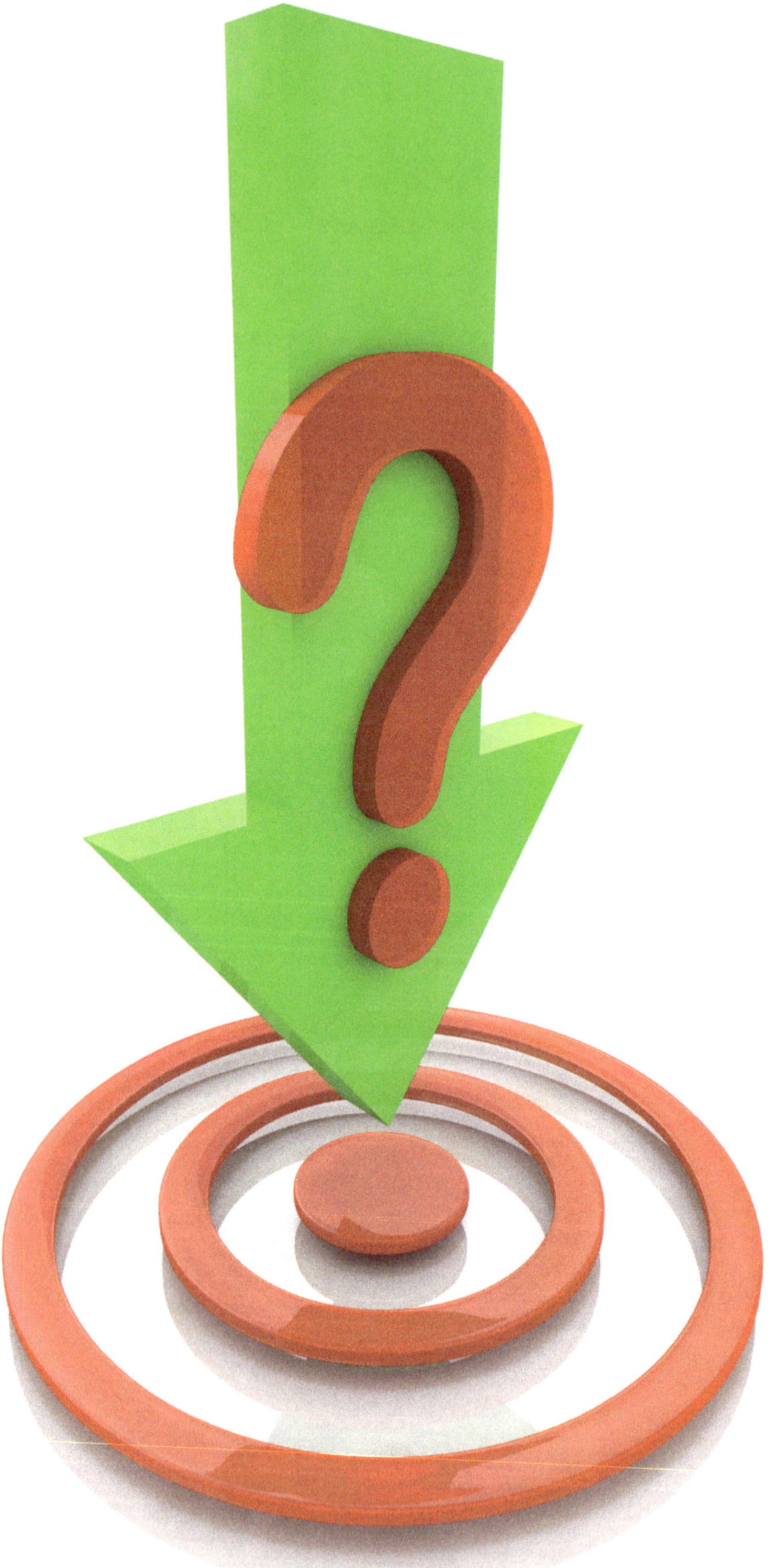

Sample Coaching Questions

1. What is the most important thing in the world to you, and why what are your 'Five Whys?' for this issue?
2. How else can I support you around your efforts to complete this?
3. If you couldn't use that excuse anymore, how would you move forward?

ACCOUNTABILITY

1. What are you willing to commit to doing/trying/changing? In what timeframe?
2. When would it make sense for us reconnect to ensure you have achieved the result you want?
3. What will things look like after you've been successful? How are you going to work your plan to get there?

VALUES AND CARE ABOUTS

1. At the end of the day, what do you want as your legacy? What is so important to you that you would stand in front of a freight train to defend it?
2. If a friend were in your shoes, what advice would you give them?
3. What is one step you could take right now that would indicate you were moving forward with what you believe in?

4. What are you most proud of?
5. Are there any important questions that have not been asked that might get you thinking your team might be going off track?

DEALING WITH TODAY'S ISSUES

1. What resources do you have access to (to fix this/to capitalize on this)?
2. What is the outcome you're looking to achieve here?
3. Can you share the specifics of what's going on?
4. What have you tried so far?
5. What's your opinion on how to handle this?
6. How have you handled something like this before? What happened?
7. Why do you think this is happening?
    a. Have you looked at the facts and data?
    b. What else can also be possible/true?
    c. What assumptions could you be making here?
8. What ideas do you have? Switch roles: How would you handle this? What's another approach that may work?
9. What's standing in your way?
10. What's another way to look at this/respond?
11. What have you done to try to solve the problem?
12. What are you doing to not achieve your goal? Are you sabotaging in any way?
13. If your main obstacle didn't exist, how would your team's efforts play out?
14. What do you need most right now?
    a. What will happen if you don't take this step?
15. What is your current biggest problem or challenge?

      a. Follow up: If this weren't a problem, what would be your next biggest problem?
16. What can you accomplish that doesn't depend on others?
17. What would you do if you had unlimited resources in your department/for this project and why/what would it give you?
18. What's important about that particular employee to you?
19. So what? What's the worst that can happen if you did try that?
20. If I wasn't here, what would you ask yourself or your people to achieve/resolve this?
21. What's the first thing you need to do to move this ball forward?
22. Practice with me: What would that conversation sound like when you talk with_____?
23. Why not?
24. What resources do you need?
25. Who else do you think needs to be involved in this?
26. What has contributed to your success so far?
27. What is working well?
      a. Follow up: Why?
28. What might keep you from getting where you want to go?
      a. Follow up: How might continuing to deal with this get in your way? How much will it cost and in what way?
      b. What would be the impact on you (and others) if things don't change?
29. What would be your next goal after you achieve your current one?
      a. Follow up: Why?

PAST SKILLS AND MOTIVATION

1. Can you tell me more about how you got here?
2. What obstacles have you faced, what did you do, and what did you learn?
3. What are your biggest mistakes and what did you learn from them?

IMAGINING THE FUTURE

1. In six months, if things were going exactly the way you want, what would you see?
2. What obstacles do you expect to face? How do you plan to approach them?
3. What does success look like?
4. What would it look like if you were entirely successful three months from now?
   a. Follow up: What would you see if you popped into a time machine and it transported you to 3 months, six months, a year and two years into the future?
   b. Follow up: What do you think you might want and what do you think you might want to learn to make today easier?

CPSIA information can be obtained
at www.ICGtesting.com
Printed in the USA
BVHW011801270219
540600BV00020B/1/P